'In this book, a group of impressive authors bring a wealth of policy, practice and theoretical knowledge to the often ignored connections between gender and child protection. The book contains an excellent range of topics, written in accessible, practical prose. It will be indispensable reading for practitioners, as well as students of child welfare and their professors.'

Professor Karen Swift, School of Social Work, York University, Canada

'This timely and innovative collection brings gender issues to the fore across a wide range of fields relevant to child welfare. The editors and authors are to be congratulated in encompassing many contemporary debates through an informative, rigorous and thought-provoking lens. This book will be vital reading for all working with children, young people and families.'

Dr Jane McCarthy, Reader in Family Studies, Department of Social Policy, Open University

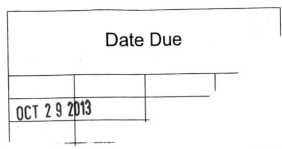

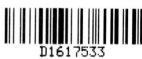

Gender and Child Welfare in Society

Edited by

Brid Featherstone
Carol-Ann Hooper
Jonathan Scourfield
Julie Taylor

WILEY-BLACKWELL
A John Wiley & Sons, Ltd., Publication

This edition first published 2010

Wiley-Blackwell is an imprint of John Wiley & Sons, formed by the merger of Wiley's global Scientific, Technical, and Medical business with Blackwell Publishing.

Registered Office
John Wiley & Sons Ltd, The Atrium, Southern Gate, Chichester, West Sussex, PO19 8SQ, UK

Editorial Offices
The Atrium, Southern Gate, Chichester, West Sussex, PO19 8SQ, UK
9600 Garsington Road, Oxford, OX4 2DQ, UK
350 Main Street, Malden, MA 02148-5020, USA

For details of our global editorial offices, for customer services, and for information about how to apply for permission to reuse the copyright material in this book please see our website at www.wiley.com/wiley-blackwell.

Library of Congress Cataloging-in-Publication Data

Gender and child welfare in society / edited by Brid Featherstone . . . [et al.].
p. cm.
Includes bibliographical references and index.
ISBN 978-0-470-68186-2 (cloth) – ISBN 978-0-470-68187-9 (pbk.)
1. Sex differences (Psychology) 2. Parenting. 3. Parent and child. 4. Child welfare.
I. Featherstone, Brid.
BF692.2.G46 2010
362.7–dc22 2009035844

A catalogue record for this book is available from the British Library.

Typeset in 11/13.5pt Minion by Aptara Inc., New Delhi, India.
Printed in Singapore by Fabulous Printers Pte Ltd.

1 [2010]

Contents

Notes on Contributors

Shereen Benjamin is a senior lecturer in primary education at the University of Edinburgh. After teaching in mainstream and special schools for many years she now teaches and researches in the field of sociology of education, with a particular interest in the intersection of gender and disability in schooling. Her books include *The Micropolitics of Inclusive Education* (Open University Press, 2002), and she is co-editor, with Suki Ali and Melanie Mauthner, of *The Politics of Gender and Education* (Palgrave, 2003).

Rosemary Carlton is a PhD candidate at the School of Social Work, McGill University. With substantial front-line practice experiences in child protection as well as a hospital-based clinic for sexually abused children, Rosemary is pursuing doctoral research that centres on the varied experiences of mothers and teenaged daughters in the aftermath of sexual abuse disclosures. With particular interest in social work practice that is reflective of and responsive to diversity, Rosemary approaches practice, teaching and research with a commitment to both feminist and anti-oppressive perspectives.

Linda Davies is Full Professor in the School of Social Work, McGill University, where she teaches in the area of clinical practice and qualitative research.

Brid Featherstone is a professor of social work and social policy at the University of Bradford. She has a particular interest in gender and child welfare issues. In recent years she has researched the issues for child welfare services in engaging fathers. Her latest book, *Contemporary Fathering: Theory, Policy and Practice*, was published by Policy Press in 2009.

Lorraine Green is a lecturer in social work and sociology at the University of Manchester. Her research and writing interests centre on and around children and child welfare, child abuse, gender, child health, sexuality, resilience and various combinations thereof. Lorraine's most recent journal articles have been written on deaf children and resilience, same sex partnership bereavement, and challenges to and opportunities for health and social care integration in the UK.

Carol-Ann Hooper is a senior lecturer in Social Policy at the University of York. Her research and teaching focus on the overlapping fields of child abuse, child protection and family support, and gender and crime. She is the author of *Mothers Surviving Child Sexual Abuse* (Routledge, 1992), co-editor with Una McCluskey of *Psychodynamic Perspectives on Abuse* (Jessica Kingsley, 2000) and co-author with Sarah Gorin, Christie Cabral and Claire Dyson of *Living with Hardship 24/7: The Diverse Experiences of Families in Poverty in England* (The Frank Buttle Trust, 2007).

Julia Krane is an associate professor in the School of Social Work, McGill University. Her teaching, practice and research endeavours centre on child welfare and violence against women in intimate relationships. Her publications engage in feminist analyses of mainstream and community child welfare practices, examinations of child protection practices that unwittingly reproduce maternal blame and responsibility for protection in cases of child sexual abuse, critical analyses of services to battered women and their children, and cautious reflections on the intersection of domestic violence and child protection interventions.

Simon Lapierre is currently a postdoctoral research fellow in the School of Social Work, McGill University. His work has focused on women's experiences of mothering in the context of domestic violence, and has provided a critical perspective on the ways child welfare policies and practices address this issue in both Canada and the United Kingdom.

Margaret McKenzie is a senior lecturer and Head of Department of Social Work and Community Development, University of Otago, New Zealand. She has extensive practice experience in child and family mental health services. Her teaching and research interests focus on family and family practice intersections with child welfare policy. She has published on family group conferences in child protection, researching with vulnerable clients and supervised contact services for fathers and is currently working on a research project to examine strengths approaches in child welfare services.

Meghan Mulcahy is a MSW candidate in the School of Social Work at McGill University researching qualitatively how mothers make meaning of a child protection encounter. Meghan has worked as an outreach worker in rural and urban Canadian communities providing strength and harm-reduction based advocacy, information and counselling support to women and adolescent girls.

Mark Rivett is Senior Lecturer in Family Therapy and Systemic Practice at the School for Policy Studies, Bristol University and a family therapist in South Wales. As well as having extensive experience in children's mental health, he has managed a domestic violence service for the NSPCC which lead him to develop an expertise in working with abusive men and also with children who have witnessed domestic violence. His publications span these specialties as well as more mainstream family therapy practice. He is the current editor of the *Journal of Family Therapy*.

Jonathan Scourfield is a Reader in Cardiff School of Social Sciences. His books include *Gender and Child Protection* (Palgrave, 2003) and *Working with Men in Health and Social Care* (Sage 2007, with Brid Featherstone and Mark Rivett). He is currently running a research project on Muslim families under the joint research council programme 'Religion and Society'.

Mark Smith is a lecturer in social work in the School of Social and Political Science at the University of Edinburgh. Formerly he was a practitioner and manager in residential childcare settings for almost 20 years. He has published widely on residential childcare and his first book, *Rethinking Residential Child Care* (2009), is published by Policy Press. He is working towards a PhD exploring changing discourses of care in Scottish residential schools.

Julie Taylor is Professor of Family Health and Head of Division, Research and Postgraduate Studies, School of Nursing and Midwifery, University of Dundee. A nurse by profession, Julie's research focuses on optimal service delivery conditions in child-care and protection practice. With Brigid Daniel, she is co-author of *Engaging with Fathers: Practice Issues for Health and Social Care* (Jessica Kingsley, 2001) and co-editor of *Child Neglect: Issues for Health and Social Care* (Jessica Kingsley, 2004). With Markus Themessl-Huber she is co-editor of *Safeguarding Children in Primary Health Care* (Jessica Kingsley, 2009).

Trish Walsh is a lecturer in social work in the School of Social Work and Social Policy, Trinity College Dublin. She practiced in child welfare and mental health social work in Dublin and London for 18 years and still takes occasional work carrying out independent court assessments in child welfare cases. Her research and teaching focus on social work education, critical discourses in social work and therapeutic interventions in mental health and family work. Her PhD (2002), a case study of the introduction of solution-focused therapy to Irish social workers, examined the diffusion of innovation in social work.

All the contributors are members of The Gender and Child Welfare Network. The network was formed in 2003 by a group of academics and consultants from all four countries in the UK with the main aim of creating a community of researchers, practitioners, policy makers and lobby groups interested in gender and child welfare issues. Since then the network has expanded to include members from the USA, Australia, Canada, the Republic of Ireland and New Zealand. Details of the Network's activities are given at www.brad.ac.uk/acad/socsci/research/genchilnet.

A Canadian branch of the Gender and Child Welfare Network was launched as a sister network in 2008. Further details are given at www.mcgill.ca/gender-child-welfare.

1

Gender and Child Welfare in Society: Introduction to Some Key Concepts

Jonathan Scourfield

A father beating his wife because he thinks she has been looking at another man while they were out in the pub; a girl being regularly kept off school to babysit her younger siblings; a mother who acknowledges ambivalent feelings towards her children being negatively judged by professionals because she is not all-giving and ever available; a teenage boy drinking daily because, in part, of his poor emotional literacy; a lesbian teenager suffering homophobic bullying in school and neighbourhood; a black boy struggling to achieve in school because he is surrounded by people expecting him not to. I could go on, of course, in listing reasons why the topic of gender and child welfare deserves a book. It does not only deserve a book; it deserves complex analysis, and therefore we have put together a collection of chapters on various different dimensions of the topic by authors from different locations and with different theoretical orientations.

Gender and Child Welfare in Society Edited by Brid Featherstone, Carol-Ann Hooper, Jonathan Scourfield, and Julie Taylor.

The book's terrain is the ways in which both relationships within families and interactions between family members and professionals are influenced by gender in interaction with other social divisions – for example, ethnicity or socio-economic status – and with other factors – for example, individual biography or professional training. The social meanings attached to being male or female are variable, contested and changing, yet they continue to influence the identities and practices of children, parents and the practitioners who work with them, and assumptions about gender (for instance, about appropriate behaviour for boys or girls, or the responsibilities of men and women as parents) often permeate interventions. Certain outcomes for children are significantly associated with gender – for example, there are higher rates of school exclusion, offending and suicide amongst boys, and higher rates of depression amongst girls, although the extent of such differences varies in different contexts and over time. Practitioners who intervene in families continue to work predominantly with mothers, reflecting traditional assumptions about gendered responsibilities for children's welfare as well as the reality that in the vast majority of families women are still the primary caregivers. However, there is a growing interest in the roles of men both as fathers and as practitioners, and interventions can either reinforce or destabilize existing gender divisions.

The book draws on current developments in thinking about gender relations to consider ways in which raising questions about gender can help researchers and practitioners better understand family relationships and issues in children's development, and both challenge and enhance interventions in the field of health and social care for children and families. We use the term 'child welfare' to locate the book's contribution within a long-standing tradition of policy and practice concern with children in the fields of health and social care, rather than as part of the more recent and definitionally circumscribed debate over 'children's well-being'. We see the book as relevant to a range of professionals who work in child welfare – social workers, health visitors and children's nurses, early years staff – as well as people studying aspects of childhood or gender relations for their own sake.

As services in the United Kingdom reorganize to reflect higher aspirations for children's well-being they also have new obligations to eliminate discrimination and promote gender equality which apply to children, parents and practitioners. We hope the book will contribute to ongoing attempts to turn these visions into reality in a variety of contexts. It will offer an overview of sociological, psychological and developmental perspectives on family relationships, child welfare outcomes and the practice/policy realities of professional interventions with families. Exploring the issues for children, mothers and fathers, as well as specific types of interventions, specific chapters will address the range of service settings, including family support, child health, education, child protection, domestic violence, 'looked after' children and youth justice.

The book will address the following questions:

- How is gender being integrated into the child welfare agenda today?
- How can children's views and experiences inform such developments?
- What are the new challenges facing women and men as parents in the context of family and societal change and diversity that policy makers and practitioners need to be aware of?
- How does gender intersect with ethnicity, religion, class, disability, age and sexuality in families?
- How are other policies such as youth justice promoting or undermining child welfare goals?
- What theoretical and practice developments are most promising in promoting both child well-being and gender equity?
- How can health and social care practitioners use information about gender to engage more meaningfully with families?
- How can the 'gender agenda' improve child safeguarding practice?

We seek to demonstrate that gender sensitivity is crucial to informed intervention across the field of child welfare, and to illustrate with examples its relevance and implications in the current context. Whereas previous books on the topic of gender and child welfare have looked at sub-themes such as family support (Featherstone, 2004) or child protection (Scourfield, 2003), or a specific group such as fathers (Daniel and Taylor, 1999), we aim for greater breadth here. This book explores contemporary childhood, mothering and fathering in the context of social policy and social interventions in several countries.

This introductory chapter aims to provide an overview of some key concepts. The overview is unavoidably partial as it reflects its author's knowledge and interests. Whilst, inevitably, many complex issues will be skated over and some even omitted altogether because of the need to be brief, I hope I can provide an *accessible* introduction both to the book and to the broader topic of the gendered dimension of child welfare. Note that at times the first person singular 'I' is used, referring to the single author of this introductory chapter. At other times, and especially when summarizing the book's content, the plural 'we' is used, with reference to the book's four editors.

Understanding gender relations

What's meant by 'gender'?

There has been a flourishing of critical writings about gender and sexuality (and the links between the two) perhaps especially in the last forty years or so, since the writings of the 1960s and 1970s, often referred to as 'second wave feminism' (the first wave being the writings and activism concerning the emancipation of women in the late nineteenth and early twentieth centuries, the suffragette movement being the most famous example). The term 'gender' is generally used to refer to 'social interpretation of reproductive biological distinctions' (Beasley, 2005: 12). That is, it refers to socially constructed identities, behaviour and institutions rather than to biological sex differences between men and women. This definition is far from being uncontested, however. Chris Beasley – the Australian academic, not the Chief Nursing Officer for England with the same name – in her very helpful overview of gender/sexuality theories, notes that there have been three principle debates about the term 'gender' within social and cultural theory (Beasley, 2005).

The first debate is about whether or not a focus on specific identities is helpful. So some commentators have argued that a conceptual focus on 'gender' draws attention away from the continuing oppression of women. Others have argued that the concept of gender prescribes rather than describes a binary social construction with 'male' and 'female' as opposite poles. The second debate is about the relationship between what is social and what is natural/bodily. Some have argued that the conventional understanding of gender sets up an artificial divide between social and natural/bodily, as if biological phenomena were fixed, when in fact ideas about biology vary across time and cultural context. Others have observed that the term is quite specific to English language literature, with French feminist writings, for example, tending to write about 'sex' and 'sexed identities' instead. Beasley herself makes pragmatic use of the term gender insofar as it is still the most commonly used in English language writings and we do the same in this book. The third debate noted by Beasley is about the links between gender and sexuality, with some seeing gender as preceding sexuality and others seeing sexuality as preceding gender. Most contemporary theorists recognize that there are at least significant conceptual overlaps between sexuality and gender. Ideas about male and female as 'opposite' characteristics are implicated in the social and cultural dominance of heterosexuality, for example, and homophobia is often about adverse reactions to transgression of gendered behaviour as much as it is about sexuality. We should acknowledge, however, that whilst we the book's editors regard sexuality and gender as strongly connected, sexuality is not to the fore in the book.

To give an overview of gender theories is a daunting task within a whole book, let alone part of one chapter. There are many possible ways of cutting the cake. One would be to organize theories according to whether they aim to treat 'male' and 'female' constructs on equal terms or emphasize the need to acknowledge differences between them – what might be called a distinction between equality feminism and difference feminism. Another possible organizing principle would be around theorists' orientations to modernism or postmodernism (see Beasley, 2005). So even within a potential single category of theories, such as radical feminism, there is a continuum of more or less modernist versions. I have decided to run with categorizing some well-recognized traditions within feminism in the full knowledge that each of these is a very broad category. Most of the following categories apply to theorizing about masculinities and femininities, but the field of masculinity theory is rather more recent than feminist theory, which primarily addresses itself to understanding the position of women. In recognition of this, I have included a separate sub-heading 'men's studies' at the end of this section.

Radical feminism

Well known radical feminist academics include Mary Daly and Adrienne Rich. Better known still, at least in the United Kingdom, are the writings of Andrea Dworkin. As I have already noted, however, a range of different stances can be found within the broad categories of theory used in this chapter. To summarize very briefly some of the most obvious characteristics of radical feminism, there is a concern with stark inequality between men and women and central to this concern would be the control of women's bodies and women's bodily integrity. So concern about domestic violence, rape and pornography would typical within radical feminism. These phenomena would be seen as rooted in patriarchy, the historical and ongoing social structural oppression of women by men. Heterosexuality would be seen as an institution based on the oppression of women by men. For most radical feminists, gender inequality is about real embodied men and real women, and there is little interest in fluidity of identities. There is generally an emphasis on women's common experience of oppression rather than on diversity between women.

In relation to child welfare, radical feminist concerns would include, for example, the (hetero)sexualization of girls, the impact of domestic abuse on women and children, men's sexual abuse of children – both within the family and outside – and female genital mutilation. Interventions might include supporting women to leave abusive men and education of men about the roots of abuse of women in patriarchy. An example of the latter would be the group work with violent men used within the Duluth model (see Pence and Paymar, 1993). This work is 'pro-feminist', with the prefix indicating that men who are supportive can help to run groups. In this programme there is an explicit message that men's abuse of women is based on a desire to control them and patriarchal views about intimate relationships. The dominant mode of engagement is educating men to accept this interpretation and to modify their behaviour via cognitive-behavioural methods. The chapter in this collection by Rivett, is critical of what he sees as the 'doctrinaire' approach of this kind of intervention with violent men. The chapter by Lapierre, however, is squarely in the tradition of radical (pro-)feminist research on domestic violence.

Liberal feminism

This approach dates back to the writings of Mary Wollstonecraft in the late nineteenth century and would in more recent times include the popular writer Naomi Wolf. The liberal feminist approach is to seek equality for women within the mainstream institutions of society. Unlike radical feminism, there is not a fundamental questioning of gender relations. Rather, liberal feminism would see society as amenable to modification so that women have a better deal from employment and education, for example. Heterosexual relationships would be seen as reformable, with the domestic division of labour addressed but heterosexual desire remaining unchallenged. This is in essence the popular face of feminism, what most people think feminism is – namely ameliorative politics to improve the lot of women within existing structures. This liberal feminist approach is by and large the face of feminism in mainstream party politics. Unlike radical feminism, liberal feminism does not involve an explicit analysis of patriarchal social structures. Also unlike radical feminism, it does not question mainstream terms of engagement in any fundamental way.

In relation to child welfare, an example of a liberal feminist approach would be to challenge an unfair focus on mothers within the child protection system. This critique would not necessarily involve fundamental questioning of the heterosexual family, but would simply point out that in very many child protection cases attention moves from initial concern about an abusive man to scrutiny of mothering (Farmer and Owen, 1998). Another example would be a concern with how girls are responded to within the youth justice system, given that they are a small minority of the client base and could therefore be rather marginalized within services which are geared towards young men. Yet another example, following the same logic, would be the marginalization of fathers from family support services. Although this concern might come from a men's rights perspective rather than a feminist one, the logic of equal opportunities for men and women within the mainstream would be the same. Whilst none of the chapters in this volume is straightforwardly written from a liberal feminist perspective, it has to be acknowledged that its version of equality does underpin many of the concerns expressed in the book about the unequal treatment of boys and girls, mothers and fathers, in the child welfare system.

An emphasis on differences between women

Under this broad umbrella I include some very diverse theories. The socialist feminist tradition prioritises class alongside gender (Hartmann, 1978). So rather than promoting women's opportunities to negotiate the inequalities required by capitalism (as it could be said that liberal feminism does), the emphasis is on social class inequalities and the ways in which working-class women are doubly disadvantaged by the labour market, for example, because of their sex and class status. Lesbian feminism was, in the 1970s and 1980s rather more associated with radical feminist critiques of heterosexuality. More recently, however, there has been a rapid development of 'queer' theory (see below under poststructuralist and postmodernist accounts), and contemporary lesbian perspectives are rather concentrated within this literature. Whatever the theoretical orientation, lesbian feminist theorizing does, again, emphasize differences between women rather than commonality. Also, approaches which emphasize both gender *and* ethnicity have been very influential. Beasley (2005) groups these approaches together as 'race/ethnicity/imperialism' perspectives, to give a flavour of the diversity – some emphasizing the experience of colour racism, others cultural difference and yet others a post-colonial perspective. Even this broad grouping does not necessarily include Muslim feminists, who may see their difference in perspective from Western feminism as more about religion than race, ethnicity or imperialism.

To give some illustrations in relation to the book's topic of gender and child welfare, socialist feminism would certainly be concerned with mothers in poverty and with policy and practice measures to structurally improve their situation. Lesbian feminists would be concerned with the well-being of lesbian, gay, bisexual, transgender (LGBT) young people, for example in relation to self-harm which has been found to be elevated in LGBT youth and associated with experience of homophobia (Rivers, 2000). An example of a child welfare issue for feminists concerned with race/ethnicity/imperialism would be the way that children are constructed as gendered and also racialized. This has been well documented in research on boys (for instance, Connolly, 1998) where, for example, South Asian boys are often found to be feminized within peer group and school cultures. Another child welfare issue where difference between women is stark is the response to young Muslim women who choose to cover their heads. We know from research such as that by Emma Tarlo that there are many different reasons why young women cover their heads (wear hijab), including a version of feminism which depends on a monotheistic world view and looks very different from a liberal (or radical) Western one:

> To the claim put forward by the French government that the hijab puts unacceptable pressure on young girls to conform to oppressive religious norms, hijab-wearing women are quick to point out the pressures placed on young girls in the West to conform to the unrealistic body images pedalled in the media, and the low self-esteem and proliferation of eating disorders they see as a result. To them, the veil is lived as a form of resistance to these pressures even if, in the process, they willingly submit to another set of discourses and disciplinary regimes concerning the female body. (Tarlo, 2007: 153)

To varying extents, all the chapters in this collection deal with differences between women and between men, including class, sexuality and ethnicity. In particular, the chapters by Benjamin, Green and Taylor and McKenzie emphasize questions of diversity, Benjamin's in considering 'special needs' (as well as class and ethnicity), Green and Taylor's in reviewing evidence about global health inequalities and McKenzie's in discussing the intersection of the politics of gender and 'race' in child welfare policy.

Poststructuralist and postmodernist feminisms

Although linking poststructuralist and postmodernist feminisms means skating over large bodies of theory and differences between various concepts, these two important developments in feminism do have some points of commonality for the purposes of this very brief overview. Both require a significant move away from the grand narratives on which earlier feminisms were based. So gone are certainties about social structure and fixed identities. Instead, the emphasis is on fluidity and complexity. In postmodernist feminism, any notion of seeking to establish truth is disavowed. Poststructuralism is very much concerned with language, and feminists influenced by Foucault use his notion of discourse as a regime of truth which circumscribes what can be known about a given issue. Poststructuralist feminists tend to talk of *multiple* gendered discourses operating simultaneously with sometimes contradictory effects. The separation of sexuality and gender is questioned, especially by queer theory, which is profoundly influenced by postmodernism. So, as noted earlier, the idea of socially constructed binaries of male and female is regarded as unhelpfully limiting theoretical possibilities and setting heterosexuality in stone. Postmodernist feminism and queer theory question any kind of identity categorization and are profoundly anti-essentialist.

Examples of applying such approaches to gender issues in child welfare might include questioning some feminist orthodoxies. So Brid Featherstone has, for example, drawn our attention to the potential for women to physically abuse children and has argued that violence in the home is not so monolithically about male power as it is often thought to be (Featherstone, 1997; Featherstone and Trinder, 1997). Parton (1998) acknowledges the inevitable uncertainty in child welfare and argues that practitioners should embrace uncertainty as a positive aspect of practice rather than vainly attempting to eliminate it by using actuarial risk measures. We also see the influence of poststructuralism in research attention to professional discourses in relation to men and women clients (Scourfield, 2003). As you would expect, poststructuralist and postmodernist approaches to gender relations have their critics. Ann Oakley has made the point that postmodernist theorizing tends to be rather distant from 'the situation of women out there in a world that definitely does exist, and that remains obdurately structured by a dualistic, power-driven gender system' (Oakley, 1998: 143).

Several contributions to this collection are influenced by poststructuralist and postmodernist ideas. An example would be Smith's chapter, insofar as he finds theories of patriarchy to be unwieldy in making sense of gender issues in residential care and instead is seeking to capture the 'complexity and contingency' of gender in practice, with power being 'multi-layered and multi-directional'.

Psychoanalytic approaches to gender

Psychoanalytic ideas with their roots in such theorists as Freud and Klein have been very influential on some feminist thinkers. To summarize very briefly, there is an important emphasis in this body of theory on the role of the unconscious and the shaping of this by early childhood experiences. Important authors who have theorized sex/gender in psychoanalytic terms include Irigaray, Kristeva and Benjamin. An example of a feminist theorist who uses both sociological and psychoanalytic ideas is Nancy Chodorow (1978). She explains the social construction of gender with reference to the infant's relationship with mother and father: dyadic (mother–child) for boys and tryadic (child–mother–father) for girls. The fact that women are largely responsible for the care of very young children helps to explain gendered identities and behaviour. Girls grow up more relationally-oriented because they retain an intense identification with their mothers. Boys repress identification with their mothers (and therefore feminine qualities) in order to become successfully masculine, making them less relational and more autonomous.

Psychoanalytic feminist ideas could be seen to be relevant to child welfare in a number of ways. Various commentators have argued the importance of the unconscious to both parenting and child development. Perhaps especially relevant in the child welfare field is the application of these ideas to understanding gendered reactions to childhood trauma and the development of abusive behaviours. The chapter in this collection by Hooper takes up this theme.

Men's studies

In truth it is rather artificial to separate out men's studies, as the same range of approaches to understanding men can be found that we can see above in relation to feminist theorizing. Indeed, there are examples given in the subsections above which relate to men and masculinities. However, there is a rather separate (and later) literature, so I briefly mention this here.

Because the range of approaches to theorizing masculinity is broad, some theorists (for example, Robert Bly) have been criticised by some feminists for being insufficiently critical of men's practices or for being essentialist about gender identities. Authors such as Connell, Hearn and Kimmel (2005) mark out a territory they call 'critical men's studies' to emphasize that they are alert to questions of power and that they are influenced by feminist critiques of masculinity. Some of these critical studies of men are focused on privilege, so they are very different from feminist research which comes from a tradition of studying the marginalized. That said, there is also considerable attention to inequalities between men, including those of race, class and sexuality. The recognition that there is more than one way of being a man has led to the plural term 'masculinities' becoming *de rigueur*.

Applications of men's studies to child welfare would include acknowledgement of the diversity of fathers and the various pressures both of tradition and change that fathers are experiencing (Featherstone, 2003). Intersectional analyses of boys' masculinities, which include an appreciation of class, race and sexuality, are important for practitioners. Frosh, Phoenix and Pattman's (2002) book provides a complex account and includes a psychoanalytic dimension. Various practitioners have sought to somehow 'make masculinity explicit' in their work with boys and men. A wide range of approaches have been used and many of these are summarized in Featherstone, Rivett and Scourfield's (2007) overview. Several chapters in the current edited collection touch on the masculinities literature. An example is the chapter by Featherstone, which draws on research evidence about the practical reality of contemporary fathering.

To round off this section on understanding gender, I shall describe Connell's (2002; 2005) sophisticated account of gender relations. It is relevant in this subsection as Connell has especially addressed herself to masculinities, but her account also, in my view, draws on the most useful aspects from a number of different feminist traditions so is more generally relevant to an understanding of gender relations. Connell does not shy away from using the concept of patriarchy. For example, she is clear that even men who oppose patriarchal beliefs and practices can gain certain social privileges simply by virtue of being men. This is the 'patriarchal dividend'. Hers is not a crude, monolithic version of patriarchy, however. She insists on the poststructuralist plurality of the term 'masculinities'. So there are multiple possible ways of being a man, and men's practices vary according to culture, class, ethnicity and sexuality as well as other mediating factors. Becoming a man is not a passive process of socialization but an active construction of an identity. Identities and practices are not freely acquired, however, but there are social structural constraints, and power relations are crucial. Gendered discursive practices configure into a hierarchy. There are multiple gendered discourses, but some are more powerful than others. So, for example, compulsory heterosexuality is an important aspect of 'hegemonic masculinity' and gay sexual identity therefore represents 'subordinated masculinity', although individual gay men are not necessarily in a position of social subordination and can draw the 'patriarchal dividend'. Men who aspire to the culturally authoritative hegemonic masculinity but cannot fulfil it because their aspirations are thwarted, perhaps because of the class system or racism, can be seen as falling into the category of 'marginalized masculinity'.

At this point I move away from gender to give an equally brief (if not briefer) overview of different ways of conceptualizing children and families, given their centrality to the book.

Understanding childhood and family life

There are other bodies of literature that could be relevant here, such as, for example, anthropological research on childhood and care, but because of space and the limitations of my own knowledge I have limited this section to three fields: developmental psychology, the sociology of childhood and the sociology of the family.

Developmental psychology

Much of child welfare practice and policy is based on a body of evidence from within the developmental psychology tradition (White, 1998). This is the biggest body of research evidence about anything to do with children. The dominant approach is to measure various aspects of children's functioning and to analyse this in terms of expected developmental pathways. There is a wealth of evidence covering a wide range of issues, from a baby's awareness of their environment to ideas about spirituality in middle childhood. The empirical basis of the science includes experimentation, observation and questionnaire-based studies. Attachment theory, based on children's attachment to primary carers, comes within the umbrella of developmental psychology. Big names in the developmental psychology field include Piaget, Kohlberg, Bowlby and Vygotsky. Developmentalism has been criticized, especially by those of a more sociological or qualitative persuasion, for seeing children as passive, for generalizing across cultures from research with white Western samples and for traditionally basing findings about family life exclusively on mothers.

As Scourfield, Dicks, Drakeford and Davies (2006) argue, some of these criticisms are rooted in caricatured versions of developmental psychology and do not take into account the sophistication of contemporary empirical and conceptual work. Critics need to accept that developmental psychology has to be part of the picture in promoting child welfare. It is essential to know what children are typically able to do at certain stages and how this might relate to child welfare, whether or not this has a gender justice angle. Just one example would be the poor developmental outcomes for children in situations of emotional neglect. There have been some interesting attempts to rescue developmental psychology from a feminist perspective. The chapter in this volume by Walsh notes that attempts to make attachment theory less exclusively focused on mothering go back several decades. Walsh points out the limitations of a traditional narrow take on attachment with reference to a specific child protection case. Chapter 6, by Krane, Davies, Carlton and Mulcahy, engages rather more positively with attachment theory, modifying it in the light of feminist criticisms.

The sociology of childhood

Within sociology there is an interest in the social construction of childhood. So the ways in which childhood is constructed within, for example, the institutions of education, health care, criminal justice and the family have been the subject of research by James and James (2004). King and Piper (1995) have written about how children are constructed in British law, using the categories of child as victim, the child as witness, the child as a bundle of needs and the child as a bearer of rights. An emphasis on the socialization of children is traditional within the sociology of childhood. This has been rather ridiculed in more recent writings, as implying a passive model of social learning and not appreciating children as social agents in their own right. However, it could still be considered a broad enough term to encompass a wide range of approaches; it simply refers to the process by which children become social beings, and that need not be theoretically limiting. There has been a tendency in recent years towards ethnographic engagement with children's everyday lives, as well as a theoretically-driven interest in this angle on childhood. An appreciation has developed of children's own cultures and of cultural variation across and within national borders.

One example of the application of the sociology of childhood to gender and child welfare is Morrow's (2006) argument that practice textbooks need wider conceptions of gender identities than are currently employed in books in which outmoded categorizations of 'all girls' and 'all boys' tend to be used instead of recognizing diversity and the contingency of identity. Another application is the research of Holland et al. (2008) on the everyday lives of children in care, focusing on the detail of how children see their own identities and social contexts. They recommend practitioners to engage in sustained listening to children's stories and work with them to construct alternative narratives where appropriate to help them promote positive change in their lives.

The sociology of the family

There is a long tradition of sociological research on the family. Earlier in the twentieth century the dominant approach was that of functionalism – attempting to explain how the family socializes people to find their role in society. For some time, 'functionalism' has been a knee-jerk pejorative term for critical social scientists who have learned the lessons of second-wave feminism and are more interested in the power dynamics within families. In recent years, the predominant emphasis within the literature on the sociology of the family has been on making sense of rapid social change. There has been a large increase, for example, in couple relationships breaking down and families re-forming with new members. Recently, there has been attention to the contemporary tendency towards 'families of choice': the building up of strong ties with friends, with whom there is no biological link, and the establishment of lesbian and gay families (Weeks, Heaphy and Donovan, 2001; Roseneil, 2004). One of the main messages of Fiona Williams's important book *Rethinking Families* is the diversity of the contemporary family, and she argues that 'policies need to be diverse and flexible enough to meet people's varying options for their living arrangements and for combining work and care in the short term' (Williams, 2004: 85).

Charles, Davies and Harris (2008), however, emphasize continuity over time in family life as well as change. They argue, on the basis of returning to research family life in Swansea, first studied in the 1960s, that considering the amount of social change in recent decades there is a surprising amount of continuity in how people 'do' family. This echoes debates about gender relations and how drastic and fundamental social change has been. Delamont (2001) addresses this question head on in her book *Changing Women, Unchanged Men?* and concludes that there is more continuity than change: 'British men and women are behaving much like their great-grandparents in 1951 and even their great, great, great, great-grandparents in 1893' (Delamont, 2001: 111).

As well as social scientific approaches to understanding gender, childhood and the family, the other important part of the book's context is social policy on child welfare and on gender equity, so it to this that we turn next.

International developments in social policy

Child welfare

In many Western countries, the history of child welfare over the twentieth century was one of a gradual move towards the professionalization of staffing and a move from voluntary sector to state provision. Residential care for children who, for various reasons, cannot be cared for by parents is an example of a service which has seen significant changes in these regards in many countries. It has struggled to shrug off a reputation for abuse of children and there has been a strong trend for moving children out of residential care and into foster families. The main English-speaking Western countries have had a common experience of a preoccupation with child abuse and child protection in the last few decades followed by attempts to refocus policy away from forensic concerns and towards effective preventative services (Lindsay, 1994; Parton, Thorpe and Wattam 1997). It should be noted that there are different trends in some European countries. Pringle (1998) characterizes the French and German child welfare systems as being much less focused on investigation of child abuse and more so on family support. In the poorest parts of the world the issues are starker: ensuring a basic primary education, especially for girls; ensuring the basic health of mothers; combating HIV; and attempting to prevent female genital mutilation in some countries (see Chapter 2 by Green and Taylor in this collection).

More recent policy moves, at least in the United Kingdom, have been based on the idea of investing in children as the workers of the future: what has been termed the 'social investment state' (Lister, 2003). Fawcett, Featherstone and Goddard (2004) have suggested there is a risk that this approach will allow some groups of children to be seen as more worthy than others. For example, there is a certain consensus that early intervention with young children, improving their opportunities for learning and play and supporting their parents, can boost health and welfare in the short term and also prevent social problems in adulthood. Older children, however, are much more likely to be demonized and criminalized. A focus of early intervention and an increasingly universal approach to safeguarding children are important aspects of child welfare policies in all the four nations of the United Kingdom. Parton (2006), with reference to English policy in particular, has characterized the New Labour approach as 'the preventive state'. Whilst there is much in this approach that could be welcomed, there is concern about excessive surveillance via extensive databases.

In relation to child health, a range of issues is of current concern in the United Kingdom, including child obesity and increasing alcohol and drug use. These are, of course, the concerns of an affluent society, although, paradoxically, the children most at risk are the most socially and economically disadvantaged. Recent education policy in the United Kingdom has emphasized raising achievement though a variety of means, including, most controversially, testing of children at 7, 11, 14 and 16 in England. Schooling is an area of policy where devolution is making a significant impact in the United Kingdom, with Wales, for example, having abandoned school league tables and significantly de-emphasized testing of children under 16, as well as bringing in a Scandinavian-style play-based curriculum for under 7s. Gender equality is a controversial issue in education (see Benjamin, Chapter 4, in this book). Especially controversial amongst feminist commentators has been the emphasis in several Western countries on the so-called under-achievement of boys. Concern has been expressed by these commentators about what have been termed 'recuperative masculinity politics' (Lingard, 2003), namely an approach which assumes men should be able to re-gain the privilege that has been dented by feminism. The feminist critics of this approach point to the continuing high achievement of middle-class boys and the greater salience of ethnicity and social class than sex for educational achievement.

Gender equality

Summarizing trends in social policy that relate to gender equality is challenging, as there is a gender angle to every area of policy. Various authors have attempted to categorize different countries' welfare states, following Esping-Andersen (1990), with reference to gender equality. Lewis (1992), for example, has grouped countries into the categories of strong, weak and modified breadwinner regimes. Hearn and Pringle (2006) have come up with the following categories for European countries.

1. The Nordic nations, which have good childcare provision, generous parental leave and make significant attempts to reconcile home and work.
2. The established EU-member nations (for example, Ireland, Italy, Germany and the United Kingdom), whose day-care provision, parental leave and home–work reconciliation policies are variable.
3. The former Soviet Eastern bloc countries which have relatively low levels of day care provision, parental and paternity leave and less developed home–work reconciliation policies.

Despite these broad distinctions, Hearn and Pringle also acknowledge that there are some apparent contradictions. For example, policies on violence against women are more developed in the United Kingdom than in the Nordic countries, despite the general trend of more proactive policies towards gender equality in Scandinavia. Daly and Rake's (2003) impressive multifactorial analysis cautions against any rush to categorize countries as considerable ambiguities exist. They too mention Sweden, however, as providing a relatively positive example of gender equality in comparison with other countries.

Approaches to tackling gender equality within state organizations are changing rapidly, in the United Kingdom at least, with gender increasingly being tackled alongside other equality issues (there is now a single equality body called the Equality and Human Rights Commission) and new responsibilities for state agencies to promote gender equality. Within the social policy literature an important development with strong gender overtones has been the emphasis on an ethic of care. Williams (2004), for example, argues for rebalancing an ethic of work and an ethic of care. She sees the United Kingdom New Labour government as having moved away from a male breadwinner model to a model in which both men and women are expected to work, and she notes that this model, whilst promoting a certain version of equality, does not sufficiently value care and personal interdependence. Shakespeare (2000: 52–65) also draws on the feminist ethic of care literature in writing about interdependence in relation to disability. He draws on Sevenhuijsen's (1998) concept of 'caring solidarity' as helping us to recognize that 'everyone is variously dependent, that disabled people are themselves often carers, and that society is based on interdependence' (Shakespeare, 2000: 65).

Having given a brief sketch of the conceptual and policy terrain of the book I will now conclude by explaining its structure and introducing its different components.

The structure of the book

The book has groups of chapters on the main sub-themes of children, mothers, fathers and interventions, and I shall summarize each of them here. We have attempted to include some breadth of coverage of policy contexts. So although most authors are from United Kingdom universities there is also some international material, with contributions from Ireland, Canada and New Zealand. Within the context of a devolved United Kingdom, there are contributions from England, Scotland and Wales. This is also, to an extent, a multidisciplinary, multi-professional endeavour. Most authors are social work academics, as you would expect with child welfare being the topic, but there are also contributions from authors whose backgrounds are in social policy, nursing and education.

Chapters 2 to 4 all focus on *children* as gendered, in relation to some key issues that are highly relevant to child welfare, namely health inequalities (Chapter 2), maltreatment and offending (Chapter 3) and schooling (Chapter 4). Chapter 2, by Lorraine Green and Julie Taylor, on gender and child health, deals with global economic inequalities. They conclude, on the basis of a review of existing research, that the gender dimension of health inequalities in children has been given relatively little academic attention to date. They note the stark health inequalities between boys and girls in the developing world but also complicate the picture by describing the less visible though nonetheless very significant gendered health inequalities in the relatively wealthy countries of the world. Some of these issues, such as eating disorders, are only likely to arise in relatively comfortable material conditions, but gendered ideologies are central to their aetiology.

In Chapter 3, on gender, maltreatment and offending, Carol-Ann Hooper considers children and young people both as victims and offenders, consistently arguing the importance of the overlap between the two categories to understanding problematic behaviour in children and intervening to prevent it. Hooper draws on a range of theory and evidence, including sociological and psycho-social work. In Chapter 4, on gender and schooling, Shereen Benjamin starts by debunking the headlines about the 'underachievement' of boys in school, in part because class and ethnicity complicate the picture in terms of exam results – the only measure that tends to be used by government to determine achievement. Benjamin insists that we need to understand the complex intersection of gender with class, ethnicity and disability to fully appreciate gendered processes in schools. She illustrates this complexity from some of her rich data on boys and girls with special educational needs in special schools.

Chapters 5 and 6 are concerned with mothering; all the authors are associated with McGill University in Montreal, where there has been some interesting work on mothering in recent years. Simon Lapierre's concern in Chapter 5, based on his qualitative research in the United Kingdom, is with mothering in the context of domestic violence. He challenges the construction of women who have experienced violence as 'bad mothers', explaining in detail the challenges that living with violence poses for their mothering and the strategies they use to keep their children safe. He also discusses the experiences – mainly negative – that these women had of social workers and the child welfare system. Chapter 6, by Julia Krane, Linda Davies, Rosemary Carlton and Meghan Mulcahy, deals with the implications of attachment theory for work with mothers. They review the foundations of attachment theory, discuss feminist critiques of it and set their discussion of social work practice in the context of Canadian policies. They then develop a detailed case study – the story of 'Amber', the 24-year old mother of three children – which illustrates the challenges of implementing therapeutic intervention in a statutory child protection context. Despite the challenges, they end with some positive suggestions for the application of attachment theory in social work practice with mothers.

Chapters 7 and 8 deal with different aspects of fathering in relation to child welfare. In Chapter 7 Brid Featherstone deals with the engagement of men in child welfare services. She starts by setting the context in various different conceptions of equality, debates about work and care and the politics of fatherhood. She then moves on to problematize some of the assumptions that seem to be underlying recent policy developments designed to promoted father involvement, asking such questions as 'Who counts as a father?' and 'What is meant by involvement?' before discussing evidence about the practical reality of contemporary fathering. Featherstone sees her chapter as asking more questions than it answers. In Chapter 8 Mark Rivett brings the focus more specifically onto working with violent fathers. He argues for a 'both/and' approach to violent male carers, which takes seriously both their abusive behaviour and their role as fathers, and he notes that interventions tend to focus on one aspect or the other. He moves on to discuss different psychological and sociological theories of men's violence and the rather ambiguous evidence about what violent fathers might mean to their children. Rivett then proceeds to review the common approaches to intervention with violent men and some of their potential shortcomings, which include neglect of fathering, the homogenization of the client group and the rejection of alternative psychological approaches. He argues for a more rounded approach to assessment and intervention for these men, addressing both their violence and their fathering.

The final group of chapters, with authors from three different countries, focuses on social interventions. The first two in this group deal in turn with specific interventions, albeit interventions that raise much wider gender issues. One of these is community-based and one residential. The final chapter discusses models of change more generally, in relation to gender concerns.

Margaret McKenzie (in Chapter 9) gives an interesting overview of the development of family group conferences (FGC) in New Zealand. It is impossible to discuss this intervention without reference to ethnicity and culture as an important part of the rationale for its promotion in New Zealand was its suitability for indigenous Maori family life. McKenzie draws attention to the problems of gender inequality that are often hidden when family group conferences are embraced as straightforwardly empowering. In fact there are several problematic features of FGC practice at ground level and McKenzie questions whether it is a suitable approach for export to non-settler societies. In Chapter 10, which looks at gender and residential care, Mark Smith considers the complexity of gender relations in residential care for children. He discusses the gendered identities of boys and girls and how these might play out in care institutions, and he tackles the positioning of male and female staff. He is keen to move beyond essentialist models of care and what he sees as the unhelpful concept of patriarchy. Smith seems to be more open than many social scientists to the possibility of some 'natural' differences between men and women, though most of his material is about the social construction of gender. Trish Walsh's chapter is both a broad consideration of therapeutic models of change and a discussion of a specific child protection case. She starts Chapter 11 by discussing the relative merits of attachment theory, crisis intervention and systems theory. She then goes on to describe in detail the case of 'Ben', a three-year-old who gets badly burnt, apparently when being showered by his older half-brother. She reflects on the therapeutic options for responding to this case, discussing various scenarios and their theoretical assumptions.

Walsh concludes that a narrow focus on maternal attachment would be less helpful than a more systemic approach which considers the roles of all relevant family members.

So the book's content is fairly diverse and wide-ranging. We hope it will be relevant to a range of different readers, including those with a professional interest, for example in social work or nursing, and those with a purely academic interest in the topic. In offering this edited collection we aim to reflect some of the diversity of thinking about gender, children and social policy that has been reviewed in this introductory chapter.

References

Beasley, C. (2005) *Gender and Sexuality: Critical Theories, Critical Thinkers.* London, Sage.

Charles, N., Davies, C. A. and Harris, C. (2008) *Families in Transition: Social Change, Family Formation and Kin Relationships.* Bristol, Policy Press.

Chodorow, N. (1978) *The Reproduction of Mothering: Psychoanalysis and the Sociology of Gender.* Berkeley, University of California Press.

Connell, R. W. (2002) *Gender.* Cambridge, Polity.

Connell, R. W. (2005) *Masculinities,* 2nd edn. Cambridge, Polity.

Connell, R. W., Hearn, J. and Kimmel, M. S. (2005) 'Introduction' in M. S. Kimmel, J. Hearn, and R. W. Connell, (eds.), *Handbook of Studies on Men and Masculinities.* London, Sage.

Connolly, P. (1998) *Racism, Gender Identities and Young Children.* London, Routledge.

Daniel, B. and Taylor, J. (1999) *Engaging Fathers.* London, Jessica Kingsley.

Daly, M. and Rake, K. (2003) *Gender and the Welfare State: Care, Work and Welfare in Europe and the USA.* Cambridge, Polity.

Delamont, S. (2001) *Changing Women, Unchanged Men? Sociological Perspectives on Gender in a Post-Industrial Society.* Buckingham, Open University Press.

Esping-Andersen, G. (1990) *The Three Worlds of Welfare Capitalism.* Cambridge, Polity.

Farmer, E. and Owen, M. (1998) Gender and the child protection process. *British Journal of Social Work,* 28: 545–64.

Fawcett, B., Featherstone, B. and Goddard, J. (2004) *Contemporary Child Care Policy and Practice.* Basingstoke, Palgrave.

Featherstone, B. (1997) What has gender got to do with it?: Exploring physically abusive behaviour towards children. *British Journal of Social Work*, 27: 419–33.

Featherstone, B. (2003) Taking fathers seriously. *British Journal of Social Work*, 33: 239–54.

Featherstone (2004) *Family Life and Family Support: A Feminist Analysis.* Basingstoke, Palgrave.

Featherstone, B. and Trinder, L. (1997) Familiar subjects? Domestic violence and child welfare. *Child and Family Social Work*, 2: 147–59.

Featherstone, B., Rivett, M. and Scourfield, J. (2007) *Working with Men in Health and Social Care.* London, Sage.

Frosh, S., Phoenix, A. and Pattman, R. (2002) *Young Masculinities.* Basingstoke, Palgrave.

Hartmann, H. (1978) The unhappy marriage of Marxism and feminism: towards a more progressive union. *Capital and Class*, 8: 1–33.

Hearn, J. and Pringle, K. (2006) Men, masculinities and children: some European perspectives. *Critical Social Policy*, 26 (2): 365–89.

Holland, S., Renold, E., Ross, N. and Hillman, A. (2008) The everyday lives of children in care: using a sociological perspective to inform social work practice. In B. Luckock, M. Lefevre (eds.), *Direct Work: Social Work With Children And Young People*, London, BAAF.

James, A. and James, A. (2004) *Constructing Childhood: Theory, Policy and Social Practice.* London, Palgrave Macmillan.

King, M. and Piper, C. (1995) *How the Law Thinks About Children*, 2nd edn. Aldershot, Arena.

Lewis, J. (1992) Gender and the development of welfare regimes. *Journal of European Social Policy*, 2 (3): 159–73.

Lindsay, D. (1994) *The Welfare of Children.* New York, Oxford University Press.

Lingard, B. (2003) Where to in gender policy in education after recuperative masculinity politics? *International Journal of Inclusive Education*, 7 (1): 33–56.

Lister, R. (2003) Investing in the citizen-workers of the future: transformations in citizenship and the state under New Labour. *Social Policy and Administration*, 37 (5): 427–43.

Morrow, V. (2006) Understanding gender differences in context: implications for young children's everyday lives. *Children and Society*, 20 (2): 92–104.

Oakley, A. (1998) Science, gender and women's liberation: an argument against postmodernism. *Women's Studies International Forum*, 21 (2): 133–46.

Parton, N. (1998) Risk, advanced liberalism and child welfare: the need to rediscover uncertainty and ambiguity. *British Journal of Social Work*, 28: 5–27.

Parton, N. (2006) *Safeguarding Childhood: Early Intervention and Surveillance in a Late Modern Society*. Basingstoke, Palgrave Macmillan.

Parton, N., Thorpe, D. and Wattam, C. (1997) *Child Protection: Risk and the Moral Order*. Basingstoke: Macmillan.

Pence, E. and Paymar, M. (1993) *Education Groups for Men who Batter: The Duluth Model*. New York, Springer.

Pringle, K. (1998) *Children and Social Welfare in Europe*. Buckingham, Open University Press.

Rivers I. (2000) Long-term consequences of bullying. In C. Neal and D. Davies (eds.), *Issues in Therapy with Lesbian, Gay, Bisexual and Transgender Clients*, Buckingham, Open University Press.

Roseneil, S. (2004) Why we should care about friends: an argument for queering the care imaginary in social policy. *Social Policy and Society*, 3 (4): 409–19.

Scourfield (2003) *Gender and Child Protection*. Basingstoke, Palgrave.

Scourfield, J., Dicks, B., Drakeford, M. and Davies, A. (2006) *Children, Place and Identity: Nation and Locality in Middle Childhood*. London, Routledge.

Sevenhuijsen, S. (1998) *Citizenship and the Feminist Ethics of Care: Feminist Considerations of Justice, Morality and Politics*. London, Routledge.

Shakespeare, T. (2000) The social relations of care. In G. Lewis, S. Gewirtz and J. Clarke (eds.), *Rethinking Social Policy*. London, Sage.

Tarlo, E. (2007) Hijab in London: metamorphosis, resonance and effects. *Journal of Material Culture* 12 (2): 131–56.

Weeks, J., Heaphy, B. and Donovan, C. (2001) *Same Sex Intimacies: Families of Choice and Other Life Experiments*. London, Routledge.

White, S. (1998) Interdiscursivity and child welfare: the ascent and durability of psycho-legalism. *Sociological Review*, 46 (2): 264–92.

Williams, F. (2004) *Rethinking Families*. London, Calouste Gulbenkian Foundation.

2

Exploring the Relationship between Gender and Child Health: A Comparative Analysis of High and Low Economic Resource Countries

Lorraine Green and Julie Taylor

This chapter examines the relationship between child health and gender through an analysis of relevant international multidisciplinary literature. Initially, the theoretical context is situated through an examination of the differences between the terms 'sex' and 'gender' and the positioning of gender as a socially constructed rather than a biologically innate phenomenon. The paucity of literature dealing with gender and child health is then evidenced and contrasted with research on gender and adult health. Gendered child health differentials and inequalities in the developing countries (of lower economic resource) are then considered, many of these arising from sexist cultural practices. These are juxtaposed against the substantively different and seemingly more subtle gender health differentials emerging in Western post-industrial nations (of higher economic resource).

The embryonic research analysed here reveals gender as highly significant in terms of children's self perceptions about health and health

Gender and Child Welfare in Society Edited by Brid Featherstone, Carol-Ann Hooper, Jonathan Scourfield, and Julie Taylor.

care, their cultural and social risk behaviours, and how they are perceived and treated by parents and professionals. Looking laterally at gender and child health also suggests it cannot be fully understood unless seemingly unrelated adult behaviour is taken into account, domestic violence being a key example of how both parental and professional gendered behaviour can impact negatively on children's health. In the conclusion the key themes are summarized and the surprising parallels between high and low economic resource countries are highlighted. The findings that emerge cumulatively reveal how globally gendered power significantly impacts upon the health of women (as child bearers and primary childcarers) and children, predominantly girls, in low economic resource countries. This discrimination is tangible and can be evidenced. However, to assume conversely gendered power does not have notable or enduring effects in countries of high economic resource, is misconceived. Although gendered discrimination and inequalities in child health are less visible in Western countries and there is less apparent overt physical force or violence used to discriminate against girls, more ideological and productive forms of gendered power (often involving identity and self surveillance) operate (Foucault, 1979; Bartky, 1990). These have unacknowledged and often unrecognized effects on the behaviour and beliefs of both adults and children, leading to significant but different gendered health risks/problems for both boys and girls.

Analysing sex and gender

The terms 'sex' and 'gender' are often regarded by the media and the general public as synonymous and interchangeable and are assumed to refer to biologically derived physical and personality differences between the sexes (Green, 2004). The social sciences since the 1970s have, however, clearly differentiated the two. Sex is seen as biological, that is as being defined by different reproductive systems and average physical differences. Gender, conversely, has been construed as the socially constructed perceived differences between the two sexes, in terms of personal characteristics, roles, identities and social position. Thus, men are assumed to be more rational, intellectual, aggressive, better leaders and 'tougher' than women; women, more caring, passive, irrational and emotionally vulnerable than men (Lindsey, 1990). More recent theorization, however, suggests it is harder to clearly divide sex and gender than was previously thought as our understanding of biological sex is based unequivocally upon our socially constructed and embodied experience of growing up gendered. It therefore may be impossible to conceptualize sex without overlaying it with our 'lived' and corporeal understandings of gender (Butler, 1990; 1993; Laqueur, 1990).

Most posited gendered differences of personality, intellect and behaviour are revealed as inaccurate or as having little statistical significance in Western countries, despite strenuous disciplinary and socialization practices encouraging conformity (Connell, 2002; Foucault, 1979). The one exception appears to be that Western men show more overt, unprovoked aggression than women (Connell, 2002), although Thorne's 1993 US study of schoolchildren found girls could be aggressive too, but in a more covert, less physical manner than boys. However, despite few strong statistical individual differences being discernable in the West, power structures associated with the social construction of global patriarchies seem to have a strong negative influence on women's life chances (Hearn, 1992). This occurs because men as a class have more power and resources than women and act through wider social systems and structures as well as individually (sometimes with limited awareness) to perpetuate that power and advantage. This behaviour is then reflected in gendered inequalities in poverty, employment, health and other spheres (Green, 2004). These inequalities are more pronounced in many countries of low economic resource, where females are devalued and subordinated consistently and are likely to live in poverty and receive inequitable resources, including health care resources.

Additionally, terms applied to one sex or another may indicate superficial manifestations from which deeper rooted differences are wrongly assumed to exist. For example, labelling women as the caring and emotional sex may reflect their greater socialized preparedness to expose vulnerability, as well as their work in caring and emotion within private and public spheres (Hochschild, 1983; Adkins, 1992), but not a biologically inevitable or desirable trait. If men are less likely to reveal distress publicly, it cannot be assumed they are inwardly unemotional. These problematic assumptions therefore need to be considered when analysing apparent sex and gender differences in child health, particularly help-seeking behaviour. For example, if boys do not report illness when questioned, it can not be assumed they are, or subjectively feel, in good health.

The absence of gender in child health literature and the importance of social constructionism

This section evidences the frequent absence of gender in literature and research about child health from most disciplinary/professional and policy perspectives. The complexity of the issue is then demonstrated by showing how a parochial analysis of the relationship between child health and gender is not sufficient for an in-depth understanding, but how social constructions of childhood also need to be incorporated into the equation.

Gender is frequently theoretically under-represented in discussions of adult health inequalities in Western nations in the health and medical literature, although there may be some statistical recording and discussion in relation to sex differences. Gender does, however, receive more theoretical attention in social science literature (for example, Wilkinson and Kitzinger, 1994; Foster, 1995). This focuses largely on female experience and disadvantage, relating to perceptions of health, access to treatment and the health care experience (for example, Doyal, 2001; Kuh and Hardy, 2003; Prior, 1999). This contrasts strongly with the generic health of 'mankind' being researched almost exclusively and 'invisibly' through the study of white men in biomedical research, with the findings often uncritically extrapolated to women, black people and children (Epstein, 2004). Increasing numbers of papers on men's health and gender are, however, now appearing in journals such as *Social Science and Medicine* with small specialist audiences. These show that men are very reluctant to seek help for health issues (Williams, 2007; Cranshaw, 2007), particularly for mental health problems and particularly if they are young men, because they feel it contravenes acceptable masculinity (O'Brien, Hunt and Hart, 2005). However, reluctance may be overturned if more valued aspects of masculinity, such as retaining one's ability to work in a prestigious occupation or restoring 'sexual performance', are considered. In addition, some of men's health problems are not linked to 'naturally occurring diseases' but to 'tough' masculine identities involving competitive risk taking (Doyal, 2001). These often manifest themselves in car accidents, male violence and substance misuse. Men in the United Kingdom are also nearly twice as likely to commit suicide as are women and are more likely to die from accidental or violent deaths than from disease or internal causes (National Statistics Online, 2004).

The expectation that literature searches of databases would elicit significant amounts of research and theorizing on children, gender and health was, consequently, not unreasonable, but this was not the case. Medical, nursing and social sciences literature databases, Medline, CINAHL and ASSIA, from between 1980 and 2008 were all extensively searched. Combination search terms were used in relation to title, keyword and abstract, such as health, illness, morbidity, mortality, well-being; gender, sex, sex differences; and children, childhood, adolescents, young people and youth. Very few relevant articles relating to Western countries were found, and health journals, including key nursing journals (see Taylor and Green, 2008), rarely considered gender as a major or a peripheral issue. Sex differences were occasionally superficially analysed in health and social science literature but were rarely accompanied by any understanding of gender as socially constructed, although there were occasional exceptions (for example, Sweeting, 1995; McCarthy et al., 2000). Searches by keyword were inadequate and more in-depth searches, online and offline, were necessary because of the paucity of literature available and the relative lack of nuanced themes or conclusions that could be drawn from it. Many journals and key texts or more specialist books (which dealt either partially or entirely with child health from a social science, or a more clinical, perspective) were therefore purposively sampled to ascertain whether gender was included. Different social constructions and understandings of childhood, of gender and of health and illness, discussed in the proceeding section, compound the difficulty of successful systematic searching.

Many public-health oriented books that were analysed took multifarious social, public-health and environmental concerns into consideration regarding children, such as fast food, pollution, bullying and dangerous roads, but often ignored gender as a variable (for example, Hall and Elliman, 2003). Similarly, popular clinical textbooks for health practitioners often seemed unaware of gender (for instance, Waterston, Helms and Platt, 2006; Glasper and Ireland, 2000; Gott and Moloney, 1994), with the exception of occasional chapters in edited books which looked at teenagers' sexual health (such as Smith, 2000; Rees et al. 2000). A relatively recent chapter in a multidisciplinary/multi-professional childhood studies textbook, written more from a social science than from a medical angle, analysed almost every conceivable social and environmental factor that might impact on young children's health (such as social class, poverty and unemployment, housing, diet, ethnicity, parenting and family diversity), but omitted gender (Kelly, 2004).

Gender-neutral research in relation to children's health and illness in the United Kingdom evidences that over the past 50 years child physical morbidity and mortality has declined, mainly due to the better environmental conditions and diet and to a lesser extent because of the eradication of many infectious diseases in countries of high economic resource (Pearn, 1997). Psychological illness, conversely, has increased over several decades (Roberts, 2002; Collishaw et al. 2004). This runs counter to morbidity and mortality rates in poorer countries, where poverty-linked resistant malaria, diarrhoea, malnutrition and HIV/AIDS contribute to high morbidity and mortality (Pearn, 1997). Poverty also exacerbates poor child health in the United Kingdom (Roberts, 2002, Department of Health, 2004). Deaths from external and domestic accidents remain the highest child killers in the United Kingdom after a child reaches 12 months of age; here, too, the likelihood of death from these causes is influenced by socio-economic status and poverty, as are neonatal and infant death rates (Roberts, 2002). Major risks in the paediatric literature are cited as asthma, allergies, to a lesser extent diabetes and also the possibility of obesity and related health risks (Pearn, 1997), but environmental and social health risks and the impact of gender, are rarely considered. One US study, however, found that culturally-influenced adolescent behaviours, such as sexual activity, substance use and smoking accounted for 74 per cent of the difference in healthy and unhealthy behaviours and that gender was a key factor (Kulbok and Cox, 2002). It therefore seems important that gendered attitudes and behaviour emanating from children, parents and professionals are analysed and that health risks are examined, as well as the impact of gender on specific illnesses and conditions.

Policy documents, such as the English *National Service Framework for Children, Young People and Maternity Services* (NSF) (a plan aiming at improving the quality and interconnectedness of health and social care services), seem to ally themselves with a perception of children as important in their own right (Department of Health, 2004). However, there is little understanding of children's embodied state (Mayall, 1998) and that their experience of pain is more conjoined than that of adults, or of possible sexed and gendered determinants of child health and illness (Green, 2006a). Adults very often invoke false binary distinctions between body and mind in their conceptualizations of pain and illness. However, children, particularly small children, who are less socialized into societal norms and ideas, are less dualistic (Prout, 2000). They may also be much more fixated by the experience of, for example, routine (but new and important to them) scratches and bruises on their bodies, experiences which adults often disregard and negate (Christensen, 2000), and gender may affect such behaviour.

The above points suggest the importance of incorporating into this analysis the socially constructed nature of childhood. This refers to constantly changing and often contradictory historical and cultural perceptions in relation to how adults represent childhood and treat children; adults' overall generational and structural power vis-à-vis children; and, ultimately, how these factors impact on children themselves (James, Jenks and Prout, 1998; Gittins, 1998; Wyness, 2000; Lee, 2001). The Dionysian and Apollonian conceptions of children, whereby children may be seen as corrupt or innocent and thus as requiring control or protection, or paradoxically both simultaneously (Jenks, 1996), are key examples. These binaries are also linked with whether children are seen as incomplete, passive, easily mouldable mini 'adults in waiting' or as competent, cognisant and agentic social actors. However, the social construction of childhood also needs to be understood in relation to other social constructions in this analysis – of health and illness and of gender. Coppock's (2002) work on the rise in diagnoses of attention deficit hyperactivity disorder (ADHD) in the United Kingdom and the United States, alongside the increased medicalization of children's behaviour, is an example of how society may be constructing notions of health. ADHD is a 'new' medical condition whose diagnostic validity and ontological existence has been challenged. Claims of vested agendas operating (in relation to the power and profit of multinational pharmaceutical companies) in conjunction with the often unchallenged hegemony of the medical model have been prevalent (Breggin, 1998). The apparent desire to control and pacify 'disruptive' children chemically rather than reflecting on what the potential structural or psychological causes of their difficulties might be, or what the long-term effects of using drugs such as Ritalin may be on children, is also of concern. ADHD therefore reflects the socially constructed nature of both childhood and health and illness. As will be discussed later, diagnoses of and responses to ADHD also tend to be influenced by both the gendered behaviour of children and the gendered preconceptions and judgements of adults.

Child health and gender in countries of low economic resource

Extensive demographic health surveys reveal gendered power is significant in terms of child health in developing countries and some of the developed countries (Hill and Upchurch, 1995). Not only may girls be directly and covertly discriminated against, but women may themselves be devalued and treated differentially, their subsequent poor health therefore impacting on the health status of born and unborn children of both sexes. In many countries of low economic resource, son preference and daughter devaluation has led to increased female morbidity and mortality. As well as being brought about through purposive female infanticide (gendercide) and sex selective abortion this is the result of generalized abuse and neglect of girls and mothers and of boys being more likely to receive medical attention than girls, (Renzetti and Curran, 1999; Seagor, 2003). This section of the chapter will consequently analyse issues associated with gender, nutrition and medical treatment and their impact. It will flag up and discuss the ambiguous and unclear relationship between greater societal or parental affluence and/or education and greater gender equality in child health care. The sexual exploitation of girls and young women and their greater propensity to develop the human immunodeficiency virus (HIV) is also examined, as are ongoing practices in some cultures of genital infibulation and of the marriage of girl children at such a young age that it may compromise their health.

In some countries, young women who require greater nutrition than men and boys because they are pregnant or breastfeeding do not receive it (Seipel, 1999). Studies from Albania, Nigeria, Nepal, Egypt, South India, the former Yugoslavia (and even Greece and Ireland), show that women, for a variety of reasons, eat less and more infrequently than men and boys. These practices are embedded in familial and societal structures of male dominance and female deference (Santow, 1995). The research of Khan et al. (1989) in Uttar Pradesh found baby girls were breastfed less often and less intensively than boys. If the first child was female the parents would immediately try for a son, and, if successful, wean the girl prematurely. If the first child was male, they would become sexually abstinent to protect him during the breastfeeding period. In Bangladesh, sequencing was also important, for although average mortality rates were 54 per cent higher for girls than boys, if girls had older sisters, it was 84 per cent greater, but only 14 per cent greater if they did not (Muhuri and Preston, 1991). Later research appears to confirm continuation of this pattern in rural China and in India (Li, 2004; Whitworth and Stephenson, 2002). This maltreatment of females is exacerbated by sexist, cultural and religious norms and practices. These include the one child policy in China, the dowry tradition in India and those practices invoked by religious fundamentalism in the Middle Eastern Crescent, although sometimes it is how the messages of religious texts are interpreted and culturally appropriated that may be the problem rather than the texts themselves. However, maltreatment varies cross-nationally and cross-culturally according to a number of factors.

One Indian study showed girls were overall less likely to be hospitalized than boys, controlling for all other factors, including health needs and that rising economic status and maternal education had little impact on gendered differences in hospitalization rates (Bhan et al., 2005). However, contradictorily, another Indian study showed girls with literate mothers were more likely to be immunized and receive a nutritious diet (Borooah, 2004). A further study in Kerala in India showed a link between greater overall gender equality and less gendered discrimination in health care from both parents and professionals, although gender bias did affect whether help was sought from allopathic or alternative health systems (Pillai et al., 2003). A study of China through the 1990s found prices and maternal education to be the most significant determinants of child immunization, but showed girls to be a highly vulnerable population as health costs rose (Xie and Dow, 2005). Holmes (2006) has optimistically suggested utilizing Alderman and Gertler's (1997) gender specific model of human capital investment in countries with significant gender disparities. Holmes contends, for example, that inequitable gendered distribution of food and medication could be mitigated by instituting policies which provide food subsidies and more accessible and affordable community health facilities. However, with rare exceptions, neither parental education nor elevated socio-economic status have been found to alleviate high rates of girl mortality and morbidity in developing countries (Hill and Upchurch, 1995; Seagor, 2003; Bhan et al., 2005). This suggests it is not only the accessibility and costs of food and resources that are important, but that wider and more entrenched cultural attitudes that devalue girls and condone their ill-treatment need to change substantially. Further the specific micro- and macro-context needs to be subject to rigorous examination.

The high incidence of children developing fetal HIV/AIDS, particularly in sub-Saharan Africa is also related to women's low status and men's assumed 'right' of sexual access without contraceptive use (Seagor, 2003). Cultural acceptance of men having multiple sexual partners, including prostitutes, is, furthermore, relevant to HIV transmission (De Bruyn, 1992). Additionally, some HIV positive men rape and infect babies because they claim sex with an unaffected child will cure them (McGreal, 2001), a practice similar to that of some men in Victorian England who justified the rape of children under the pretext of it curing them of syphilis. Young girls are perceived as safe sexual partners in the global sex trade, an ironically self-destructive abuse in the case of sub-Saharan Africa where orphaned girls are particularly prone to sexual exploitation and trafficking and thus to HIV infection. The skewed ratio of girls to boys in countries where gendercide is routinely practised has also led to a shortage of women and to increased kidnapping and sex trafficking of young girls (Seagor, 2003). Furthermore, studies in South Africa have shown HIV/AIDS and teenage pregnancies are exacerbated by teenage girls' sense of limited agency vis-à-vis men, and by mothers representing sex as a dangerous activity and proscribing open dialogue (Jewkes, Penn-Kekana, and Rose-Junius, 2005).

Girls in some countries often marry and become pregnant, according to cultural norms, at such a young age that their growth and development can be compromized and they can suffer nutritional and health risks (UNICEF, 1998). Even where the sexual health of girls is considered – for example, through the provision of sexual health clinics for teenagers in Northern Thailand – sexual double standards are evident. In Thailand, teenage girls, but not boys, have reported threatening, judgemental comments from service providers and violations of confidentiality (Tangmunkongvorakul, Kane and Wellings, 2005). Female circumcision is also practised in some developing countries (Seagor, 2003; McKie, 2003). This is a dangerous painful procedure, frequently performed in unsanitary conditions and without anaesthetic. Its aim is to eradicate female sexual satisfaction and limit female infidelity. It can also engender significant health problems through the girls' lives and pose risks to unborn children and to the mothers during childbirth (Santow, 1995). Although adult initiation into some tribal cultures may for boys involve circumcision, this is rarely as dangerous, with the exception of the Ghisu in Eastern Uganda. There circumcision is regarded as a phenomenally painful, gruelling experience, it is only inflicted on older youths, who are thought to be able to stand the pain, and involves not only cutting the foreskin but also removing the subcutaneous fat around the *glans* penis (Heald, 1982).

Child health and gender in high economic resource countries

Elevated girl mortality and morbidity rates in countries of low economic resource are to some extent acknowledged by the wealthier nations, even if there is little understanding of the socially constructed nature of gender. However, there has been little research into the impact of gender upon children's health in countries of high economic resource. This could be linked to recognizing inequality solely in terms of social class morbidity and mortality differentials (Townsend and Davidson, 1980; Acheson, 1998), as gender differences within socio-economic inequalities, even with adults, have largely been ignored (Matthews, Manor and Power, 1999). However, other potential reasons could include the dominant biomedical model within health, which treats multilayered social factors as peripheral. Children could additionally be incorrectly assumed to be sex/gender undifferentiated prior to puberty, despite the fact that their peers and adults display and police gendered behaviour. Also, because females in most wealthy countries 'appear' symbolically and through law to have gender, educational and occupational equality with males (Connell, 2002), then gendered practices and inequalities in child health may be disregarded or inaccurately assumed not to exist, particularly given that they are not as easy to detect as the stark sex/gender differences in physical morbidity and mortality in less resourced countries.

Research looking at the interaction between race/ethnicity and sex and gender in Western countries shows an equalizing impact upon child physical health in some areas but not others. One study of white British and British Asian children found no sex differences in immunization rates (Martineau, White and Bhopal, 1997). This could suggest greater gender equality in the migrant country which is taken on board by Asian families but could also be more pragmatically related to access and free immunization in the United Kingdom, or conversely more official child health monitoring and surveillance, or a combination of all these factors. Female circumcision, often referred to as female genital mutilation (FGM), also occurs in Western countries which have migrant populations from countries where it is the norm. In the United Kingdom an estimated 4,000 girls per year are subjected to FGM; despite the fact that it has been banned since 1985 and that there has recently been stringent legislation and policy and practice guidance not a single prosecution has occurred. The problem is so acute in France that in areas with high African populations girls are medically examined annually (Kasekei, 2007).

The majority of this section of the chapter will now deal with purported but unclear gender differences in health, particularly psychological health, showing how difficult it is to come to a firm conclusion as to whether it is boys or girls who suffer the most ill health physically or psychologically either before or after adolescence. The complexities and methodological difficulties in reaching firm conclusions in relation to sex/gender differences and the barriers to doing so will be evident. Gendered practices which could lead to psychological and physical ill health are also analysed, such as girls' preoccupations with body image and weight and the linked disordered eating practices and boys' reluctance to seek help when ill and their dangerous risk-taking practices linked to hegemonic constructions of masculinity. Research demonstrating gendered and sexualized bullying of both girls and gender atypical girls and boys may also impact upon the victims' psychological and physical health, and this body of evidence is also therefore seen as important.

One relevant, but now dated, hallmark review article analysed multidisciplinary and official 'Western' literature relating to sex/gender differences in child health, concentrating on children between 7 and 15 years of age. It revealed that, according to referral to health services and documented illnesses, young boys seemed to suffer more illness than girls. From adolescence onwards girls then predominated, particularly with psychological illness (Sweeting, 1995). A later empirical study examining sex differences in health at 11, 13 and 15 in a large Scottish school-based cohort, presented further evidence that between 11 and 15 a significant female excess in general psychological ill health, as well as poor self-rated physical health emerges, which intensifies by age 15 (Sweeting and West, 2002). Sweeting (1995) herself, however, tentatively suggested that boys may suffer as much psychological illness as girls but manifest it in different ways, for example, via excess alcohol or drug consumption or violence.

Recent cross-national statistical analysis of 29 European and North American countries also shows higher prevalence of reported subjective physical and psychological ill health in adolescent girls across all countries. However, the relationship is mediated strongly both by higher ratings on the Gender Development Index (GDI), which focuses on achievements in the areas of education, health and income, and by overall greater political and social gender equality, with a much slighter gender difference and lower number of reported complaints for boys and girls in countries with higher levels of both. This suggests greater gender equality is beneficial for boys and girls (Torsheim et al., 2006). In the United Kingdom, another large-scale statistical research project on the mental health of 5–15-year-olds involved 10,348 structured interviews with children, parents and professionals. It showed the proportion of 'medically diagnosable' mental disorder overall was greater for boys (10 per cent in those aged 5–10 and 13 per cent in those aged 10–15) than girls (6 per cent and 10 per cent, relatively). Rates of emotional disorders, according to the WHO International Classification of Diseases standard diagnostic manual (10th revision) (ICD-10) classifications, were fairly similar, but boys were twice as likely to have conduct disorders. Mental health was also affected by other factors including social class, income and housing, ethnicity and family structure and the interaction between gender and these factors (Meltzer and Gatward, 2000). A US study also suggested that children's mental health may be mediated not only by gender but also by a complex but unclear relationship involving both ethnicity and parental gender. This study, involving 2,966 respondents with an average mean age of 15 years, found that the degree of closeness in the father–daughter relationship strongly impacted on the daughter's suicidal ideation, regardless of race or age. However, with boys, a father's influence declined with age and there were differences according to race (Liu, 2005). Closeness with the mother had little effect except with Asian American girls.

There is some contested literature that suggests younger boys are more genetically vulnerable than girls to physical illness prior to adolescence (Schaffer, 1996). This could explain their over-representation in official statistics, and if this is the case it may apply to low economic resource countries too. Therefore, young boys may be taken for medical attention by parents when they need (but do not necessarily want) to go. Conversely, following the pattern of countries of low economic resource, they may be given preferential attention and medical treatment in comparison to their female peers. However, it may also be that the putative neglect of girls is not illuminated in statistics because illnesses and health problems in wealthier nations are generally less severe and life threatening than in poorer countries. What little gender sensitive research has been conducted suggests younger and older boys are less likely than girls to admit to pain or ask for help regarding health problems (Mayall, 1994; Brannen et al., 1994; Benjamin, 2001). Adolescent males may, therefore, have significant physical and psychological problems but be less likely to disclose them because of their increasing autonomy as teenagers, alongside their striving towards hegemonic (powerful and preferred) masculine identities and behaviours (Connell, 1995). Health problems may, then, only be identified in extreme situations, such as in life threatening illnesses, conduct disorders and suicide attempts, or where alcohol/substance abuse or risk-taking masculine behaviour engenders serious consequences (Connell, 2002), thus paralleling the previous research with adult males.

A recent statistical 25-year study of 15–16 year olds, using three general population samples and examining them at three different time points, 1974, 1986 and 1999, confirmed that psychological problems had increased in both sexes and amongst all social classes and ethnicities by 70 per cent, but that boys were more likely than girls to have 'conduct disorders' or behavioural problems (Collishaw et al., 2004). These studies suggest boys rarely voluntarily request help, and it is only when their issues adversely affect others that they are noticed. However, even conduct disorders, such as ADHD, have been shown to be influenced by gendered diagnoses. Girls are more likely to be seen as suffering from or diagnosed with ADHD when actually exhibiting different symptoms fewer boys and fewer of them (Abikoff et al., 2002; Bluhm, Nolfi and Sciutto, 2004; Jackson and King, 2004), possibly because disruptive behaviour is 'naturalized' and more tolerated from boys than girls. It is also important not to assume such behaviour always masks psychological problems or that they can be used to justify it. Rising rates of suicide amongst young men in the last decades of the twentieth century in the United Kingdom (Benjamin, 2002) suggested undetected psychological problems. A recent time-trend study, however, asserts that since the 1990s rates of suicide in young men have declined generally, and study shows that this is so in all the common methods of suicide amongst this group, by 2005 they were at their lowest level (Biddle et al., 2008). Risk-taking behaviour linked to approved masculinity and resulting in poor health and accidents is also a major health issue. In a 26-country study, the highest causes of mortality for 15–34-year-old males were motor vehicle accidents, murder and suicide. Adolescence was the time when these fatal risk behaviours began to be prominent (Heuveline and Slap, 2002). In another Italian study, risky driving behaviours were particularly pertinent between the ages of 14 and 17 for boys and were also accompanied by other risky behaviours (Bina, Graziano and Bonino, 2006).

No evidence exists to suggest women are more constitutionally vulnerable to psychological or physical problems than men (Busfield, 1996). However, biological differences may converge with gendered inequalities to exacerbate girls' health problems. For example, if women's and girls' greater biological predisposition to sexually transmitted diseases (STDs) is coupled with social constraints, such as little power to control sexual access or the use of contraception, it poses a serious health risk. Sexual health is one rare area where sociological research in the United Kingdom has documented teenaged girls' increased psychological and physical health risks. These relate to coerced sex and a lack of mutuality. Such factors linked to a sexual double standard and female fears about acquiring a 'bad' reputation' then lead to lower expectations of personal sexual pleasure, esteem and agency and result in increased STDs and unwanted pregnancies, which are also often class related (Lees, 1993; Halson, 1991; Holland, 1998). Single teenage mothers are often also stigmatized by the media and within political rhetoric. Such problems are exacerbated in countries such as Ireland where religiously based moral conservatism leads to women having less reproductive autonomy than in other Western European countries (Smyth, 2006).

Sweeting (1995) notes that the area of psychopathology in the United Kingdom with the greatest adolescence sex difference and potentially serious health consequences is that of eating disorders, with 90 per cent of patients being female. Also, currently emerging research increasingly suggests strong links between gender, body image and disordered eating/eating disorders, even with very young children (Smolak and Murnen, 2004; Phares et al., 2004). One Swedish study showed that being female and overweight at both 16 and 21 was related to lower future work and class position for girls, but not boys, suggesting girls' prioritization of body image reflects the reality of their social context (Hammerstrom and Janlert, 2005). Many teenage boys also tend to see positive mental health as equating with self achievement, whereas girls associate it with a slender body image (Armstrong, Hill and Secker, 2001) to the extent that some girls are now reported as taking steroids to achieve this (*Sunday Times*, 20 June, 2005). Teenage boys are more likely than girls to associate health with fitness and to engage with sport and attend sports centres (Brannen, Dodd, Oakley and Storey, 1994). In Iceland, where organized sport is still primarily organized by men and targets men and boys, girls' lower involvement accounted for their much lower overall physical activity (Vilhjalmsson and Kristjansdottir, 2003).

Girls' overwhelmingly socially-influenced concern with body image and weight may therefore only mirror society's own messages, conveying girls' accurate understandings of the enduring social and economic, as well as health disadvantages associated with being overweight and female. The advantages that having a 'thin' eating disorder can bring may therefore be seen to outweigh the different disadvantages and health risks associated with such a disorder. Thus a double bind and paradoxical situation emerges for girls, whereby appearance and sexual desirability become a key indicator of global self-esteem. This is not to say 'eating' disorders are not relevant for boys, but they are less frequent and tend to emerge when boys are objectively overweight or do not conform to notions of hegemonic masculinity or heterosexuality (Muise, Stein and Arbess, 2003).

Some studies also suggest an interaction between gender and ethnicity when looking at problematic eating and body image. A rare statistical British study examining overweight 5–7-year-old children born between 1991 and 1999 in East Berkshire found although statistically boys as a group were more overweight than girls, South Asian boys were markedly more overweight or clinically obese than both South Asian girls and white boys (Balakrishnan, Webster and Sinclair, 2008). Although hypothetical reasons for increasing obesity in South Asian child populations in the United Kingdom were posited, such as diet change related to migration, there is no attempt to explain why boys might be more at risk than girls generally or any discussion of the interaction between gender and race/ethnicity. One possible explanation could again be son preference, demonstrated in more food being given to boys, as is the case in the low economic resource countries (or possibly it is because of a lack of constraining parental behaviours in relation to boys and dietary intake). A US study based on a national longitudinal dataset of adolescents' health involving 4,100 males and 4,302 females additionally found not only that at a mean age of 14.9 years adolescent girls were significantly more likely to be dieting than their male counterparts, but that Hispanic and white girls were more likely to be dieting (at 58 per cent and 55.2 per cent) than their African American counterparts (51.1 per cent) (Field et al., 2007). Girls who dieted were also likely to have higher BMI ratings and be more at risk of obesity later in the study than those not dieting. The ethnic pattern of males mirrored that of the girls, but overall, and according to each ethnic group, a much smaller proportion of boys were dieting. These findings would seem to fit with earlier studies suggesting greater tolerance of larger body size by African American females, ironically alongside high dissatisfaction with their bodies (Wilfley et al., 1996; Caldwell, Brownell and Wilfley, 1997) but accompanied by more accurate perceptions than white women of the body shape men typically find attractive (Demarest and Allen, 2000). Although these were studies from the United States similar issues may be relevant in the United Kingdom. Such evidence suggests that in the current climate, where there is almost hysterical concern about a rise in obesity amongst children and young people, unless policy makers and practitioners respond to such difficulties in a gender and ethnically sensitive manner, they may merely exacerbate the problem, and one form of disordered eating may be replaced by another.

Girls' concerns about, and negative views of, their bodies were further fuelled by the gendered treatment they received from peers and adults in other areas. A UK study of menarche showed it to be a lonely, shameful and unsettling experience for many girls where it remained a guarded private secret between mother and daughter, or amongst close friends. Girls reported being teased by boys about menstruation, an experience worsened by societal messages such as menstruation being 'a curse', unclean and polluting (Prendergast, 2000). An ethnographic study of primary school children in the United Kingdom further revealed extensive gendered, heterosexist and homophobic bullying. Boys pulled the bra strings of 9/10-year-old developing girls, pummelled girls' breasts and called them names such as 'big tits', 'period bag' and 'slag', although girls were frequently too embarrassed to report such harassment (Renold, 2002). Gender atypical children (both boys and girls) have also been found to endure significant bullying and harassment from their peers along homophobic and transphobic lines (Wilson et al., 2005). These studies seem to offer further evidence that girls are bombarded with constraining, controlling and negative gendered images about their bodies, which could impact severely on their psychological and physical health. Boys who do not conform to notions of hegemonic heterosexual masculinity could similarly suffer psychological and physical problems. It therefore seems very difficult to come to a conclusion as to whether Western boys or girls suffer more physical or psychological health problems, but the studies presented and analysed above do seem to provide emerging evidence that gender and the social context are very important factors in relation to child and adolescent health, and help-seeking behaviour.

A lateral look at gender and child health in the West: analysing the gendered behaviour of relevant adults and its impact on child health

Although gender discrimination and inequalities impacting on child health do not seem so overt in Western countries, their impact is still highly significant, as the previous section evidenced. If one looks more obliquely at issues of gender in terms of gendered parental and professional behaviours, then further problematic and somewhat surprising issues emerge. For example, sex selection via termination appears rare and is banned in many high resource countries (although public opinion in the United States surveys show it is increasingly seen as more acceptable, and that boys are favoured over girls, see Renzetti and Curran, 2003). Furthermore, in an online survey of assisted reproductive technology clinics in the United States (190 clinics responded), 42 per cent had offered non-medical sex selection to parents (Baruch, Kaufman and Hudson, 2007). This section therefore examines the gendered health maintenance and care behaviour of both parents and child health/welfare professionals and its impact on child health, as well as taking two examples of violent and frequently gendered behaviour, domestic violence and child sexual abuse, to show their impact on the children concerned and their health.

Women, predominantly mothers (Mayall, 1994) but also health and social care professionals (Robb, 2004) such as nurses, doctors and social workers, are disproportionately involved in training children to acquire health care skills, monitoring children's health and dealing with health care and related social problems. Historically, school health education also seems to have been focused on predominantly working-class girls and 'body work' in relation to hygiene, childcare femininity and housewifery as Pilcher (2007) shows through her socio-historical documentary analysis of official health education publications and reports from 1870 to the late 1970s. Girls' bodies are also positioned as troublesome in later documents in relation to puberty, sexuality, contraception and 'venereal disease'. Brannen et al. (1994) and Brannen and Storey (1996), in their more contemporary sociological, family-situated research on the health and general well-being of children aged 11–12 and 15–17, found mothers were overwhelmingly responsible for children's overall care, health and ill health. Fathers were neither expected to contribute nor actively did so, except on very rare occasions.

Mothers, in one study of chronic childhood illness, were the main childcarers but ironically exhibited less confidence when dealing with their children and, more understandably, greater fatigue than their husbands (Knafl and Zoeller, 2000), evidencing gendered parental inequality in child health care and differential understandings of what that care involves. A US study involving 22 interviews with fathers of chronically ill children found they were profoundly emotionally affected by their children's illness and saw it as a reason to be more involved in a broad range of parenting behaviours. The findings from this study, however, do not necessarily contradict the previous study's findings, as many felt the mother was 'naturally' the most important parent and did not claim to be the primary carer or to share parenting equally (McNeill, 2007). A recent review of the literature in relation to gender and parenting a child with a health problem showed more evidence of anxiety and mental health problems in mothers, although, as the previous discussion has shown, fathers may manifest their distress in different ways. Mothers had high expectations in relation to their childcare role which the fathers did not have. Mothers also dealt with stress differently, through seeking emotional support, whereas fathers often utilized more cognitive and action/task-oriented strategies (Pelchat, Lefebvre and Levert, 2007). Another study revealing the importance of the interaction between race/ethnicity and gender in parental care was a qualitative study of 10 Canadian mothers of African and Caribbean descent, raising children with sickle cell disease (SCD). The daily challenges mothers endured around fears for their children's health were exacerbated not only by 'a perceived gendered parenting role expectation that mothers endure most of the caregiving responsibilities and stress' but by the societal stigma linked to SCD and by racism (Burnes et al., 2008).

More research needs to be conducted in the area of how parents and professionals respond to and deal with children's health and overall well-being in gendered ways in relation to chronic and acute illnesses as well as everyday illness and health care more generally. Boys seem to face less parental surveillance and constraint than girls. This could lead to parents condoning, or perhaps unwittingly encouraging, boys' masculine competitive, risk-taking behaviours, without an awareness of the potentially negative health consequences. Boys' sexual health and education within the family furthermore tends to be left to fathers, and it is often neglected (Brannen et al., 1994; Brannen and Storey, 1996). This neglect could be related to boys' expectations and the taking of responsibility in relation to sexuality and the impact and influence this also has on girls and their male peers.

Domestic violence, a disproportionately male to female phenomenon, also represents a huge problem in countries of both high (McKie, 2003) and low (Seagor, 2003) economic resource. It impacts psychologically on the children, is often perpetrated during pregnancy and can cause miscarriage (Richardson et al., 2002). Children in families in which domestic violence takes place are also more likely to be directly abused or neglected (Humphreys, 2001). UK studies of health visitors (McKie, 2003; Peckover, 2002) found that these predominantly female professionals received little support, organizationally or from direct line management, for dealing with families in which men perpetrate domestic violence, although they are ideally placed to investigate and support women and children. As a result of the men's aggression, combined with little agency support or guidance, such professionals frequently avoided the men's responsibility and culpability. They tended to focus solely on the women's ability to protect and care for their children in isolation from the violence. Such behaviour not only relates to issues of fairness but suggests a failure to directly address the risk involved. Male social workers also tend to distance themselves from male service users' violence, except if intervening in a 'heroic macho manner' as protector of female social workers. This may encourage, not defuse, further potential violence, whilst simultaneously disempowering the female professionals (Green, Parkin and Hearn, 2001; Christie, 2006). It is clear that, internationally, major societal shifts in attitude, practices and effective legislation are necessary to really make a difference. The situation is not helped by research which demonstrates that even in countries of high economic resource, many women as well as men believe it is acceptable for men to hit their partners (Seagor, 2003).

Child abuse, particularly child sexual abuse, which has significant probabilistic links to poor psychological and physical health through the lifespan, has also been found to have a number of gendered facets. Men are disproportionately (90 per cent or more) more likely to be perpetrators than women (May-Chahal, 2006) and employ gendered characteristics in the abuse, such as aggression. Girls are statistically more likely to be abused than boys and are often eroticized in a gendered manner, although rates of abuse for boys are still highly significant (Green, 2006b). Furthermore, recent research from the United States involving undergraduates asserts that the relationship between child sexual abuse and poor adult mental health is not gender specific and that males are no less affected than females (Young et al., 2007). How children and adults, including professionals, interpret and understand the abuse in relation to constructions of gender is, however, important for detection and recovery (Hooper and Warwick, 2006). For example, a boy may not disclose because he feels being abused reveals weakness or because he fears being labelled homosexual by peers and adults and subsequently victimized and harassed. The findings from research into abuse in residential children's homes, albeit an atypical setting, showed in this institutional microcosm these fears were borne out (Green, Parkin and Hearn 2001).

The ability of even well-educated health and welfare professionals to deal with gender discrimination effectively is also cast into doubt by Hunter's (2005) work on the ambivalence, defended subjectivities and psychological defence mechanisms employed by health professionals to deny or suppress how sexism impacted upon them personally in their workplaces. Such research suggests some women may behave similarly to some men through semiconsciously accepting and internalizing discrimination against them, and thus are at risk of simultaneously perpetuating it against others.

Conclusion and Implications

To summarize the key themes, in many countries of low economic resource, girls receive iniquitous health care, but they can often also be aborted, neglected, raped, starved, contract STDs or be genitally mutilated, all of which occur in the wider context of gross gendered social and economic inequalities. Where health care and other resources are limited, these practices are pronounced. However, even when greater parental education and affluence and sufficient health resources are present, girls do not always receive equal treatment. Also, teenage girls generally feel unable to refuse men's sexual advances or insist on the use of condoms. These discriminatory practices and their manifestations and effects generally have high visibility. The research focus in low income resource countries therefore seems to be different from high resource countries insofar as it often concentrates on overt discriminatory gendered practices, frequently associated with physical violence or deliberate neglect. These tangible practices tend to have concrete effects and are often statistically measurable. More covert gendered practices – for example, childhood psychological difficulties impacted upon by gender – may be neglected because they are more difficult to research or because of limited awareness. It could also be argued that the most discriminatory practices in low resource countries need to be challenged before seemingly less pressing areas can be researched. However, as this chapter has shown, unless gendered ideologies and practices are challenged successfully on a wider societal scale, in terms of both attitudes and enforceable legislation, then it may be difficult to eradicate even the more tangible manifestations of gender inequality.

In post-industrial Western countries, although girls do not seem to receive inequitable health resources there are still significant, but more covert, problems. Ironically, eating disorders predominate in Western countries, particularly amongst teenage girls, but increasingly amongst some younger girls, who continually monitor weight or starve themselves despite having adequate food. This behaviour is related to women's societal subordination alongside the emphasis the media place on an emaciated pre-adolescent image as being the pinnacle of adult female beauty and identity. Sexual health and mutuality within sexual practices in Western countries are also significantly affected by gendered power inequalities, the corresponding sexual double standard and the different expectations boys and girls hold of their responsibilities and of what sex is or should be about.

Although methodological and definitional problems abound and research findings are contradictory as to whether it is girls or boys who are likely to be more at risk, both adolescent girls and boys in Western societies appear to be experiencing an increase in psychological difficulties. These problems may be partially linked to increasing individualization within high modernity and the stress associated with uncertain transitions between childhood and adulthood (Furlong and Cartmel, 2007). However, how these stresses are experienced and manifest themselves is gendered, as is whether they are expressed internally or externally and whether help is sought. With boys, macho stereotypes which focus on concealing vulnerability (including health problems), and on unnecessary risk taking, for example fast car driving and proving bravery in the peer group context, need to be addressed, and their links to health and illness made explicit. Domestic violence and child sexual abuse are also gendered phenomena predicated on power inequalities. These have significant implications for the health of both boys and girls, how they express health and distress, as well as for the health and parenting capabilities of parents, particularly mothers.

Patriarchal violence and control (and their direct as well as trickle-down effects) have therefore been a key global theme, whether or not such violence is covert or overt, intended or unintended, or is manifested structurally or individually. The clear parallels between high and low economic resource countries, in terms of the end product of gendered disadvantage in relation to child health, are surprising and hitherto unnoticed. The minimal sexual agency of young females in the wealthy nations bears striking resemblance to teenage girls' experiences in lower economic resource countries, although HIV is currently less prevalent. Furthermore, sex selection via termination and *in vitro* fertilization (IVF) is requested and practised in some wealthier nations, although it attracts little attention and discussion compared to low resource countries. A preference for male children therefore exists in many countries, although is not necessarily universal. Men also disproportionately sexually abuse both male and female children globally, although research agendas, media representations and considerations differ across countries. The well-documented fact that it is predominantly men who are the perpetrators of violence is rarely made explicit and therefore questions about why these men are violent and how such behaviour may be prevented are rarely directly asked. Baby girls are still found to be fed less and less often in some European countries as well as in many lower economic resource countries, and a not insignificant number of girls are subjected to genital mutilation in Europe, despite increasingly stringent legislation. Furthermore, although there is no economic reason why teenage girls should be starving in high economic resource societies, many actually are because of ideological and societal messages that place value on Western women largely according to prescribed ideals in appearance.

The research analysed here suggests the relationship between gender and child health is of paramount significance for health and social care academics, professionals and policy makers globally. However, social work practitioners and academics in the United Kingdom are increasingly subsumed under the rubric of health care (and therefore medicine) in terms of policy and education, despite different disciplinary origins, methodological preferences and debates about what constitutes evidence or worthwhile knowledge (Barnes, Green and Hopton, 2007). It is therefore possible that this ongoing process may lead to the neglect of a holistic social science perspective which embraces gender within a wider social context. The paucity of current research also indicates specific prescriptive suggestions for different professionals, academics and policy makers are difficult to give. In terms of responding appropriately and professionally to child health, at the very least an understanding of sex and gender and social and structural patriarchies needs to be present, alongside a willingness to challenge gendered and generational power abuse and inequalities. To be successful, organizational, legislative and societal support also needs to be available. However, if we believe that gender issues and inequalities exist in society for children in the same way that socioeconomic and cultural disparities do, and that gender is an important explanatory factor in child health, then we have a duty to explore further the theoretical, practice and policy-based consequences and implications.

References

Abikoff, H. B., Jensen, P. S., Arnold, E. L., et al. (2002) Observed classroom behaviour of children with ADHD: Relationship to gender and comorbidity. *Journal of Abnormal Child Psychology*, 30: 349–59.

Acheson, D. (1998) *Independent Inquiry into Health Inequalities: The Acheson Report.* London, Stationery Office.

Adkins, L. (1992) Sexual work and the employment of women in service industries. In M. Savage and A. Witz (eds.), *Gender and Bureaucracy.* Oxford, Blackwell.

Armstrong, C., Hill, M., Secker, J. (2001) Young people's perceptions of mental health. *Children and Society*, 14: 60–72.

Balakrishnan, R., Webster, P. and Sinclair, D. (2008) Trends in overweight and obesity among 5–7 year old white and South Asian children born between 1991 and 1999. *Journal of Public Health*, 30 (2): 139–44.

Barnes, H. M., Green, L. and Hopton, J. (2007) Guest editorial. Social work theory, research, policy and practice – challenges and opportunities in health and social care integration. *Health and Social Care in the Community*, 15 (3): 191–4.

Bartky, S. (1990) *Femininity and Domination: Studies in the Phenomenology of Oppression*. London, Routledge.

Baruch, S., Kaufman, D. Hudson, K. L. (2007) Genetic testing of embryos: practices and perspectives of U.S. IVF clinics. *Fertility and Sterility* available online 19 September 2007 (doi:10.1016/j.fertnstert.2007.05.048).

Benjamin, A. (2001) The weaker sex: health services fail to reach young men. *Guardian Unlimited* (12 December 2001).

Benjamin, A. (2002) Open to change: Novel ways of reaching out to young men in Dorset have helped to reverse suicide rates. *Guardian Unlimited* (6 November 2002).

Bhan, G., Bhandari N., Taneja S., *et al.* (2005) The effects of maternal education on gender bias in care-seeking from common childhood illnesses. *Social Science and Medicine*, 60: 715–24.

Biddle, L., Brock, A., Brookes, S. T. and Gunnell, D. (2008) Suicide rates in young men in England and Wales in the 21st century: Time trend study. *BMJ*, 336: 539–42.

Bina, M., Graziano, F. and Bonino, S. (2006) Risky driving and lifestyles in adolescence. *Accident Analysis and Prevention*, 38: 472–81.

Bluhm, C., Nolfi, C. J., Sciutto, M. J. (2004) Effects of child gender and symptom type on referrals for ADHD on elementary school teachers. *Journal of Emotional and Behavioural Disorders*, 12: 247–53.

Borooah, V. K. (2004) Gender bias among children in India in their diet and immunisation against disease. *Social Science and Medicine*, 58: 1719–31.

Brannen, J., Dodd, K., Oakley, A., Storey, P. (1994) *Young People, Health and Family Life*. Buckingham, OUP.

Brannen, J. and Storey, P. (1996) *Child Health in Social Context*. London, Health Education Authority.

Breggin, P. (1998) *Talking back to Ritalin: What Doctors Aren't Telling You About Stimulants for Children*. Monroe, Common Courage Press.

Burnes, D. P. R., Antle, B. J., Williams, C. C. and Cook, L. (2008) Mothers raising children with sickle cell disease at the intersection of race, gender, and illness stigma. *Health and Social Work*, 33 (3): 211–20.

Busfield, J. (1996) *Men, Women and Madness: Understanding Gender and Mental Disorder*. Basingstoke, Palgrave Macmillan.

Butler, J. (1990) *Gender Trouble: Feminism and the Subversion of Identity.* London, Routledge.
Butler, J. (1993) *Bodies That Matter: On the Discursive Limits of Sex.* London, Routledge.
Caldwell, M. B., Brownell, K. D. and Wilfley, D. E. (1997) Relationship of weight, body dissatisfaction and self esteem in African American and white female dieters. *International Journal of Eating Disorders*, 22: 127–30.
Christensen, P. H. (2000) Childhood and the cultural constitution of vulnerable bodies. In A. Prout (ed.), *The Body, Childhood and Society.* Basingstoke, Macmillan.
Christie, C. (2006) Negotiating the uncomfortable intersections between gender and professional identities in social work. *Critical Social Policy*, 26: 390–411.
Collishaw, S., Vaughan B., Goodman R and Pickles A. (2004) Time trends in adolescent mental health. *Journal of Child Psychology and Psychiatry*, 45: 1350–62.
Connell, R. (1995) *Masculinities.* Cambridge, Polity.
Connell, R. (2002) *Gender.* Cambridge, Polity.
Coppock, V. (2002) Medicalising children's behaviour. In B. Franklin (ed.), *The New Handbook of Children's Rights.* London, Routledge.
Cranshaw, P. (2007) Governing the healthy male citizen: Men, masculinity and poor health in *Men's Health* magazine. *Social Science and Medicine*, 65 (8): 1606–18.
De Bruyn, M. (1992) Women and AIDS in developing countries. *Social Science and Medicine*, 34: 249.
Department of Health (2004) *National Service Framework for Children, Young People and Maternity Services.* London, Department of Health.
Demarest, J. and Allen, R. (2000) Body image: Gender, ethnic and age differences. *The Journal of Social Psychology*, 140 (4): 465–72.
Doyal, L. (1999) *Women and Health Services: An Agenda for Change.* Buckingham, Open University Press.
Doyal, L. (2001) Sex, gender and health: The need for a new approach. *BMJ*, 323: 1061–3.
Epstein, S. (2004) Bodily differences and collective identities: The politics of gender and race in biomedical research in the United States. *Body and Society*, 10: 183–203.
Field, A. E., Aneja, P., Shrier, L. A., de Moor, C. and Gordon-Larsen, P. (2007) Race and gender differences in the association of dieting and gains in BMI among young adults. *Obesity*, 15 (2): 456–64.
Foster, P. (1995) *Women and the Healthcare System: An Unhealthy Relationship.* Buckingham, Open University Press.
Foucault, M. (1979) *Discipline and Punish.* London, Penguin.

Furlong, A. and Cartmel, F. (2007) *Young People and Social Change: New Perspectives.* Buckingham, Open University Press.

Gittins, D. (1998) *The Child in Question.* Basingstoke, Macmillan.

Glasper, A. and Ireland, L. (eds.) (2000) *Evidence Based Child Health Care: Challenges for Practice.* Basingstoke, Macmillan.

Gott, M. and Moloney, B. (eds.) (1994) *Child Health: A Reader.* Oxford, Radcliffe Medical Press.

Green, L. (2004) *Gender.* In G. Taylor and G. Spencer. (eds.), *Social Identity: Multidisciplinary Approaches.* London, Routledge.

Green, L. (2005) Theorising sexuality, sexual abuse and residential children's homes: Adding gender to the equation. *British Journal of Social Work*, 35 (4): 453–81.

Green, L. (2006a) An unhealthy neglect? Examining the relationship between child health and gender in research and policy. *Critical Social Policy*, 26 (2): 450–66.

Green, L. (2006b) An overwhelming sense of injustice? An exploration of child sexual abuse in relation to the concept of justice. *Critical Social Policy*, 26: 74–100.

Green, L., Parkin, W. and Hearn, J. (2001) 'Power' in E. Wilson. (eds.) *Organizational Behaviour Reassessed: The Impact of Gender.* London: Sage.

Hall, D. M. and Elliman D. (2003) *Health for All Children*, 4th edn. Oxford, Oxford University Press.

Halson, A. (1991) Young women, sexual harassment and heterosexuality: Violence, power relations and mixed sex schooling. In P. Abbott and C. Wallace. (eds.), *Gender Power and Sexuality.* Basingstoke, Macmillan.

Hammerstrom, A. and Janlert, U. (2005) Health selection in a 14 year follow-up study – A question of gendered discrimination? *Social Science and Medicine*, 61: 2221–32.

Heald, S. (1982) The making of men: the relevance of vernacular psychology to the interpretation of a Gisu ritual. *Africa*, 52: 15–36.

Hearn, J. (1992) *Men in the Public Eye: The Construction and Deconstruction of Public Men and Public Patriarchies.* London, Routledge.

Heuveline, P. and Slap, G. B. (2002) Adolescent and young adult mortality by cause: Age, gender and country, 1955–1994. *Journal of Adolescent Health*, 30 (1): 29–34.

Hill, K. and Upchurch D. M. (1995) Gender differences in child health: Evidence from the demographic health surveys. *Population and Development Review*, 21: 127–51.

Hochschild, A. (1983) *The Managed Heart: Commercialization of Human Feeling.* Berkeley, CA, University of California Press.

Holland, J. (1998) *Male in the Head: Young Women, Heterosexuality and Power.* London, Tufnell Press.

Holmes, J. (2006) Do community factors have a differential effect on the health outcomes of boys and girls? Evidence from rural Pakistan. *Health Policy and Planning*, 21: 231–40.

Hooper, C. A. and Warwick, I. (2006) Gender and the politics of service provision for adults with a history of childhood sexual abuse. *Critical Social Policy*, 26 (2): 467–79.

Humphreys, C. (2001) The impact of domestic violence on children. In P. Foley, J. Roche and S. Tucker. (eds.) *Children in Society: Contemporary Theory, Policy and Practice.* Basingstoke, Palgrave.

Hunter, S. (2005) Negotiating professional and social voices in research principles and practice. *Journal of Social Work Practice*, 19: 149–62.

Jackson, D. A. and King, A. R. (2004) Gender differences in the effects of oppositional behaviour on teacher ratings of ADHD symptoms. *Journal of Abnormal Child Psychology*, 32: 215–24.

James, A., Jenks, C. and Prout, A. (1998) *Theorizing Childhood.* Cambridge, Polity.

Jenks, C. (1996) *Childhood.* London, Routledge.

Jewkes, R., Penn-Kekana, L. and Rose-Junius, H. (2005) 'If they rape me, I can't blame them': Reflections on gender in the context of child rape in South Africa and Namibia. *Social Science and Medicine*, 61: 1809–20.

Kasekei, J. K. (2007) A cut too far. (9 May 2007) *Guardian.* <www.guardian.co.uk> accessed 25 October 2008.

Kelly, A. (2004) Child health. In T. Maynard and N. Thomas. (eds.) *An Introduction to Early Childhood Studies.* London, Sage.

Khan, M. E., Anker, R., Ghosh Dastidar, S. K. and Bairathi, S. (1989) Inequalities between men and women in nutrition and family welfare services: An in-depth enquiry in an Indian Village. In J. C. Caldwell, and M. G. Santow. (eds.), *Selected Readings in the Cultural, Social, and Behavioural Determinants of Health.* Canberra, The Health Transition Centre, The Australian National University.

Knafl, K. and Zoeller, L. (2000) Childhood chronic illness: a comparison of mothers' and fathers' experiences. *Journal of Family Nursing*, 6: 287–302.

Kuh, D. and Hardy R. (2003) *A Lifecourse Approach to Women's Health.* Oxford, Oxford University Press.

Kulbok, P. A. and Cox, C. L. (2002) Dimensions of adolescent health behaviour. *Journal of Adolescent Health*, 31: 394–400.

Laqueur, T. (1990) *Making Sex: Body and Gender from the Greeks to Freud.* London, Harvard University Press.

Lee, N. (2001) *Childhood and Society: Growing up in an Age of Uncertainty.* Buckingham, Open University Press.

Lees, S. (1993) *Sugar and Spice: Sexuality and Adolescent Girls.* Hutchinson, London.

Li, J. (2004) Gender inequality, family planning, and maternal and child care in a rural Chinese county. *Social Science and Medicine*, 59: 695–708.

Lindsey, S. (1990) *Gender Roles: A Sociological Perspective.* London, Sage.

Liu, R. (2005) Parent-youth closeness and youth's suicidal ideation: the moderating effects of gender, stages of adolescence, and race or ethnicity. *Youth and Society*, 37 (2): 145–75.

McCarthy, P. L. and the Committee on Pediatric Research (2000) Race/ethnicity, gender, socioeconomic status – Research exploring their effects on child health: A subject review. *Pediatrics*, 105: 1349–51.

McGreal, C. (2001) AIDS myth drives South African baby-rape crisis 'due to aids myth'. *Guardian Unlimited* (3 November 2001).

McKie, L. (2003) Review article. Gender, violence and health care: Implications for research, policy and practice. *Sociology of Health and Illness*, 25: 120–31.

McNeill, M. (2007) Fathers of children with a chronic health condition. *Men and Masculinities*, 9 (4): 409–24.

Martineau, A., White, M. and Bhopal, R. (1997) No sex differences in immunisation rates of British South Asian children: The effects of migration? *British Medical Journal*, 314: 642.

Matthews, S., Manor O. and Power C. (1999) Social inequalities in health: Are there gender differences? *Social Science and Medicine*, 48: 49–60.

May-Chahal, C. (2006) Gender and child maltreatment: The evidence base. *Social Work and Society*, 4: 1–17.

Mayall, B. (1994) *Negotiating Health: Primary School Children at Home and School.* London, Cassell.

Mayall, B. (1998) Towards a sociology of child health. *Sociology of Health and Illness*, 20: 269–88.

Meltzer, H. and Gatward, R. with Goodman, R. and Ford, T. (2000) *Mental Health of Children and Adolescents in Great Britain.* London, The Stationery Office.

Muhuri, P. K. and Preston, S. H. (1991) Effects of family composition on mortality differentials by sex among children in Matlab, Bangladesh. *Population and Development Review*, 17: 415–34.

Muise, A. M., Stein, D. G. and Arbess, G. (2003) Eating disorders in adolescent boys: A review of adolescent and young adult literature. *Journal of Adolescent Health*, 3: 427–35.

National Statistics Online <www.statistics.gov.uk> accessed 21 June 2005.

O'Brien, R., Hunt, K. and Hart, G. (2005) 'It's cavemen stuff, but that is to a certain extent how guys still operate': Men's accounts of masculinity and help seeking. *Social Science and Medicine*, 61: 503–16.

Pearn, J. (1997) Recent advances in child paediatrics: 2 – Childhood and adolescence. *British Medical Journal*, 314: 1099.

Peckover, S. (2002) Focusing upon children and men in situations of domestic violence: An analysis of the gendered nature of British health visiting. *Health and Social Care in the Community*, 10: 254–61.

Pelchat, D., Lefebvre, H. and Levert, M. J. (2007) Gender differences and similarities in the experience of parenting a child with a health problem: Current state of knowledge. *Journal of Child Health Care*, 11 (2): 112–31.

Phares, V., Steinberg, A. R. and Thompson, A. K. (2004) Gender differences in peer and parental influences: Body image disturbance, self-worth and psychological functioning in preadolescent children. *Journal of Youth and Adolescence*, 33: 421–9.

Pilcher, J. (2007) Body work: Childhood, gender and school health education in England, 1870–1977. *Childhood*, 14 (2): 215–33.

Pillai, R. K., Williams, S. V., Glick, H. A., *et al.* (2003) Factors affecting decisions to seek treatment for sick children in Kerala, India. *Social Science and Medicine*, 57: 783–90.

Prendergast, S. (2000) To become dizzy in our turning: Girls, body maps and gender as childhood ends. In A. Prout. (ed.), *The Body, Childhood and Society*. Macmillan, Basingstoke.

Prior, P. M. (1999) *Gender and Mental Health*. Basingstoke, Macmillan.

Prout, A. (2000) Childhood bodies: Construction, agency and hybridity. In A. Prout. (ed.), *The Body, Childhood and Society*. Basingstoke, Macmillan.

Rees, J., Mellanby, A., White, J. and Tripp, J. (2000) Added power and understanding in sex education (A PAUSE): A sex education intervention staffed predominantly by school nurses. In A. Glasper and L. Ireland. (eds.), *Evidence Based Child Health Care: Challenges for Practice*. Basingstoke, Macmillan.

Renold, E. (2002) Presumed innocence: Hetero(sexual), heterosexist and homophobic harassment amongst primary school boys and girls. *Childhood*, 9: 415–34.

Renzetti, C. N. and Curran, D. J. (1999) *Women, Men and Society*, 4th edn. Needham Heights, Allyn and Bacon.

Richardson, J., Coid, J., Petruckevitch, A., Chung, W. S., Moorey, S. and Feder, G. (2002) Identifying domestic violence: Cross sectional study in primary care. *BMJ*, 324 (7332): 274–7.

Robb, M. (2004) Gender and communication. *Nursing Management*, 11: 1–11.

Roberts, H. (2002) Reducing inequalities in child health. In D. McNeish, T. Newman and H. Roberts (eds.), *What Works for Children*. Buckingham, Open University Press.

Santow, G. (1995) Social roles and physical health: The case of female disadvantage in poor countries. *Social Science and Medicine*, 40: 147–61.

Schaffer, H. R. (1996) *Social Development*. Oxford, Blackwell.

Seagor, J. (2003) *The Atlas of Women: An Economic, Social and Political Survey*, 3rd edn. London, The Women's Press.

Seipel, M. O. (1999) Social consequences of malnutrition. *Social Work*, 44: 416–27.

Smolak, L. and Murnen, S. K. (2004) A feminist approach to eating disorders. In J. K. Thompson. (ed.), *Handbook of Eating Disorders and Obesity*. Hoboken, NJ: Wiley.

Smith, R. L. (2000) Promoting adolescent sexual health: Enhancing professional knowledge and skills. In A. Glasper and L. Ireland. (eds.), *Evidence Based Child Health Care: Challenges for Practice*. Basingstoke, Macmillan.

Smyth, L. (2006) The cultural politics of sex and reproduction in Northern Ireland. *Sociology*, 40: 663–70.

Sweeting, H. (1995) Reversals of fortune? Sex differences in health in childhood and adolescence. *Social Science and Medicine*, 40: 77–90.

Sweeting, H. and West, P. (2002) Sex differences in health at ages 11, 13 and 15. *Social and Medicine*, 56: 31–9.

Tangmunkongvorakul, A., Kane, R. and Wellings, K. (2005) Gender double standards in young people attending sexual health clinics in Northern Thailand. *Culture, Health and Sexuality*, 7: 361–73.

Taylor, J. S. and Green, L. (2008) Children, health and gender: Recognition in nursing research. *Journal of Clinical Nursing*, 17: 3226–37.

Thorne, B. (1993) *Gender Play: Girls and Boys in School*. New Brunswick, NY, Rutgers University Press.

Torsheim, T., Ravens-Sieberer, Y., Hetland, J., Valimaa, R., Danielson, M. and Overpeck, M. (2006) Cross-nation variation of gender differences in adolescent subjective health in Europe and North America. *Social Science and Medicine*, 6: 815–27.

Townsend, P. and Davidson, P. (1980) *Inequalities in Health: The Black Report*. Harmondsworth, Penguin.

UNICEF (1998) *The State of the World's Children*. New York, UNICEF.

Vilhjalmsson, R. and Kristjansdottir, G. (2003) Gender differences in physical activity in older children and adolescents: The central role of organised sport. *Social Science and Medicine*, 56: 363–74.

Waterson, T., Helms, P. J. and Platt, M. W. (eds.) (2006) *Paediatrics: A Core Text on Child Health*. Oxford, Radcliffe Publishing.

Whitworth, A. and Stephenson, R. (2002) Birth spacing, sibling rivalry and child mortality in India. *Social Science and Medicine*, 59: 2107–19.

Wilfley, D. E., Schreiber, G. D., Pike, K. M., Striegel-Moore, R.,Wright, D. J. and Rodin, J. (1996) Eating disturbance and body image: A comparison of a community sample of adult black and white women. *International Journal of Eating Disorders*, 20: 377–87.

Wilkinson, S. and Kitzinger, C. (1994) (eds.) *Women and Health: Feminist Perspectives.* London, Taylor and Francis.

Williams, R. A. (2007) Masculinities fathering and health: The experience of African Caribbean and white working class fathers. *Social Science and Medicine,* 64 (2): 338–49.

Wilson, I., Griffin, C. Wren, B. (2005) The interaction between young people with atypical gender identity organization and their peers. *Journal of Health Psychology,* 10: 307–15.

Wyness, M. G. (2000) *Contesting Childhood.* London, Falmer.

Xie, J. and Dow, W. H. (2005) Longitudinal study of child immunization determinants in China. *Social Science and Medicine,* 61: 601–11.

Young, S. Y., Harford, K. L., Kinder, B. and Savell, J.K. (2007) The relationship between childhood sexual abuse and adult mental health among undergraduates: Victim gender doesn't matter. *Journal of Interpersonal Violence,* 22 (10): 1315–31.

3

Gender, Child Maltreatment and Young People's Offending

Carol-Ann Hooper

This chapter considers two issues, child maltreatment and young people's offending, bringing a gendered lens to each and to the relationship between them. That child maltreatment is associated with an increased risk of offending, amongst a range of other negative outcomes, and that a high proportion of young offenders have histories of maltreatment, has long been apparent in research. It is much less often visible in policy, at least in the United Kingdom. The organizational separation of child protection and youth justice in England and Wales inhibits recognition of the overlap (they are combined, at least to some extent, in many other countries), as do the different and implicitly gendered constructions of childhood which appear in different policy contexts. As Seaford put it 'the child moves through Whitehall growing and shrinking like Alice: in the DoH [*sic*] she is a small potential victim, at the Treasury and Department of Education [*sic*] a growing but silent unit of investment, but at the Home Office a

Gender and Child Welfare in Society Edited by Brid Featherstone, Carol-Ann Hooper, Jonathan Scourfield, and Julie Taylor.

huge and threatening yob' (Seaford, 2001: 464–5). The yob is clearly no longer an Alice, and it is not only the child's age and size which change but her gender. The chapter gives an overview of what we know about gender and child maltreatment, then explores in more detail the association between maltreatment and offending, reflecting on its gender dimensions, before considering implications for policy and practice.

Maltreatment is one factor amongst others which may contribute to troubled and troublesome young people's difficulties, a link in a chain in which multiple disadvantages may accumulate over time. It is not my intention to attribute it greater status than other issues (though that may sometimes be appropriate) or to turn young people who offend into victims, denying their agency or ignoring the other victims they may create, but to argue for its full recognition amongst other factors, with due attention to gender, to ensure appropriate resources are available to safeguard all children and promote their welfare, as required by the Children Acts of 1989 and 2004.

It is also not my intention to add further negative expectations to the challenges already faced by children who are maltreated, a possible danger of focusing on this association. There is no inevitability about negative outcomes, although an increased risk exists also of physical and mental health problems, substance misuse, self-harm, teenage parenting, homelessness and parenting difficulties. Much depends on the responses of others to the child, within their families, schools, communities and state agencies, all of whom can play a part in alleviating hurt and distress and promoting resilience and well-being. The current broadened preventative agenda for children and young people in the United Kingdom, with a 'risk and protective factor' paradigm increasingly used to focus interventions, has been subject to some adverse criticism for its orientation to children's future in the social investment state rather than their present needs and wishes (Seaford, 2001; Lister, 2006). As Uprichard (2008) argues, however, children are always both 'beings and becomings' and their futures are a concern they and their parents are likely to share with policymakers and practitioners. Those futures clearly depend on fully informed and thoughtful attention to the present, and the preventative agenda offers opportunities for justifying the development of therapeutic practices and resources on economic as well as humanitarian and social justice grounds (Spratt, 2009).

In bringing a gendered perspective to this topic, there are a number of issues I think important. First, one of the hazards of focusing on gender is the risk of reinforcing rather than undoing stereotypes. As Deborah Cameron argues in *The Myth of Mars and Venus*, whilst there has been substantial change in gender relations it remains culturally acceptable to fix ideas of gender difference in exaggerated form despite the evidence frequently showing much more similarity, overlap and change (Cameron, 2007). In the highly masculinized fields of criminology and criminal justice, both academic specialization and institutional structures can reinforce this tendency, although there is a growing body of research which can also be used to question it. Second, there remain significant gender inequalities (interwoven with inequalities of class and race) – women on average earn significantly lower incomes, are more vulnerable to poverty and bear an unequal share of childcare responsibilities. Whilst individuals are differently positioned in relation to these 'on average' issues, women's relationships with their children are also affected by the material fact that it is women who become pregnant and give birth, and by the cultural meanings of motherhood, although in much more complex ways than implied by traditional familial ideology which assumed women's nurturing and caring role to follow naturally from their reproductive role (Hollway, 2006; Gadd and Jefferson, 2007). Children's relationships with their mothers and fathers also differ, as a result not only of the individuals involved and the ways they negotiate the sharing of parenthood over time but also of the symbolic meanings of motherhood and fatherhood and the role of attachments and identifications in psycho-sexual development.

Third, whilst the diverse and changing meanings people may attach to being a girl or a boy, a woman or a man, a mother or a father, derive from culturally available discourses they may also serve defensive functions in relation to the person's own life experience, for example, investing in 'tough masculinity' to avoid the vulnerability inherent in desire for intimacy with another which may evoke painful early experiences of separation or rejection (Gadd and Jefferson, 2007). Multifaceted identities, including gender identities, may be unstable and continually reconstructed over the life course through narrative and performance in interaction with others (Butler, 1990; 2004), but defensive investments inhibit the fluidity of that process.

Gender and maltreatment – an overview

Child maltreatment is a term used to include physical abuse, sexual abuse, emotional abuse and neglect. Definitions of maltreatment are contested and changing, however, and this process itself may be affected by gendered assumptions. In practice, neglect tends to be used primarily in relation to women, reflecting the higher expectations of their care, and this now extends back before birth with the recent addition in the United Kingdom of substance abuse during pregnancy to the definition of neglect (Department of Health, 2006). Whilst recent evidence on the health of babies born to heroin-addicted mothers underlies this development, it is arguably also inflected with judgements about marginalized women behaving badly and a construction of motherhood which can sometimes reduce women's lives to their maternal role and responsibilities. There are other risky activities undertaken by pregnant women which would not attract the label neglect (Bewley, 2002), and much less attention is paid to the contribution of fathers' behaviour to fetal health with a greater reluctance to draw the conclusion that fathers should change their behaviour where links are identified (Daniels, 2002). As another example, whilst the impact on children of non-resident parents who are unreliable and often unavailable (physically and emotionally) is akin to a form of emotional abuse or neglect (Hooper, Koprowska and Milsom, 2007), this is often overlooked both in research and practice, perhaps partly because these are mostly fathers and even less is expected of them outside than within the household.

Prevalence surveys show maltreatment is much more widespread than suggested by the number of cases reported to agencies. The best source of evidence in the United Kingdom is Cawson et al.'s (2000; 2002) survey of 2,869 18–24-year-olds who were interviewed about their childhood experiences. A range of definitions were used, but using the narrowest definitions in each category of abuse, 7 per cent were assessed to have experienced serious physical abuse from parents or carers, 6 per cent serious physical neglect (absence of care), 5 per cent serious lack of supervision and 6 per cent serious emotional maltreatment. Sexual abuse – defined as sexual experiences if (1) the other person was a parent or carer, (2) they were against the person's wishes or (3) they were felt to be consensual but involved a person other than the parent who was five years older when the child was 12 or under – had been experienced by 16 per cent. There is some overlap between these groups (discussed further below) but 16 per cent of the sample as a whole were assessed to have experienced serious maltreatment by parents.

Gender affects children's vulnerability to abuse in different ways depending on the form of the abuse. The greatest variation is found in relation to sexual abuse where most studies find the risk to be between 1.5 and 3 times as high for girls. The 16 per cent of Cawson et al. (2000)'s sample who experienced sexual abuse breaks down as 21 per cent of the girls and 11 per cent of the boys. Another common finding is that girls are more likely to be abused by someone within the family, and boys by someone outside the family, partly reflecting the patterns of children's lives and the opportunities they present, since boys still tend to be less supervised than girls outside of the home (Hooper and Warwick, 2006). In the NSPCC research, however, male and female respondents were equally likely to have been abused by a parent (Cawson et al., 2000), and in a further survey of 2,420 school-aged children (ages 9–16) exploring sexual abuse by strangers only, girls were still over twice as likely to report a sexual incident involving a stranger as boys (11 per cent compared to 5 per cent) (Gallagher, Bradford and Pease, 2002). For other forms of abuse, the differences tend to be slighter, although Cawson et al. (2000) also found girls twice as likely to be emotionally abused as boys. Boys appear overall to be more vulnerable to physical abuse, although Cawson et al. (2000) found girls more vulnerable to serious physical abuse. Girls were also found to be slightly more vulnerable to serious absence of care, although again boys were more vulnerable to absence of care overall. With regard to supervision, girls were more likely to have been expected to care for younger siblings regularly, but boys more likely to have been left without supervision themselves.

Children's vulnerability to abuse is affected not only by gender, of course, but also by age, socio-economic status, ethnicity, disability and sexual orientation. In brief: babies are most vulnerable to fatal abuse and young children to physical punishment, although there is also growing recognition of the abuse of adolescents. Living in poverty brings an increased risk of physical abuse and neglect though all forms of abuse occur across class and the forms of neglect more likely to occur in middle-class families (emotional rather than physical) are probably less likely to be noticed. Black and ethnic minority children are vulnerable to racial abuse and harassment both from outside the family and sometimes from within (especially in mixed parentage families) and often witness racial abuse against other family members too. Disabled children are at greater risk of all forms of abuse, although different disabilities affect vulnerability in different ways, and disability is also sometimes the consequence of abuse. And lesbian, gay and bisexual young men and women also report higher rates of childhood abuse. These patterns are reviewed and discussed more fully in Hooper (2002; 2005).

Many children who experience one form of abuse or neglect also experience others, and there is growing recognition of the issue of multi-type maltreatment or poly-victimization. Serious 'multi-type' maltreatment by parents had been experienced by 5 per cent of Cawson et al. (2002)'s sample. Those who experienced serious physical abuse, sexual abuse by a parent or emotional maltreatment were highly likely to have experienced other forms of maltreatment at home too. Those who were maltreated at home were also more likely to have been bullied, discriminated against or made to feel different at school. A longitudinal study in the United States which included a wider range of forms of victimization, including property and violent crime, and community violence, as well as domestic violence, child maltreatment and peer/sibling abuse, found that victimization often persisted over time, with the experience of victimization at one point in time increasing the risk of victimization a year later, and poly-victimization increasing the risk of ongoing poly-victimization. High levels of anger and aggression and moving to a worse neighbourhood contributed to persistence of poly-victimization, and more good friends and a lower level of other adversities to desistance. As the authors argue, for some children victimization is more an ongoing condition than an event (as many practitioners know), and it is this group, who had experienced multiple victimization and repeat victimization, who were most at risk of trauma (Finkelhor, Ormrod and Turner, 2007a; 2007b). This has implications for assessment, and for treatment and prevention – the most apparent form of victimization should not be assumed to be the only one, although it may be. Equally, however, it should not divert attention from the unique constellations of context and meaning within which children experience the impacts of any kind of victimization.

Turning to the perpetration of abuse, all forms are committed by both men and women. Much sociological and feminist analysis has focused on explaining the preponderance of men amongst perpetrators of sexual abuse (a common estimate attributes 90–95 per cent of sexual abuse to men) (Finkelhor, 1994; Turton, 2008), and the greater propensity of men to physical violence (reflected both in the asymmetry of domestic violence, common context of all forms of maltreatment, and in physical violence towards children, when time with children is taken into account) (Radford and Hester, 2006). Gender is only one part of the complex web of influences behind any incident of abuse, but gender divisions within families (regarding, for example, expectations of authority and responsibility, control over reproduction and emotion work), gendered patterns of experience of emotional expression and caring for children, and identities invested in particular discourses of masculinity and femininity may all play a part. Each parent's own experience of childhood, their access to material resources and social support and, at a broader level, the cultural value accorded to childhood and its consequences, are common interwoven aspects of context.

A strand of feminist thinking originating with Nancy Chodorow (1999), has explored the consequences of women's role in childbearing and early maternal care for the psychological development of boys and girls and their subsequent capacity to care for others. Chodorow's argument that girls grow up more oriented to others' needs (and hence to mothering) because mothers tend to identify more with daughters than sons, keeping them close and discouraging separation, whilst boys are pushed into separating earlier and consequently tend to defend more against connection has been developed and complicated by Benjamin (1995) and Hollway (2006) to take into account the wider range of identifications children form with the adults in their lives (men and women) and the different ways separation may be managed for both boys and girls. Clearly men as well as women may give good enough care to children, but gender continues to matter, in ways affected by specific biography and family history as well as continuity and change in gender relations more broadly. If, as Hollway (2006) argues, capacity to care depends on both the ability to imagine the child's experience and to see the child accurately as different from oneself in order to respond to their needs, it is likely that women's development tends to equip them better for the first, but not necessarily for the second. The ability to develop and retain a sense of self as a 'subject in one's own right', which is required in order to see the child as separate, distinct and differentiated, has not traditionally been as prioritized for girls as for boys and is often undermined by the expectations of self-sacrifice associated with motherhood.

Feminists have tended to emphasize risks to children from men, which was both vital to constructing an accurate picture and a corrective to the previous assumption of women's responsibility for all matters of child welfare. When motherhood is so easily and extensively pathologized (with the blanket problematization of all teenage mothers, for example, many of whom parent well despite difficult circumstances) it is tempting to avoid dwelling on the risks that do exist. But if fathers may be resources as well as risks for children (as is commonly emphasized now) the same is true (if in reverse) of mothers (Reich, 2005). The balance appears gender-differentiated – to cite one suggestive statistic, in Cawson et al. (2000), 20 per cent of respondents (both boys and girls) reported being 'sometimes really afraid' of their fathers/stepfathers compared with 7 per cent reporting similar fear of mothers/stepmothers. It is crucial for professionals to recognize the contexts of deprivation and multiple adversity (including their own past and ongoing victimization) within which many women struggle with the huge responsibilities of motherhood and neither to lose sight of the impact of such contexts through overfamiliarity (Hooper et al., 2007) nor to judge marginalized women against middle-class standards, ignoring the logic of their practices in context (Gillies, 2007). It is equally important, however, to recognize that whilst 'bad mothering', like 'bad fathering', is socially constructed, and they are defined very differently and occur in significantly different contexts, children's health and well-being may be adversely affected by both.

There are gender dimensions too to children's help-seeking and to the impacts of maltreatment. The growing body of research on who children turn to for help has been usefully summarized by Featherstone and Evans (2004). Having someone they can talk to about their concerns is central to children's safety, and the vast majority do have someone they can generally turn to, although a small minority do not. Mothers tend to be the preferred person for young children, and young people also tend to find it easier to talk to their mothers than their fathers, although such statistical generalizations should not be used as a substitute for attention to children's particular preferences.

Older children increasingly turn to their friends, alongside siblings and a wider range of adults, although girls are more likely than boys to have the kind of friendships within which worries are confided. Boys are less likely to talk to anyone about their problems than girls (Gorin, 2004; Featherstone and Evans, 2004).

Children's decisions to tell about sexual abuse, which relies on disclosure more than other forms of maltreatment since it usually occurs in secret, are complex. Disclosure is often difficult, both in childhood and later, especially where a parent is involved, affected by threats and loyalties and by the impacts of abuse, which may include shame and stigma, guilt and self-blame, low self-worth, lack of trust in others or sense of entitlement to help, and dissociation. Many children still tell no one. Whilst boys are less likely to be sexually abused than girls they are also less likely to tell anyone; the 'male ethic of self-reliance' and, if they were abused by men, the effects of homophobia (either their own or that which they anticipate from others) and poorer recognition amongst professionals, compound the barriers to seeking help (Hooper and Warwick, 2006). It is likely also that the very small number of girls and boys sexually abused by their mothers are least able to tell anyone, given that abuse in this context is combined with both attachment to and intense dependence on the person likely to have been the child's primary caregiver from birth (and life support before) and the internalization of idealized and asexual cultural images of motherhood. The confusion generated by threat coming from the person most children turn to first for help and denial and minimization from others can compound these children's isolation (Turton, 2008). Children sexually abused by other women may also face disbelief or trivialization of their experience from others as well as a sense of betrayal influenced by cultural expectations of women, although many impacts are similar to sexual abuse by men (Denov, 2004).

There is a vast literature on the emotional and psychological impacts of maltreatment, which, in addition to those mentioned above, may include fear and anger, anxiety and depression, insecure attachment, post-traumatic stress disorder (PTSD) and complex PTSD (Herman, 1992). It is commonly noted that girls are more likely to internalize their distress (expressed, for example, in depression or self-harm), boys to externalize and display 'hypermasculine compensation' (Lisak, 1995), for example, aggression, antisocial behaviour, violence to others and homophobic behaviour, though this pattern may be changing somewhat as the constraints imposed by social constructions of gender change, resulting in more open expression of anger and aggression from girls and some increase in self-harm amongst boys (Hooper and Warwick, 2006). Physiological impacts may include not only physical injury but the impacts of trauma and early deprivation of care and emotional containment on brain development, which can leave ongoing difficulties in regulating emotions (Gerhardt, 2004).

Recent sociological work on personal life – emphasizing the role memory plays in constructing a sense of self and identity, the embeddedness of individuals in webs of relationship through which shared memories are formed, and the 'stickiness' of family relationships even if contact is discontinued (Smart, 2007) – also casts useful light on the challenges that may face children who have experienced maltreatment as they grow up. Whilst many become estranged from their families of origin, for those in continued contact with relatives, silences, conflicts over family history and distortions of reality often persist, especially where sexual abuse is not disclosed to, or is denied by, some family members (Hooper, Koprowska and Milsom, 1999; Hooper et al., 2007). The shared narrative which helps to sustain a coherent identity may therefore be difficult to achieve. In addition, for those who go into the care system, networks of relationship within it are frequently tenuous and disrupted, offering little if any opportunity for developing a sense of self embedded in trusted relationships over time (Coy, 2007). The more relational orientation of girls, together with expectations of greater closeness with mothers and of their involvement in 'kin and caring work' may make it more difficult for girls than boys to separate from conflictual and invalidating family networks, and perhaps also to bear their lack. Culture may be an influence too however – African Caribbean girls have been found more autonomous than white girls (Lees, 2002) – and girls may also find validation for their experiences elsewhere more easily than boys given the tendency for them to have more confiding friendships. Girls do appear to be more vulnerable to negative outcomes as a result of being in care (Hobcraft, 1998), although it is not clear how much this is the result of their experience prior to, or in, care. That young girls, most of whom have been sexually abused before coming into care, within or outside their families, are very vulnerable to being exploited again in mixed-sex children's homes, where staff sometimes appear to condone sexually aggressive behaviour from boys (Farmer and Pollock, 1998; Green, 2000), may play a part in this pattern too.

To reiterate the point made earlier, negative outcomes are by no means inevitable for children who are maltreated. The growing literature on resilience shows that the presence of a non-abusing parent and/or siblings in particular contributes significantly to children's ability to be well and do well despite adverse experiences, including maltreatment, as can other supportive adults and peers. Schools and communities can also contribute to developing children's resilience through the opportunities they offer, and therapeutic interventions can do much to restore health and well-being. However, if the expanding preventative agenda is to fulfil its potential, recognition of the extent and impacts of maltreatment is essential. The next section focuses on an issue where this is often lost sight of – young people's offending – and explores the complexity of the interaction of gender with other influences.

Maltreatment and offending – a complex and gendered pathway

The underrecognition in policy of a relationship between maltreatment on the one hand and antisocial behaviour or offending on the other has many interwoven roots. In a political context where a show of toughness is a ritual part of virtually all policy announcements on crime, whatever their content, to recognize that offenders (young or older) may also have been victims themselves smacks of making excuses for them and denying or downplaying their responsibility. The tendency to think of victims and offenders as mutually exclusive identities – 'hoodie or goodie' as the title of a recent report from Victim Support (2007) unhelpfully put it – reinforces this. Whilst victimization and offending are more usefully considered to be life experiences amongst other life experiences, which may or may not coexist (and where they do, may or may not be related), it is arguable that the cultural gendering of offending and victimization further fuels resistance to considering their overlap. Less powerful groups in society are more easily perceived as victims (Christie, 1986). Hence, though the patterns of different forms of victimization vary, victimization is culturally feminized – the consequences of this for both girls and boys who are sexually abused have been discussed elsewhere (Hooper and Warwick, 2006). Offending is masculinized, reflecting both the reality of the much higher rates of offending and antisocial behaviour amongst boys and men, and social constructions of masculinity from which it is a shorter step to criminal behaviour (especially violent and aggressive forms) than from femininity – hence the greater interest often shown by the media in girls' offending, since it involves greater transgression of social norms.

Social constructions of gender may also contribute to the tendency to attribute more competence and responsibility at a given age to the antisocial or offending child (implicitly male) than to the child of children's services, a pattern charted through recent developments in Scotland by Tisdall (2006). Feminist criminologists have noted that in the courts' treatment of adult offenders, there is a tendency to attribute greater agency and culpability to men, with victimization or mental health problems being given less weight than for women (Gelsthorpe, 2001). Similarly, whilst the bidirectionality of parenting (that children influence their parents as well as vice versa) is increasingly recognized, the relevance of children's behaviour to their own maltreatment is a stronger theme in the pathways to offending literature (traditionally and still predominantly concerned with boys) than in the maltreatment literature.

The relative invisibility of maltreatment

Recognizing the overlap between maltreatment and offending is crucial both to fully understanding pathways to offending in order to reduce it and to considering the implications of criminal justice system (CJS) responses for the health and well-being of the children and young people who encounter them. There is, in fact, growing recognition of the overlap in reviews of research, largely in relation to young offenders and women offenders (see, for example, Youth Justice Board, 2005; Farrington and Welsh, 2007; Hill et al., 2007; Corston,

2007; Margo and Stevens, 2008), but very little in policy (for example, HM Government, 2008). There are a number of ways in which the research literature still contributes to the relative invisibility of the issue. First, there is often a lack of clarity about current definitions of maltreatment in the offending literature. Hence one review concludes that there is 'abundant evidence . . . that coercive, hostile, critical, punitive parenting style is associated with an increased risk for anti-social behaviour' (which is reminiscent of the 'low warmth/high criticism environments' now thought most damaging to children in the child maltreatment field) yet downplays the issue of abuse and neglect which is discussed in a different section (Rutter, Giller and Hagel, 1998). Second, whilst methodologies to explore the prevalence of maltreatment have become increasingly sophisticated, research with offender populations is rarely informed by current thinking on how to research these issues most reliably. Hence a single question is often asked relying on a shared definition of 'abuse' where multiple questions to explore specific behaviours and experiences are needed for a thorough assessment; or measures based on reported cases or a sub-sample of them (for example, child protection registrations) are used when prevalence studies show only a tiny minority of cases are reported to any agency.

Third, large-scale longitudinal studies commonly also either under-research maltreatment (by using limited questions or measures, as above, and/or by the common omission of sexual abuse) or under-recognize it, using more neutral terms for issues that would elsewhere be recognized as maltreatment, such as poor supervision (which may constitute neglect) and parental conflict (much of which may be domestic violence). Fourth, whilst there have been a series of papers on the overlap between victimization and offending (Smith, 2004; Smith and Ecob, 2007; Victim Support, 2007), these tend to take a foreshortened perspective, focusing on recent experience only. Hence they usually attribute the overlap – those young people who have been victims of crime over the previous year, are also more likely to have offended, and vice versa (see also Roe and Ashe, 2008) – to lifestyle, routine activities, and retaliation (direct or displaced) which result in the roles of victim and offender being easily interchangeable. Family context tends to fade into the background, contributing to the risk of the overlap occurring but not being a source of victimization itself, although even with limited questions, assaults by family members are often evident (Roe and Ashe, 2008). That victimization increases the risk both of further victimization and of offending is recognized, therefore, but we do not know when the cycle started, which may sometimes be very early. Raine, Brennan and Sarnoff (1994) found, in a sample of 4,000 males, that significantly higher rates of violent offending between the ages of 17 and 19 were associated with a combination of birth complications and maternal rejection either pre-birth or during the first year of life.

The association between maltreatment and offending

There is a substantial body of research clearly indicating the overlap between child maltreatment and offending. Retrospective studies have found very high rates of abuse and neglect amongst young people who come into contact with the youth justice system – four to five times the rates found in the NSPCC survey discussed above, where methodologies are sufficiently thorough to justify comparison (for example, Boswell, 1997; Hamilton, Falshaw and Browne, 2002; Youth Justice Trust, 2004). Prospective studies which follow up a population of children over time also show a significant increase in risk of antisocial behaviour and offending associated with maltreatment independent of other variables, alongside a more open picture with diverse outcomes and much evidence of resilience – the majority of maltreated children do not go on to offend (Widom, 1989; Spohn, 2000; Bowen, Heron and Steer, 2008). The pathway between maltreatment and offending may be a long one – in Pitts (2004) study of young people in contact with an inner London borough youth offending team (YOT), 35 per cent of the persistent offenders had been on the child protection register between the ages of 1 and 5 years – with many other influences along the way, including the care system. Placement in care may reduce the risk of offending in some circumstances but increases it in others, particularly where multiple placements are involved (Jonson-Reid and Barth, 2000; McMahon and Clay-Warner, 2002; Haas et al., 2004; Ryan and Testa, 2005; Jonson-Reid, 2004; McConville, 2003). And whilst some specific links are particularly strong (for example, between child sexual abuse and involvement in prostitution for women, though this might now be seen more as a form of revictimization than offending), the association is relevant to a wide range of offending behaviour. Pitts' (2004) study cited above found 58 per cent of first-time offenders, as well as 41 per cent of persistent offenders had previously been on the child protection register.

There is some evidence that the increased risk of offending amongst maltreated children is intensified by neighbourhood disadvantage, probably by a combination of the greater risks associated with lack of supervision or effective parenting in such contexts, the lack of resources available to build resilience, and/or the frustration and resentment generated by lack of opportunity to escape abusive families and community stigma (Schuck and Widom, 2005). Multiple forms of victimization can also increase risk (Salter et al., 2003; Cuevas et al., 2007), although this is not always the case. Some research has found that amongst parental forms of maltreatment, neglect alone is the most significant influence for boys (Spohn, 2000), though this may be partly the effect of neglect being more strongly associated with socio-economic deprivation than other forms of abuse and hence with other risks in the neighbourhood context. Another study found rejection to be the strongest influence (McCord, 1983). Domestic violence (a common context of neglect) is also often omitted. Amongst a sample of sexually abused boys, neglect, emotional deprivation and domestic violence against the mother were all associated with an increased risk of becoming a perpetrator, as was sexual abuse by a woman (Salter et al., 2003).

Engendering the picture

Whilst a history of maltreatment is common amongst young offenders, and especially but not only serious and persistent offenders, higher rates of maltreatment are commonly found amongst female offenders, young and adult, especially of sexual abuse, ongoing violence from a partner, and multiple and repeat victimization (Hamilton, Falshaw and Browne, 2002; Singleton et al., 1998). To give just one indicative statistic, in Loucks's (1997) study of women in Cornton Vale prison, 11 per cent had been sexually abused by a parent, compared with 1 per cent in the recent NSPCC survey (Cawson et al., 2000).

The conclusion sometimes drawn from large-scale quantitative research that risk factors are the same for boys and girls is seriously undermined by the common absence of attention to sexual abuse in such research. Studies which do address gender sometimes simply add being female to resilience factors, and being male to risk factors (Bowen, Heron and Steer, 2008). Research designed to explore the connection between maltreatment and offending thoroughly, however, has found both similarities and significant gender differences – in brief, higher levels of victimization (including ongoing violence from partners) and/or lower levels of offending amongst girls (Silverthorn and Finch, 1999; Spohn, 2000; Cuevas et al., 2007). Offending remains more the norm for boys, whether for biological reasons such as the higher rates of neurocognitive deficits and hyperactivity amongst boys (Moffitt et al., 2001) or sociological reasons – the tighter social constraints on women's behaviour, and the thinner dividing line between masculinity and crime (Steffensmeier, 1996) – or more likely a combination of the two. Hence, it 'takes more' to turn girls to offending, and that 'more' is often maltreatment, disadvantage (social and economic) (Farringdon and Painter, 2004) or both.

The higher levels of maltreatment and victimization amongst girls who offend contextualizes the finding that girls' violence is more likely to be against someone they know well, often a close relative or partner, with boys' violence more commonly against friends or strangers (Herrera and McCloskey, 2001; Budd et al., 2005). Girls may therefore be using violence in somewhat different ways from boys – whether to establish boundaries for self-protection and respect (in ways that notions of self-defence as traditionally conceived or retaliation may not capture) (Batchelor, 2005), or to express emotions that they are unable to contain (Hart et al., 2007), although there may also be similarities. Neighbourhood disadvantage has been found less significant for girls than for boys in the association between maltreatment and offending, which may also reflect this pattern, with the immediate social context more relevant than the broader context to girls' violence (Chauhan and Reppucci, 2008).

There is more also to engendering resilience than noting the simple fact of gender. Attachment to fathers has been found to increase resilience for boys but reduce it for girls (Bowen, Heron and Steer, 2008), directing attention to the quality of relationships and their meaning rather than simply the presence or absence of a father (the common focus of political rhetoric emphasizing the positive potential of fathers in preventing youth crime). There is some evidence that resilient girls tend to show autonomy, and resilient boys to be emotionally expressive, socially perceptive and nurturant, suggesting that children of both sexes do better with a broader range of personal resources than is fostered by traditional gender stereotypes (Bauman, 2002). Girls' greater ability to seek help for their problems, from friends, family or other adults, is also a significant contributor to their resilience (Hart et al., 2007; Salzinger, Rosario and Feldman, 2007).

Alongside the evidence of gender differences, there is a widespread view that girls' offending is becoming more like boys. However, despite some real increase in female offending over the last 25 years, an exaggerated impression of change is often given by short-term trends in reported statistics, which use broad categories that may conceal differences of severity, and which, given the low baseline for female offending, generate high proportional increases very quickly. Changing social attitudes and policing practices may also be a significant contributor to the increase in reported cases, and the media enthusiasm for stories involving girls' violence to the exaggerated impression. Self-report studies show only fairly modest change occurring. The idea that as gender inequalities decrease in other areas of life so they will in offending is not new, the current 'mean girl discourse' being a successor to the 'liberated female crook thesis' of the 1970s (Silvestri and Crowther-Dowey, 2008). The evidence, however, suggests that where girls' offending is increasing it has much more to do with continued class inequality than increased gender equality. Hansen's (2006) interesting reanalysis of the Offending, Crime and Justice Survey 2003 data found the gender gap greater for the youngest cohort, who grew up during the 1990s and 2000s, than for the oldest, the reverse of what might be expected. However, when the data was broken down by education as well as gender, the picture was more mixed, the gap having increased amongst those with most education, but declined for those with no qualifications to the extent that gender was no longer statistically significant once other known risk factors were controlled for in the latter group. The loosening social control of girls and their increased street presence contributes both to changes in behaviour through new opportunities (increased drinking, for example), and to social anxiety at the loss of girls' traditional civilizing influence on boys

(Gelsthorpe and Sharpe, 2005), but they remain a small minority of offenders.

Is 'race' relevant?

There is very little research that has addressed the way the association between maltreatment and offending may be influenced by ethnicity, and even less that addresses both ethnicity and gender as cross-cutting rather than separate factors. What research there is has mostly been conducted in the United States, a different context for diversity in many ways from the United Kingdom. The existing research is also limited by small black and minority ethnic (BME) samples (and the tendency to combine them into a single group – 'ethnic lumping' – or to reduce much greater heterogeneity to a few categories); by a tendency to rely on official records which means discriminatory criminal justice system responses may distort the picture; and/or by the use of measures which may not be interpreted similarly by all groups (Taussig and Talmi, 2001; Chitsabesan et al., 2006).

It is clear that the increased risk of offending associated with maltreatment occurs across ethnic groups. Where differences have been found they are not always consistent in extent or direction, but are likely to be the result of differences in family networks (which may make parental role more or less significant for different groups), family income, peer group norms (and the opportunities they offer for belonging through pro-social or antisocial behaviour), experiences of care (including the overrepresentation of BME young people in the care system and different patterns of placement and reunification), and/or community contexts (including exposure to stressors such as community violence, poverty and racism, the demands of acculturation for immigrant young people, experience of schools and access to services) (Perez, 2001; Taussig and Talmi, 2001; Taussig, 2002; Fagan, 2005; Wall et al., 2005; Lansford et al., 2007). A rare study addressing 'race' amongst girls in the juvenile justice system found physical abuse by parents a stronger influence on violence in white girls, and witnessing violence a stronger risk factor for black girls. Black girls were more likely, in this study, to live in disadvantaged neighbourhoods, and it may be that neighbourhood context was more significant for black than for white girls (Chauhan and Reppucci, 2008).

Processes in the pathway from maltreatment to offending

The impacts of maltreatment discussed earlier are relevant to the somewhat gendered pathways by which some children who are maltreated go on to offend. Difficulty regulating emotional states as a result of the impact of early deprivation on brain development may make it harder to manage anger without resort to violence (Gerhardt, 2004) whilst coercive family interactions may also teach that aggression pays. Insecure attachment or lack of attachment may result in lasting difficulties in forming supportive social relationships, lack of empathy and a sense of alienation and anger, all of which easily contribute to joining with peers involved in antisocial behaviour (in gangs or otherwise) for a sense of belonging, and/or vulnerability to exploitative relationships. Post-traumatic stress disorder and complex PTSD can involve heightened distress; reduced ability for restraint; high levels of risk-taking, including drug, alcohol and sexual risk-taking as part of a compulsion to relive and master danger; and alternation between reliving the sense of powerlessness that victimization may involve and attempting to find relief from it through aggression and control (Herman, 2002; Feiring, Miller-Johnson and Cleland, 2007). Dissociation and depression may affect the ability to resist temptation or pressure, interfere with thinking about the consequences of actions and inhibit the ability to develop pro-social lifestyles.

Additional issues include stigmatized identities, survival strategies and the fundamental human need for respect and recognition. Where abuse leaves children with a sense of difference and badness as a way of explaining an intolerably painful experience, a stigmatized identity often reinforced by the care system (Coy, 2007), the transition from this 'primary deviant identity' to offending is a smaller step than for others, after which school and CJS interventions may easily reinforce a 'secondary deviant identity' which further entrenches problems (Spohn, 2000; Robinson, 2005). Survival strategies at the intrapersonal level (for example, resort to drugs or alcohol to dull pain) or the interpersonal level (running away from home to escape abuse and being drawn into prostitution or selling drugs to survive on the streets or, at a lesser level, carrying weapons) may increase vulnerability to temptation, exploitation or revictimization. The use of violence to gain respect and recognition, which it may offer in some community, as well as family, contexts, may be fuelled by long-term experience of their lack, as well as by a retaliatory impulse, either direct or displaced.

Whilst all these issues may occur in both sexes, patterns of offending and victimization, the contexts of offending and its motivations reflect the tendency for boys to externalize distress and girls to internalize it, and the greater relational orientation of girls, amongst other influences. In terms of patterns, boys and men are prone to more serious violence and aggression, and girls and women more vulnerable to violent partners and more likely to direct violence at known people. In terms of contexts, ongoing relationships with coercive or exploitative partners often play a significant role in initiating girls into offending behaviour, especially into prostitution – as a result they tend to find it harder than boys to escape prostitution. In terms of motivations, women's risk-taking is more often orientated to maintaining relationships than is that of men, as is reflected in women's accounts of 'doing it for love' of their partner or children. The responses of schools, communities, the criminal justice system and other agencies may also reflect gendered assumptions and/or have gendered impacts, with a risk that the 'mean girl discourse' and the myth of equality may now justify harsher responses to the most vulnerable and disadvantaged young women.

The centrality of relationships to women's identity, and thus motivation, does not necessarily translate into empathy, either for themselves or others, unsurprisingly given female offenders' own common lack of experience of empathic caregiving in childhood. Indeed, psychological research has found the psychological profiles of women offenders to be closer to those of men (offending and non-offending) than of non-offending women (personal communication, Jane Clarbour, 2008). It may be that some girls with traumatic histories may invest, like boys, in the toughness associated with masculinity to defend against their own vulnerability (Miller, 2001), especially where the poor relationships with their mothers common amongst female offenders (Howden-Windell and Clark, 1999) have generated ambivalence about their own gender identities, reinforced by unsafety and the devaluing of femininity in the wider world. Identifications occur across as well as within gender (Hollway, 2006), and so too may investments in gendered discourses.

Whilst the processes involved in pathways to offending are a complex mix of biological, social and environmental influences, a gendered perspective on the role of maltreatment has implications for theory, policy and practice. Theoretically, two trajectories of offending are commonly distinguished: childhood-onset offending, which is more likely to become serious and persistent and to which childhood and family factors are more relevant (where the gender gap is widest as this is predominantly boys), and adolescent time-limited offending, which is influenced by a wider range of factors, including peer groups and youth transitions (Smith, 2007). (A more complex typology of five trajectories has also been developed by Fergusson and Horwood (2002).) Girls' adolescent offending is associated with many of the same correlates as childhood onset offending for boys, however, and Silverthorn and Finch (1999) suggest this reflects a pattern they call 'delayed-onset', where the impacts may be present earlier but do not manifest in antisocial behaviour until adolescence. Whilst female offending careers are usually shorter than those of males, unresolved histories of maltreatment may also prolong them – a recent longitudinal study found female adolescent offenders with histories of physical and sexual abuse by parents to be more likely to continue offending at a relatively high level as adults than others (alongside high levels of ongoing victimization) (Cernkovich et al., 2008).

In terms of policy and practice, it is clear that female young offenders are a particularly vulnerable group. A recent health needs assessment of young women in Young Offender Institutions found over a third had self-harmed in the last month and over two-thirds had some level of psychiatric disturbance (Douglas and Plugge, 2006). At the same time, experiences of trauma with their common consequences for mental health occur amongst both male and female young offenders (Cuevas et al., 2007) and there are therefore many young people, men and women, in custodial situations, where the culture of neglect, coercion and punishment they have already adapted to is simply continued, carrying a high risk of retraumatization (Detrick et al., 2008).

Conclusion and Implications

To reiterate, maltreatment is only one factor influencing offending amongst many others, including gender, age (the vast majority of offending begins in adolescence and most of those involved desist as they get older), social inequality (with which there is a strong association both cross-nationally and locally – Wilkinson, 2005), loss and bereavement, parental conflict (not all of which involves domestic violence) and lack of supervision (not all of which constitutes neglect), educational failure and community deprivation. Whilst it is more relevant to girls' offending than to boys, the greater focus on victimization which is characteristic of research on women's offending also raises issues relevant to all young offenders. This final section reflects on some implications of the literature reviewed in this chapter.

First, the role of trauma in pathways to offending has been given little attention in the criminological literature, except in recent work by feminist criminologists on women offenders. It merits more attention, as do the implications for policy and practice. To recognize young people's victimization is not to deny their agency, but to understand better how it is experienced and exercised, including the way defensive investments in offending identities and lifestyles may protect against painful experiences of neglect, rejection, abuse and loss. As Coy puts it of young women drawn into prostitution from care, they had 'learned to resist their othering by embracing the role of an outsider' (2007: 11). Unless young offenders with histories of trauma are offered opportunities to make sense of their lives and resolve the emotional impacts, at least to some extent, their ability to make sufficient changes to construct a pro-social lifestyle embedded in the healthy relationships known to facilitate desistance is likely to be impaired. Creative ways of working with troubled young people are developing in many contexts, both in the community (Batmangelidjh, 2006; 2008) and in care (Boddy et al., 2005; Coy, 2007), and there is much to be learnt from them, most crucially the need for reliable, caring adults who are present for the whole young person and believe in them, with whom they can develop relationships of trust, and the considerable time the process may take. Alongside the high priority now given in the rehabilitation and resettlement of offenders to paid work (and education and training to enhance employability), more space needs to be made for the care and relationship-based approaches necessary to resolve trauma.

Despite some growth of attention to young offenders' welfare needs, including via the presence of social workers with responsibilities under the Children Act 1989 in youth offending teams and Young Offender Institutions, in a climate of public fear and political punitiveness, a preoccupation with risk and responsibilization frequently trumps considerations of children's welfare. Hence, broader grounds for custodial sentences for 12–14-year-olds introduced in 1994 resulted in an increase in the numbers of children under 15 sentenced to custody from 100 in 1992 to 824 in 2005–6 (Prison Reform Trust, 2008), despite a decline in recorded offending over the period. Custody may meet some needs – for example, for shelter, food, access to education and mental health services (Chitsabesan et al., 2006; Barrett and Byford, 2006) – but it carries a serious risk of retraumatization, and recidivism rates are high. A commitment to children's well-being requires as a minimum not only stronger efforts to divert those vulnerable from unresolved trauma (not just those with a formal diagnosis of mental illness (Baker et al., 2003)) away from custody, but also an expansion of therapeutic residential institutions, community-based alternatives such as intensive fostering, community mental health provision for young offenders (via forensic child and adolescent mental health services (CAMHS)) and properly constructed and resourced community supervision (McNeill, 2005) with attention to continuity of care across contexts. Youth courts should be informed with thorough assessments of traumatic experiences (which may underlie common patterns such as impulsivity, poor peer relationships, risk-taking) and their ongoing impacts. Use should be made of the provision in the Offender Management Act 2007 (Section 34) for young people on detention and training orders to be placed in non-custodial establishments (including specialist treatment facilities and residential schools). Where other considerations such as risk to the public make custody necessary, custodial institutions should avoid retraumatization (for example, via the use of strip searching and painful physical restraint procedures) where at all possible, and staff should be sufficiently trained and motivated to establish relationships with young people which can help them to manage their emotional lives and change their behaviour, with a stronger personal officer system developed to facilitate this.

Second, more attention is needed to gender in policy and practice with young offenders. The Youth Justice Board (YJB) (2005) recognizes that boys offend more than girls but dismisses gender as 'completely unmodifiable' and gives it no further attention, thus shutting its eyes to several decades of feminist and social scientific effort. As gender relations change, so too may the familiar gendered patterns of offending, but gender identity is too important to psycho-social development, and gender too culturally laden with meaning, for it easily to become irrelevant. Assumptions about gender, whether of similarity or difference, need continually to be checked against evidence. In recent political rhetoric on youth crime much emphasis has been placed on the positive potential of fathers' roles, though this is supported by research only for boys. Where gender is recognized in work with young men it is often simply by relying on traditionally gendered interests, football, for example, to engage them (Featherstone, Rivett and Scourfield, 2007). Valuable though such activities and other sports may be, opening up different ways of 'doing gender' may also help to build resilience and create space for change.

Because women offenders (young and adult) are a relatively small and particularly vulnerable group, often overlooked in criminological research, and because the prison service is by and large organized in a gender segregated way, a series of reports and recommendations have focused specifically on women (Prison Reform Trust, 2000; Corston, 2007). Although some progress has been made this way, it is slow, partly because such recommendations are easily perceived as preferential treatment for women, and resisted as being in tension with a commitment to equality. Whilst the orientation of the new gender equality duty to equality of outcome rather than equal treatment is helpful in requiring attention to different needs, care must be taken to distinguish between those needs which are clearly gender-specific (such as the needs of women offenders associated with menstruation, sexual health and pregnancy) and those that are interwoven with but not reduceable to gender (such as those associated with victimization, trauma and mental health problems). To address the latter only in relation to women offenders is to reflect the cultural resistance to mapping victimization onto masculinity, and hence to reinforce rather than deconstruct group differentiation (Fraser, 1997).

Finally, the association between maltreatment and offending needs to be set in broader context if it is not to reinforce the punitive, responsibilizing and remoralizing agenda for parents in policy on antisocial behaviour. In practice this focuses mostly on mothers who are struggling to manage children (mostly boys) with antisocial behaviour problems, whilst too often ignoring the contexts of multiple adversity (including their own past and present victimization) in which they are doing so (Squires, 2006; Hooper et al., 2007). Both some forms of maltreatment (physical abuse and neglect) and offending amongst young people are associated with poverty, and social inequality is clearly relevant to both (Wilkinson, 2005). Poverty, unemployment, poor housing, high-crime neighbourhoods and poor services, including long waits for mental health services for adults and children, the persistent experience of disrespect and high levels of uncertainty, may all undermine parents' capacity to fulfil their own aspirations in relation to their children. In this context, whilst parenting programmes, intensive family intervention projects and other whole family approaches are clearly helpful for some (Parr, 2008; Zeedyk, Werritty and Riach, 2008; Social Exclusion Unit, 2008), and should be fully informed about both the impacts of adversity on parenting and the diversity of values and meanings brought to it (influenced by class, gender and ethnicity), increasing use of compulsion and punishment with parents whose children offend is only likely to increase their alienation and sense of injustice (Hooper et al., 2007).

Furthermore, comparative research suggests that the association between maltreatment and young people's offending is not just a failure of parents and families but of governments in their commitment to children's rights and to policies to support families. The Nordic countries with more child- and family-friendly policies and political cultures than most Anglophone countries also have lower levels of childhood and youth aggression and violent crime (Covell and Howe, 2009). Some progress has been made in the United Kingdom with reference to a children's rights framework, but there is considerably further to go in relation both to child protection and to youth justice. The recommendations of the United Nations Committee on the Rights of the Child (2008) that corporal punishment be prohibited in all contexts, that resources to facilitate children's recovery from maltreatment and social reintegration be extended across the country, that the principle of the 'best interests of the child' be incorporated across policy including criminal justice, that detention be used only as a last resort facilitated by increased investment in alternatives, and that the age of criminal responsibility be raised (from its present level of 8 in Scotland and 10 in England, Wales and Northern Ireland) all deserve serious consideration. Much is still to happen in adolescence in terms of ongoing brain development, hormonal change and the development of reflective capacity (Rutter, Giller and Hagel, 1998), even without the impacts of trauma on development, as most parents know. Whilst issues of responsibility for young people's behaviour – of individual, family, community, society – are complex, the individualized and punishment-oriented response of the criminal justice system is profoundly at odds with our knowledge of child development, the promotion of children's well-being and the protection of their rights.

References

Baker, K. et al. (2003) *The Evaluation of the Validity And Reliability of the YJB's Assessment for Young Offenders.* Centre for Criminological Research, Oxford.

Barrett, B. and Byford, S. (2006) Mental health provision for young offenders: service use and cost. *British Journal of Psychiatry*, 188: 541–6.

Batchelor, S. (2005) Prove me the bam! Victimisation and agency in the lives of young women who commit violent offences. *Probation Journal*, 52: 4.

Batmanghelidjh, C. (2006), *Shattered Lives: Children Who Live with Courage and Dignity.* London and Philadelphia, Jessica Kingsley.

Batmanghelidjh, C. (2008) ASBOs don't work. The power of calm can, *The Times*, 2 June 2008.

Bauman, S. S. M. (2002) Fostering resilience in children. In C. L. Juntunen and D. R. Atkinson (eds.), *Counselling across the Lifespan*, Sage.

Benjamin, J. (1995) *Like Subjects, Love Objects – Essays on Recognition and Sexual Difference.* New Haven, Yale University Press.

Bewley, S. (2002) Restricting the freedom of pregnant women. In D. L. Dickenson (ed.), *Ethical Issues in Maternal-Fetal Medicine*, Cambridge: Cambridge University Press.

Boddy, J., Cameron, C., Mooney, A., Moss, P., Petrie, P. and Statham, J. (2005) *Introducing Pedagogy into the Children's Workforce: Children's Workforce Strategy: A Response to the Consultation Document.* TCRU, Institute of Education, University of London.

Boswell, G. (1997) The backgrounds of violent young offenders: the present picture. In V. Varma (ed.), *Violence in Children and Adolescents*, London, Jessica Kingsley.

Bowen, E., Heron, J. and Steer, C. (2008) *Anti-social and Other Problem Behaviour among Young Children: Findings from the ALSPAC*. Home Office Online Report no. 02/08. <www.homeoffice.gov.uk/rds>

Budd, T., Sharp, C., Weir, G., Wilson, D. and Owen, N. (2005) *Young People and Crime: Findings from the 2004 Offending, Crime and Justice Survey*. London: Home Office Report no. 20/05.

Butler, J. (1990) *Gender Trouble: Feminism and the Subversion of Identity*. London, Routledge.

Butler, J. (2004) *Undoing Gender*. London, Routledge.

Cameron, D. (2007) *The Myth of Mars and Venus: Do Men and Women Really Speak Different Languages?* Oxford, Oxford University Press.

Cawson, P. (2002) *Child Maltreatment in the Family*. London, NSPCC.

Cawson, P., Wattam, C., Brooker, S. and Kelly, G. (2000) *Child Maltreatment in the UK: A Study of the Prevalence of Child Abuse and Neglect*. London, NSPCC.

Cernkovich, S. A., Lanctot, N. and Giordano, P. C. (2008) Predicting adolescent and adult antisocial behaviour among adjudicated delinquent females. *Crime & Delinquency*, 54 (1): 3–33.

Chauhan, P. and Reppucci N. D. (2008) The impact of neighbourhood disadvantage and exposure to violence on self-report of antisocial behaviour among girls in the juvenile justice system. *Journal of Youth and Adolescence*, 38 (3): 401–16.

Chitsabesan, P., Kroll, L., Bailey, S., Kenning, C., Sneier, S., MacDonald, W. and Theodosiou, L. (2006) Mental health needs of young offenders in custody and in the community. *British Journal of Psychiatry*, 188: 534–40.

Chodorow, N. J. (1999). *The Reproduction of Mothering: Psychoanalysis and the Sociology of Gender*, 2nd edn. Berkeley, University of California Press.

Christie, N. (1986) The ideal victim. In E. Fattah, *From Crime Policy to Victim Policy*. London, Macmillan.

Corston, J. (2007) *The Corston Report: A Review of Women with Particular Vulnerabilities in the Criminal Justice System*. London, Home Office.

Covell, K. and Howe, R. B. (2009) *Children, Families and Violence: Challenges for Children's Rights*. London, Jessica Kingsley.

Coy, M. (2007) Young women, local authority care and selling sex: findings from research. *British Journal of Social Work*, 38 (7): 1408–24.

Cuevas, C. A., Finkelhor, D., Turner, H. A. and Ormrod, R. K. (2007) Juvenile delinquency and victimization: a theoretical typology. *Journal of Interpersonal Violence*, 22: 1581–602.

Daniels, C. R. (2002) Between fathers and fetuses: the social construction of fatherhood and the politics of fetal harm. In D. L. Dickenson (ed.), *Ethical Issues in Maternal-Fetal Medicine*, Cambridge: Cambridge University Press.

Denov, M. S. (2004) The long-term effects of child sexual abuse by female perpetrators: a qualitative study of male and female victims. *Journal of Interpersonal Violence*, 19: 1137–56.

Department of Health (2006) *Working Together to Safeguard Children: A Guide To Inter-Agency Working to Safeguard and Promote the Welfare of Children*. London, Home Office.

Detrick, S., Abel, G., Berger, M., Delon, A. and Meek, R. (2008) *Violence against Children in Conflict with the Law*. Amsterdam, Defence for Children International – The Netherlands.

Douglas, N. and Plugge, E. (2006) *A Health Needs Assessment for Young Women in YOIs*. London, Youth Justice Board.

Fagan, A. A. (2005) The relationship between adolescent physical abuse and criminal offending: support for an enduring and generalized cycle of violence. *Journal of Family Violence*, 20 (5): 279–90.

Farmer, E. and Pollock, S. (1998) *Sexually Abused and Abusing Children in Substitute Care*. Chichester, Wiley.

Farrington, D. P. (2007) Childhood risk factors and risk-focussed prevention. In M. Maguire, R. Morgan and R. Reiner (eds.), *Oxford Handbook of Criminology*. Oxford, Oxford University Press.

Farrington, D. P. and Painter, K. (2004) *Gender Differences in Risk Factors for Offending*, London, Home Office Research Development Statistics Directorate.

Farrington, D. and Welsh, B. (2007) *Saving Children from a Life of Crime*. Oxford, Oxford University Press.

Featherstone, B. and Evans, H. (2004) *Children Experiencing Maltreatment: Who Do They Turn To?* London, NSPCC.

Featherstone, B., Rivett, M. and Scourfield, J. (2007) *Working with Men in Health and Social Care*. London, Sage.

Feiring, C., Miller-Johnson, S. and Cleland, C. M. (2007) Potential pathways from stigmatization and internalizing symptoms to delinquency in sexually abused youth. *Child Maltreatment*, 12 (3): 220–32.

Fergusson, D. M. and Horwood, L. J. (2002) Male and female offending trajectories. *Development and Psychopathology*, 14: 159–77.

Finkelhor, D. (1994) The international epidemiology of child sexual abuse. *Child Abuse & Neglect*, 18 (5): 409–17.

Finkelhor, D., Ormrod, R. K. and Turner, H. A. (2007a) Poly-victimization: a neglected component in child victimization. *Child Abuse & Neglect*, 31 (1): 7–26.

Finkelhor, D., Ormrod, R. K. and Turner, H. A. (2007b) Revictimization patterns in a national longitudinal sample of children and youth. *Child Abuse and Neglect*, 31: 479–502, and commentary by S. N. Hart 'Reflections on the implications of revictimization patterns of children and youth as clarified by the research of Finkelhor, Ormrod and Turner', 473–77.

Fraser, N. (1997) From redistribution to recognition? Dilemmas of justice in a 'postsocialist' age. In N. Fraser, *Justice Interruptus: Critical Reflections on the 'Postsocialist' Condition*. London, Routledge.

Gadd, D. and Jefferson, T. (2007) *Psychosocial Criminology*. London, Sage.

Gallagher, B., Bradford, M. and Pease, K. (2002) The sexual abuse of children by strangers: its extent, nature and victims' characteristics. *Children & Society*, 16: 346–59.

Gelsthorpe, L. (2001) Critical Decisions and Processes in the Criminal Courts. In E. McLaughlin and J. Muncie (eds.), *Controlling Crime*. London: Sage/OU.

Gelsthorpe, L. and Sharpe, G. (2005) Gender, youth crime and justice. In B. Goldson and J. Muncie, *Youth Crime and Justice*, London: Sage.

Gerhardt, S. (2004) *Why Love Matters: How Affection Shapes a Baby's Brain*. London, Brunner-Routledge.

Gillies, V. (2007) *Marginalised Mothers: Exploring Working-Class Experiences of Parenting*. London, Routledge.

Gorin, S. (2004) *Understanding What Children Say about Living With Domestic Violence, Parental Substance Misuse or Parental Health Problems*. York, JRF Findings.

Green, L. (2000) Silenced Voice/Zero Choice – Young Women in Residential Care. In L. Green, P. Cox, S. Kershaw and J. Trotter (eds.), *Child sexual assault: feminist perspectives*. London: Palgrave.

Haas, H., Farrington, D. P., Killias, M. and Sattar, G. (2004) The impact of different family configurations on delinquency. *British Journal of Criminology*, 44: 520–32.

Hamilton, C. E., Falshaw, L. and Browne, K. D. (2002) The link between recurrent maltreatment and offending behaviour. *International Journal of Offender Therapy and Comparative Criminology*, 46 (1): 75–94.

Hansen, K. (2006) Gender differences in self-reported offending. In F. Heidensohn (ed.), *Gender and Justice: New Concepts and Approaches*, Devon: Willan Publishing.

Hart, J. L., O'Toole, S. K., Price-Sharps, J. L. and Schaffer, T. W. (2007) The risk and protective factors of violent juvenile offending: an examination of gender differences. *Youth Violence and Juvenile Justice*, 5: 367–84.

Herman, J. (1992) *Trauma and Recovery*. London, Pandora.

Herrera, V. M. and McCloskey, L. A. (2001) Gender differences in the risk for delinquency among youth exposed to family violence. *Child Abuse & Neglect*, 25 (8): 1037–51.

Hill, M., Lockyer, A. and Stone, F. (2007) Introduction: the principles and practice of compulsory intervention when children are 'at risk' or engage in criminal behaviour. In M. Hill et al. (eds.), *Youth Justice and Child Protection*, London: Jessica Kingsley.

HM Government (2008), *Youth Crime Action Plan*. London, Home Office.

Hobcraft, J. (1998) *Intergeneration and Life Course Transmission of Social Exclusion*, Working Paper 28, LSE Centre for the Analysis of Social Exclusion.

Hollway, W. (2006) *The Capacity to Care: Gender and Ethical Subjectivity*. London, Routledge.

Hooper, C. A. (2002) The maltreatment of children. In J. Bradshaw (ed.), *The Well-being of Children in the UK*. London. Save the Children/University of York.

Hooper, C. A. (2005) Child maltreatment in J. Bradshaw and E. Mayhew (eds.), *The Well-being of Children in the UK 2005*, vol. 2. London: Save the Children/University of York.

Hooper, C. A., Gorin, S., Cabral, C. and Dyson, C. (2007) *Living with Hardship 24/7: The Diverse Experiences of Families in Poverty in England*. London, The Frank Buttle Trust.

Hooper, C. A., Koprowska, J. and Milsom, R. (1999) *Research on Adult Survivors of Childhood Sexual Abuse: Report on Experiences of Services*, North Yorkshire Mental Health Co-ordinating Group.

Hooper, C. A. and Warwick, I. (2006), 'Gender and the politics of service provision for adults with a history of childhood sexual abuse', *Critical Social Policy*, Special Issue on Gender and Child Welfare, 26: 467–79.

Howden-Windell, J. and Clark, D. (1999) *Criminogenic Needs of Female Offenders*. London, HM Prison Service.

Howe, A. (2008) *Sex, Violence and Crime: Foucault and the 'Man' Question*. Routledge-Cavendish, Abingdon.

Jonson-Reid, M. (2004), Child welfare services and delinquency: the need to know more. *Child Welfare*, 83 (2): 157–73.

Jonson-Reid, M. and Barth, R. P. (2000) From maltreatment report to juvenile incarceration: the role of child welfare services. *Child Abuse & Neglect*, 24 (4): 505–20.

Lansford, J. E., Miller-Johnson, S., Berlin, L. J., Dodge, K. A., Bates, J. E. and Pettit, G. S. (2007) Early physical abuse and later violent delinquency: a prospective longitudinal study. *Child Maltreatment*, 12 (3): 233–45.

Lees, S. (2002) Gender, ethnicity and vulnerability in young women in local authority care. *British Journal of Social Work*, 32: 907–22.

Lisak, D. (1995) Integrating a critique of gender in the treatment of male survivors of childhood abuse, *Psychotherapy: Theory, Research, Practice, Training*, 32 (2): 258–69.

Lister, R. (2006) Children (but not women) first: New Labour, child welfare and gender. *Critical Social Policy*, 26 (2): 315–35.

Margo, J. and Stevens, A. (2008) *Make Me a Criminal. Preventing Youth Crime.* Institute for Public Policy Research, London.

McConville, S. (2003) *The Use of Punishment.* Devon: Willan.

McCord, J. (1983) A forty year perspective on effects of child abuse and neglect. *Child Abuse & Neglect*, 7: 265–70.

McMahon, J. and Clay-Warner, J. (2002) Child abuse and future criminality: the role of social service placement, family disorganization and gender. *Journal of Interpersonal Violence*, 17 (9): 1002–19.

McNeill, F. (2005) Community supervisions: context and relationships matter. In B. Goldson and J. Muncie (eds.), *Youth Crime and Justice.* London: Sage.

Miller, J. (2001) *One of the Guys: Girls, Gangs and Gender.* Oxford, Oxford University Press.

Moffitt, T. E., Caspi, A., Rutter, M. and Silva, P. A. (2001) *Sex Differences in Antisocial Behaviour: Conduct Disorder, Delinquency and Violence in the Dunedin Longitudinal Study.* Cambridge, Cambridge University Press.

Parr, S. (2008) Family intervention projects: a site of social work practice. *British Journal of Social Work.* <bjsw.oxfordjournals.org/papbyrecent.dtl> accessed 1 July 2009.

Perez, D. M. (2001) Ethnic differences in property, violent, and sex offending for abused and nonabused adolescents. *Journal of Criminal Justice*, 29 (5): 407–17.

Pitts, J. (2004) An examination into the connection between child protection registration and subsequent offending. *Research Matters*, April–October: 79–88.

Prison Reform Trust (2000) *Justice for Women, The Need for Reform: Report of the Committee on Women's Imprisonment chaired by Professor Dorothy Wedderburn.*

Prison Reform Trust (2008), *Bromley Briefings Prison Factfile.* June. <www.prisonreformtrust.org.uk>

Radford, L. and Hester, M. (2006) *Mothering through Domestic Violence.* London, Jessica Kingsley.

Raine, A., Brennan, P. and Sarnoff, A. M. (1994) Birth complications combined with early maternal rejection at age 1 year predispose to violence crime at age 18 years. *Archives of General Psychiatry*, vol. 51: 984–8.

Reich, J. A. (2005) *Fixing Families: Parents, Power and the Child Welfare System.* London, Routledge.

Robinson, R. (2005) 'Crystal Virtues': seeking reconciliation between ideals and violations of girlhood. *Contemporary Justice Review*, 8 (1): 59–73.

Roe, S. and Ashe, J. (2008) *Young People and Crime: Findings from the 2006 Offending, Crime and Justice Survey*. London, Home Office Statistical Bulletin.

Rutter, M., Giller, H. and Hagel, A. (1998) *Anti-social Behaviour by Young People*. Cambridge, Cambridge University Press.

Ryan, J. P. and Testa, M. F. (2005) Child maltreatment and juvenile delinquency: investigating the role of placement and placement instability. *Children and Youth Services Review*, 27 (3): 227–49.

Salter, D., McMillan, D., Richards, M., Talbot, T., Hodges, J., Bentovim, A. et al. (2003) Development of sexually abusive behaviour in sexually victimised males: a longitudinal study. *The Lancet*, 361 (9356): 471–6.

Salzinger, S., Rosario, M. and Feldman, R. S. (2007) Physical child abuse and adolescent violent delinquency: the mediating and moderating roles of personal relationships. *Child Maltreatment*, 12 (3): 208–19.

Schuck, A. M. and Widom, C. S. (2005) Understanding the role of neighbourhood context in the long-term criminal consequences of child maltreatment. *American Journal of Community Psychology*, 36 (3): 207–22.

Seaford, H. (2001) Children and childhood: perceptions and realities. *The Political Quarterly*, 72 (4): 454–65.

Silverthorn, P. and Finch, P. J. (1999) Developmental pathways to antisocial behaviour: the delayed-onset pathway in girls. *Development & Psychopathology*, 11 (1): 101–26.

Silvestri, M. and Crowther-Dowey, C. (2008) *Gender and Crime*. London, Sage.

Singleton, N., Meltzer, H., Gatward, R., Coid, J. and Deasy, D. (1998) *Psychiatric Morbidity among Prisoners in England and Wales*. London, The Stationery Office.

Smart, C. (2007) *Personal Life: New Directions in Sociological Thinking*. Polity Press, Cambridge.

Smith, D. (2004) *The Links between Victimization and Offending*. Briefing paper no. 5, Edinburgh Study of Youth Transitions and Crime.

Smith, D. J. (2007) Crime and the life course. In M. Maguire, R. Morgan and R. Reiner (eds.), *The Oxford Handbook of Criminology*, 4th edn. Oxford: Oxford University Press.

Smith, D. J. and Ecob, R. (2007) An investigation into causal links between victimization and offending in adolescents. *British Journal of Sociology*, 58 (4): 633–59.

Social Exclusion Unit (2008) *Think Family: A Literature Review of Whole Family Approaches*. London, UK Social Exclusion Unit.

Spohn, R. E. (2000) Gender differences in the effect of child maltreatment on criminal activity over the life course. In G. Fox Litton (ed.), *Families, Crime and Criminal Justice*. Stamford, CT, JAI Press.

Spratt, T. (2009) Identifying families with multiple problems: possible responses from child and family social work to current policy developments. *British Journal of Social Work*, 39 (3): 435–50.

Squires, P. (2006) New Labour and the politics of anti–social behaviour. *Critical Social Policy*, 26: 144–68.

Steffensmeier, D. (1996) Gender and crime: towards a gendered theory of female offending. *Annual Review of Sociology*, 22: 459–87.

Taussig, H. N. (2002) Risk behaviours in maltreated youth placed in foster care: a longitudinal study of protective and vulnerability factors. *Child Abuse & Neglect*, 26 (11): 1179–99.

Taussig, H. N. and Talmi, A. (2001) Ethnic differences in risk behaviours and related psychosocial variables among a cohort of maltreated adolescents in foster care. *Child Maltreatment*, 6: 180–92.

Tisdall, E. K. M. (2006) Antisocial behaviour legislation meets children's services: challenging perspectives on children, parents and the state. *Critical Social Policy*, 26 (1): 101–20.

Turton, J. (2008) *Child Abuse, Gender and Society*. London, Routledge.

Uprichard, E. (2008) Children as 'beings and becomings': children, childhood and temporality. *Children & Society*, 22: 303–13.

Victim Support (2007) *Hoodie or Goodie? The Link between Violent Victimisation and Offending in Young People: A Research Report*. London, Victim Support.

Wall, A. E., Barth, R. P. and the NSCAW Research Group (2005) Aggressive and delinquent behaviour of maltreated adolescents: risk factors and gender differences. *Stress, Trauma and Crisis*, 8: 1–24.

Widom, C. S. (1989) Child abuse, neglect and violent criminal behaviour. *Criminology*, 27 (2): 251–71.

Wilkinson, R. G. (2005) *The Impact of Inequality: How to Make Sick Societies Healthier*. London, Routledge.

Youth Justice Board (2005) *Risk and Protective Factors*. London, Youth Justice Board.

Youth Justice Trust (2004) *On the Case: A Survey of over 1,000 Children and Young People under Supervision by Youth Offending Teams in Greater Manchester and West Yorkshire*. Manchester: Youth Justice Trust.

Zeedyk, M. S., Werritty, I. and Riach, C. (2008) One year on: perceptions of the lasting benefits of involvement in a parenting support programme. *Children & Society*, 22: 99–111.

4

Gender and Schooling

Shereen Benjamin

Introduction

Every year, when the results of the United Kingdom's school examinations[1] are made public, attention is drawn to the relative underperformance of boys. A reasonably well-informed observer of education in the United Kingdom, and indeed throughout much of the minority world, might be forgiven for thinking that boys' 'underachievement' is the most pressing – or even the only – issue in gender and education. It would seem that the question of the times

[1]The constituent countries of the United Kingdom all have different education and examination systems. In England, 'high-stakes' testing features prominently when children are 7, 11, 16 and 18. In Scotland, Wales and Northern Ireland, the process is arguably less intense than in England, though results of school-leaving exams are still widely publicized.

Gender and Child Welfare in Society Edited by Brid Featherstone, Carol-Ann Hooper, Jonathan Scourfield, and Julie Taylor.

for educators is how to enable boys to raise their game. The August 2008 *Guardian* headline, 'SATS results reach plateau as boys struggle with reading' (Curtis 2008) is typical of the many news stories that feature in national and local media each summer. There are, however, many reasons why we should treat such claims with caution. First, if we unquestioningly accept that boys are underachieving, we are, implicitly, accepting without challenge a regime of high-stakes testing as the only way to measure, and accord value to, education. Second, the notion of boys' underachievement can obscure important questions about which groups of boys are doing badly in education and which groups are really doing rather well – and can likewise obscure important questions of which girls are doing well, and which girls are not. Third, we risk constructing boys as the problem of education upon whom policy initiatives must focus, and constructing girls as straightforward and 'easy' to educate. It is worth spending a little time considering each of these in turn.

High-stakes standardized testing of schoolchildren in the United Kingdom dates from the late 1980s. The 1980s saw the schooling systems of the United Kingdom gripped by a panic about the educational and behavioural standards being achieved by schools and their pupils. This panic took on its own distinctive formulations in the United Kingdom but was also linked to the restructuring of education systems in most minority world countries in the wake of globalization and changes to the global labour market.[2] Restructuring in the United Kingdom was legitimized through the combination of two distinct ideological positions. On the one hand was a 'traditional' conservative view that values such as discipline and respect for authority were being eroded along with the neglect of traditional skills such as arithmetic and spelling. And on the other hand, but running alongside that view in sometimes uneasy juxtaposition, was the neo-liberal perspective that a public sector monopoly within schooling was no longer capable (if it ever had been) of delivering an appropriately skilled workforce for the increasingly competitive global economy (see, for example, Johnson 1991). Local education

[2]'Minority world' refers to those rich and powerful countries where a minority of the world's population live. I have used it here as an alternative to 'Western' and 'developed' because it is more accurate, and draws attention to the inequalities between rich and poor nations.

authorities (LEAs) and teachers, it was argued, were failing to act as the guarantors of standards and were indoctrinating children instead of educating them (Ball 1990; Jones and Mahony 1989). This systematic undermining of LEAs (especially those led by Labour) and of teachers created the conditions in which the Education Reform Act of 1988 was passed. The Education Reform Act effectively brought quasi-market conditions into schooling through the introduction in England and Wales of a National Curriculum according to which children could be tested. Standard assessment tasks[3] and tests would provide 'objective', measurable results through which the performance of children, and through them, their teachers and schools, could be judged. 'Good' schools (that is, those whose pupils performed well in the tests) would prove attractive to parents, and would, according to the laws of the marketplace, grow and flourish. 'Bad' schools, where pupils did not do so well, would wither and die. Budgetary control was largely taken out of the hands of the LEAs and redistributed to schools, paving the way for subsequent moves towards marketization, privatization and commercialization of schooling in England. Scotland and Northern Ireland followed England and Wales with similar, though perhaps less intensive, processes, and the structural reforms in these countries have not yet been as far-reaching. Teachers were reconstructed as deliverers of a curriculum decided at national level, and their performance could now be measured and made public in local 'league tables' of school examination results. High-stakes testing – that is, testing and examination regimes where there is more at stake than simply informing individual children's education – is therefore 'linked to a mistrustful regulation of teacher work' (Hayes, Mills, Christie and Lingard 2006: 82) in the name of accountability. It has also been widely argued (see, for example, Reay and Lucey 2000; Slee, Weiner and Tomlinson 1998; Tomlinson 1994) that the National Curriculum and its attendant testing regimes reduce the complex business of learning to that which can be quantified, and reduce the complex craft of teaching to a set of arid techniques. This reductive approach to education leaves out, or renders invisible, much of what is learnt in classrooms. It also blunts what should be a nuanced understanding of the interplay of social

[3] When standard assessment tasks for 7-year-olds were introduced in England and Wales the name was abbreviated to 'SATS'. The name stuck and remains in popular use for what are formally called 'national tests'.

differences and the way these shape children's and young people's experiences of schooling: for instance, making it appear as if boys, as a homogenous group, are performing poorly in school. This takes us to the second problem with the 'underachieving boys' narrative.

Since the late 1990s, critical commentators have likened the concern around boys' 'underachievement' to a moral panic in which the rhetoric oversimplifies and exceeds the reality. This is not to say that some boys' attainment within and engagement with schooling is not a legitimate cause for concern. Francis and Skelton (2005: 6) suggest that 'it is clear that *generally* boys are doing less well than are girls in terms of exam performance, and that in spite of much effort on the part of policy-makers and many teachers, this gap remains significant (particularly in relation to language and literacy subjects)'. But the same authors go on to show that social class and, to a lesser extent, 'race', are the most significant variables in school achievement, whilst Burgess et al. (2008: 9) argue that what they call the 'poverty gap', as measured by the number of pupils in a school eligible for free school meals, has a much greater impact than the gender gap. In other words, whilst girls from disadvantaged backgrounds tend to outperform boys from similar backgrounds in school examinations, both are outperformed by boys from better-off backgrounds. When pupil ethnicity is taken into account, the picture is complicated further, with some groups doing far better than others. For instance, in 2005, 77.1 per cent of boys from Chinese backgrounds (the highest-attaining ethnic group) achieved five or more GCSE passes at grade C or above, whilst only 54.1 per cent of girls from Pakistani backgrounds, and 20 per cent of girls from Gypsy Roma backgrounds (the lowest-attaining ethnic group) did so (Department for Education and Skills 2006). Closer analysis of the statistics demonstrates the importance of reading socio-economic status, gender and ethnicity together, as these do not operate separately. For example, taking free school meal entitlement (FSM) as a proxy measure for poverty, 'although still one of the lowest attaining groups at GCSE (a quarter of Black Caribbean and Black Other FSM boys achieve 5+A*–C), the attainment of White British FSM boys is even lower, at 21%, compared to 66% of Chinese FSM boys and 48% of Indian FSM boys' (Department for Education and Skills 2006: 64). It is also important to remember that the pattern is not consistent across all school subjects. Burgess et al. (2008: 7) show that the perceived gender gap in GCSE examinations taken by pupils at age 16 is driven by English: in Maths and in Science, girls' and boys' attainment is roughly equal, with boys slightly outperforming girls at the very top of the grade spectrum. There are, therefore, important questions to be asked about which boys and which girls are underachieving and why; I will return to these later in the chapter. What it is important to note here is that the notion of boys' underachievement deflects attention away from the intersecting network of social differences through which children and young people experience schooling.

This brings me to the third of the problems I outlined, and to the construction of boys as the problem of education. Epstein et al. (1998) identify three distinct narratives that have emerged through the overarching discourse of boys' underachievement: a 'pity the poor boys' narrative that positions boys as the victims of a society and a schooling system that places more value on girls and their capacities; a 'failing schools failing boys' narrative associated with the more generalized panic about school standards already discussed here, in combination with the idea that schools have become feminized places which are therefore less accessible to boys; and a 'boys will be boys' narrative that sees boys as innately less capable than girls of doing well at school. None of these narratives are likely to prove helpful for boys or girls. On the one hand, they continue to elide the question of how gender operates in conjunction with multiple differences to produce the contexts in which children and young people experience schooling. And, on the other hand, they render girls unproblematic and therefore invisible. If schoolgirls are achieving, then they no longer require our concern. Nor do we have to engage with the consequences for girls of some boys' anti-school orientation: consequences which include the enduring phenomenon of boys' domination of physical space and teacher time. As Francis and Skelton (2005: 5) note, 'to suggest that all girls are now achieving, or all boys underachieving, and proceeding on that basis, clearly risks ignoring (and hence potentially exacerbating) the continuing underachievement of particular groups of girls'. This, indeed, is what appears to be happening: what we are now seeing is a failure to allocate time and resources to girls' needs in school, and a failure to address the consequences of boys' domination of schools and classrooms (Francis 2005; Osler and Vincent 2003).

There are, therefore, three sets of interrelated problems with the dominant notion of boys' underachievement. I have outlined them separately here, but in reality it is important to consider them together: a reductive approach to what counts as 'achievement' in schooling, the elision of multiple and intersecting social differences such as social class and 'race', and the positioning of boys as the problem and girls the success story of schooling all combine to produce the contexts in which schools currently operate. In the next section of this chapter, I will try to put the jigsaw together, using theories of gender to explore the question of what counts as a 'successful' education for boys and girls in England and Scotland, and drawing on narrative data collected in English and Scottish schools. I will consider in particular the gendered construction of special educational needs (SEN)[4] in the context of what counts as success. Finally, I will outline the implications of some wider societal changes for policy, practice and research in gender and education.

Masculinities and Schooling: what counts as 'success' for boys?

In England, the public policy story of what counts as success in schooling is clear, and it is apparently ungendered. The marker of success for schools and their pupils and students is the attainment of the 'benchmark' levels of success: National Curriculum Level 4 at age 11, Level 5 at age 14 and 5 GCSE passes at grades A*-C at age 16. In Scotland things are somewhat less clear-cut. School pupils take the level A–E tests relating to the Curriculum Guidelines when their schools deem them ready. School leavers customarily take a cocktail of Standard Grades, Intermediate 1 and 2, Highers and Advanced Highers. Nonetheless, the local and national press in Scotland, like

[4]The term 'special educational needs' was introduced in the United Kingdom in 1981 following the publication of the Warnock Report (1978), which had criticized the old terminology of 'handicap'; it was intended to suggest that difficulties in school were not simply the result of within-child deficit but could also be environmental. In Scotland, the term was replaced with 'additional support needs' in 2005, with the intention of moving even further from a within-child deficit model. However, since England, with its much larger school population, still uses SEN, I have used it here.

the local and national press in England, construct 'league tables' of school performance based on pupils' and students' examination results.

But this public policy story is only part of the picture. Boys in schools are engaged in a much bigger project: that of learning to be men in the communities in which they find themselves. Success or otherwise in meeting the formal requirements of schooling is part of that project. For some boys, the formal requirements of schooling sit unproblematically alongside the larger project of becoming the kind of man they want to be. For many boys, however, tensions and contradictions emerge. To explain some of these contradictions, there has been a tendency for sociologists of education to turn to work on masculinities (see, for example, Connell 1995; Connell 2002; Haywood and Mac an Ghaill 1996; Kenway, Kraack and Hickey-Moody 2006; Martino 2001) to help understand the contradictory demands and desires faced by schoolboys. Jackson (2006: 11) sums up the explanation suggested in this body of work:

> Evidence suggests . . . that academic work is perceived by many young people as 'feminine' . . . Hegemonic masculinity is constructed in opposition to femininity, and so boys must *avoid* any activities associated with femininity. Therefore, if schoolboys want to avoid the physical and verbal abuse attached to being labelled as 'feminine', they must *avoid* academic work, or at least they must *appear* to avoid academic work. If boys want to undertake academic work, but they want to do so without harassment, they must work covertly.

Although such an explanation is far from perfect (it does not, for example, explain why some boys *do* want to engage with academic work), it is worth unravelling a little further. In a 2006 episode of the reality TV show *Strictly Come Dancing*,[5] one of the judges remarked to a celebrity contestant following his performance of the Paso Doble,[6] 'You *reek* of masculinity'. What she meant was clear. She was using a visceral metaphor to tell the contestant and the viewers that he was

---

[5]The format of *Strictly Come Dancing* consists of celebrities performing classical and Latin dances with their professional partners/coaches. Each performance is marked and commented upon by a panel of expert judges before a public elimination vote is cast.
[6]The *Paso Doble* is the Spanish bullfighter dance. The man stamps, commands, struts and throws the woman around the floor.

(amongst other things) dominant, virile, heterosexually attractive, physically strong, powerful and commanding. Such characteristics, argue many sociologists, are associated with what have been called 'hegemonic' (dominant, or ideal) versions of masculinity in most Western societies. Whilst there is no one definition of masculinity, there does seem to be agreement that masculinities – different ways of being boys and men – relate to identifiable social and cultural ideals, and are hierarchically ordered. For Connell (1995: 77), hegemonic masculinity 'can be defined as the configuration of gender practice which embodies the currently accepted answer to the problem of the legitimacy of patriarchy, which guarantees (or is taken to guarantee) the dominant position of men and the subordination of women'.

In the same work, Connell goes on to outline a four-part relational pattern, characterized by four overarching versions of masculinity. Standing in opposition to hegemonic masculinity, he argues, is subordinated masculinity: the 'dumping ground' of everything that hegemonic masculinity is not. Thus, if hegemonic masculinity is associated in a particular community with dominance, virility, heterosexual attractiveness, physical strength, power and command/control, then subordinate masculinity will be associated with submission, lack of virility, homosexuality or lack of heterosexual attractiveness, physical weakness or vulnerability, powerlessness and subordination to another's command/control. Adjacent to hegemonic masculinity, complicit masculinities allow men and boys to 'reap the patriarchal dividend' (that is, realize the advantages that accrue to men and boys in a society still largely run by men) without the need to embody the hegemonic ideal. Marginalized masculinities, on the other hand, include some of the embodied characteristics of hegemonic masculinity (such as toughness and physical strength) but without the societal and cultural authority of hegemonic masculinity. Connell associates this version of masculinity with communities marginalized through 'race' and social class. As Paechter (2007) and others have pointed out, each individual man and boy constructs his own masculinity in relation to these configurations, but the point is that he does not do so in a vacuum. Individual masculinities are much more varied than any typology might suggest. However, they all stand in relation to the hegemonic ideal.

Where, then, does this take us with respect to boys and schooling? Crucially, what such an analysis does is draw our attention to the negotiation of power relations which, though absent from public policy discourse on what counts as success in education, in reality shapes and produces boys' and girls' engagement with schooling. Studies of working-class schoolboys from the 1970s onwards have shown that such boys can be more interested in demonstrating their anti-authority and anti-school orientations than in engaging with the formal goals of the school (see, for example, Benjamin 2001; Dalley-Trim 2007 and many others; Mac an Ghaill 1994; Willis 1977). The argument here is that boys from more marginalized communities lack the authority and legitimacy associated with hegemonic masculinity; their attempts to dominate and control are not, for the most part, recognizable as powerful beyond their immediate circles, and will not, for the most part, translate into the occupation of positions of power in adulthood. Therefore, it is argued, schoolboys will come to desire, embody and perform some of the characteristics of hegemonic masculinity, such as physical strength and domination of space, in what has variously been called hyper-masculinity, protest masculinity and marginalized masculinity. These masculinities, whilst they may not confer in the long term the power associated with hegemonic masculinity, do at least enable boys to demonstrate their distance from the powerlessness associated with subordinated masculinities. Such an explanation has much to commend it, not least because it begins to enable us to understand the connections between gender, social class, 'race' and other social differences. It is important, however, to see such an explanation as the beginning of an account, and not as an over-determinant of the experiences of *all* boys from disadvantaged or marginalized communities, nor as *the* account for all boys who do not do well at school.

To take just one example, Ryan (not his real name) did not have an easy ride through his first years of schooling. According to the formal policy discourse, he was unsuccessful. The normative benchmarks for attainment were inaccessible to him, and he was identified in Year 3 (when aged 7) as having SEN. Having spent most of his primary years in a mainstream school, he transferred to the special education sector at the beginning of Year 5, soon after his ninth birthday. He took with him an unhappy history of failing to make discernible academic progress and of failing to make friends with other children as he progressed through the mainstream school. By the end of his first half-term in a small, all-age special school, he declared himself to be much happier and began to make academic progress, albeit not at a rate that would enable him to attain the national benchmarks for 'success'. Ryan's mother described how she made sense of the changes in Ryan's engagement with schooling:

> We didn't want to put Ryan into a special school, but now that he's here, our family life, well, our family life has changed beyond recognition, he's like a changed boy, and the battles we used to have every morning to get him to come to school, every morning he whined and whined and wouldn't get out of bed, there's just nothing like it now . . . In [mainstream] school, all he could think about was playtime, it was a complete nightmare for him, you know, he couldn't make the football team, let's face it, he couldn't begin to even kick the ball or even know which goalpost to aim for, and his playtimes were a complete nightmare, so he never wanted to go to school. It wasn't even that they bullied him, the teachers there were very good, they didn't allow bullying, it was just, I don't know, in the atmosphere somehow, between the children . . . He obviously wasn't a clever boy, not in the usual sense of the word, and the boys were either clever or good at football, it had to be one or the other, and poor Ryan, well, he just didn't fit in. There was another child in his class, she was a sweet little thing, Ryan used to like her, they sat on the same table, and they both went to [the Learning Support Unit] together, and she used to play with the little infants at playtime, but Ryan could hardly do that, could he, a boy his size? (interview, all-age special school, England)

It is no coincidence that Ryan's mother attributes Ryan's disposition towards schooling largely to his inclusion or otherwise in playground football. Sport in general, and football in particular, is one of the foremost sites for the production of masculinities in English primary schools. It is on the football field (or, in most urban schools, the allotted corner of the tarmac playground) that boys struggle over their hold on dominant versions of masculinity (Benjamin 1998; Gard 2001; Renold 1997; Skelton 2001; Smith 2007). The version of masculinity being struggled over is one of physical strength and skill, where physical strength is associated with the considerable material rewards of top footballers, with the ability to win fights and with heterosexual prowess and attractiveness to girls (Benjamin 2001; Epstein and Johnson 1998). As Thorne (1993) and others have noted, failure to excel in playground football is associated, for even very young boys, with 'gayness', and seen as the antithesis of successful masculinity. This failure is particularly marked for those boys whose hold on hegemonic masculinity is the most tenuous and fragile. Thorne observed that very successful boys – those who have many resources 'in the bank' on which to draw – can afford to be least invested in continual demonstrations of 'macho' masculinity since their hold on success is secure. The opposite is true for boys such as Ryan who cannot lay claim to many of the traditional markers of success. But it would be an over-simplification to assume that for boys who cannot lay claim to those traditional markers a hyper-masculine 'laddishness' is the inevitable outcome. Other variables, such as physical dexterity and size in this case, complicate the picture. For Ryan, not only are powerful hegemonic masculinities out of reach, but the contingently powerful marginalized or hyper-masculinities are equally unavailable. What is interesting here is the interplay between the formal school discourses of what counts as 'success' and the informal or microcultural peer group versions of what counts as 'success': both contributed to the construction of a position in his mainstream primary school that Ryan and his family had found hard to live with.

As I will argue in more detail in the next section, SEN, associated with neediness, is also associated with vulnerability and femininity. This meant that Ryan was constantly fighting an uphill (and often losing) battle to be recognized as 'properly' masculine. As Ryan's mother remarked, he was not in a position to go and play with the younger children in his previous school, unlike his 'sweet little' girl classmate. For a boy whose hold on masculinity was already tenuous such an action would have been unthinkable as it would have inscribed him as feminine, and positioned him firmly within the subordinate version of masculinity. But Ryan's physical characteristics – he was heavily built and his severe dyspraxia meant he was clumsy and lacked physical strength and dexterity – made it impossible for him to use the site of the football game to perform the hyper-masculinity apparently necessary for a boy with so little 'in the bank'. Ryan's response to the masculinities available in his mainstream primary school had been a withdrawal from peer group activity as far as possible, leading to a dislike and fear of school.

Following Ryan's mother's account, it might be thought that the special school, unlike the mainstream school, was a gentle place in which boys could perform a wider range of masculinities. Ryan certainly found it a more hospitable environment, so maybe this was true to an extent. However, it did not mean that hyper-masculinities were absent. Indeed, a large proportion of the boys at the special school habitually took up hyper-masculine behaviours. The Year 6 (10–11-year-old) boys, for example, had developed a contamination chasing game, in which the chaser would be designated as 'gay', and in which he would pass the 'gayness' on through touching someone else, the object of the game being to avoid the chaser's touch. They also routinely engaged in collective appreciation of girls they deemed to be attractive, and in collective derogation of girls deemed unattractive, often using extremely (hetero)sexist language, and readily engaging in fighting over the girls of their choice. Through such acts – the explicit performance of heterosexualized identities – the boys would attempt to distance themselves from all things effeminate. Davies might argue that their chasing game and ritualized pursuit of 'desirable' girls acted as a signifying practice:

> Boys, for example, to be recognised as appropriate boys, must perform themselves as heterosexual before they can know what that might mean. In order to be recognisable as heterosexual, they may engage in signifying practices through which they abject the 'other', cast it out from the self. They may revile girls and 'sissy boys', for example, in attempts to signal, 'this is what I am not'. They accomplish this through acts that signal, 'this disgusts me'. Through such practices they may gain for themselves a sense of being heterosexual. (2006: 428)

I am not arguing here that *only* boys considered to have SEN take up hyper-masculinities. To the contrary, Davies is arguing that such practices are widespread amongst schoolboys. But these boys' inability to access the formally-sanctioned, dominant sites of male power – and in particular their failure to make the linear progress associated with the incrementally-developing boy – together with their inscription into the 'neediness' connoted by SEN, apparently made informal hyper-masculine performances such as the 'you're gay' chasing game particularly imperative for those boys who were physically able to perform them. The point here is that popular conceptualizations of 'laddishness', and exhortations from the media and from politicians that boys should raise their game and schools should make them do so, do not adequately explain the complex and intricate processes through which boys negotiate the intersecting web of differences (such as class, 'race', disability, physical appearance and so on) in the context of local and systemic relations of power.

Femininities and schooling: what counts as 'success' for girls?

As suggested earlier, discourses of underachieving boys connote also their opposite: high- (or over-) achieving girls. Usually, this connotation is unspoken: although the successful girl is the commonsense corollary to the underachieving boy, she goes unmentioned and remains implicitly in the shadow of the boys. Ringrose's (2007) powerful analysis of what she calls the 'post-feminist, neoliberal discourses of educational achievement and gender equality' demonstrates the ways in which the neo-liberal, meritocratic fantasy that everyone can be successful if they only work hard enough and aim high enough, is projected onto the fantasy ideal of the successful, high-achieving girl, who has never had it so good.

> The successful girls discourse has a widening scope and powerful reach, spreading in complex ways through the realm of globalised popular culture inspiring, on the one hand, dread and anxiety over the 'feminization' of culture, and confirming and co-constructing, on the other, the girl as metaphor for neoliberal discourse of personal performance, choice and freedom, and its auxiliary and mutually reinforcing discourse or 'rationale' of individual responsibility for self-failure in the 'global education race'. (Ringrose 2007: 481)

If boys are now the problem for education, girls are the 'proof' that current insistence on a narrow conceptualization of standards and a crude system of measuring those standards is working. The apparent success of large numbers of girls in attaining benchmark levels in school examinations enables policy-makers to claim that standards are rising and that their policies must therefore be the right ones. But positioning girls as the success story is fraught with problems. Just as the dominant narrative of boys' underachievement obscures the complexities of which boys might be doing well and which boys might be doing badly, so does its opposite, the high-achieving girl narrative, elide questions of which girls are not doing well. In addition, this dominant narrative allows us to evade the question of what the costs might be for high-achieving girls, and draws attention away from the lived realities of schooling for girls in boy-dominated environments.

As discussed earlier, gaps in school achievement according to socio-economic status and ethnicity are more significant than those of gender, and all are co-constructed. The implicit suggestion that if all boys are currently underachieving then all girls must be overachieving is a serious mistake, and, as suggested earlier, carries the risk that the underachievement of girls from particular groups will be at best ignored (Francis and Skelton 2005: 5). Walkerdine, Lucey and Melody (2001: 4) argue that, despite the slipperiness of social class as a marker of difference, 'it is clear that in new millennium Britain class is just as important as it ever was'. In their longitudinal study of girls' and young women's trajectories through schooling, they show that social class, more than anything else, explains their distinct experiences of school. Whether one accepts the slippery conceptualizations of social class, or prefers to concentrate on more easily measurable phenomena, such as economic disadvantage and (in schools) eligibility for free school meals as a measure of poverty, what is inescapable is that girls from more advantaged families tend to do better than girls from less advantaged families.

Does that necessarily mean that all is well for these high-flying girls from advantaged backgrounds? This is far from clear, and there is evidence to the contrary. In the study referred to above, Walkerdine et al. argue that high-achieving middle-class girls found it much more difficult to be proud of their performance than did working-class girls whose achievements were far more modest, and that despite hard evidence in the form of superlative examination grades, these high-achieving girls felt they were never 'good enough'. The costs for these young women of having been high-achievers all the way through their schooling was a perpetual sense of inadequacy, and an internalization of failure (or the fear of failure) as 'a personal one that could only be overcome by working harder and harder' (Walkerdine, Lucey and Melody, 2001: 180). Furthermore, as Ali (2003) points out, the production of a 'successful' schoolgirl self involves achievement that includes but also surpasses academic success: it would seem that successful schoolgirl femininities are produced through an intersection of perceived academic ability, social class, 'race', access to popular culture, material wealth evidenced through ownership of particular brand names, and (heterosexually-coded) attractiveness. A tough set of requirements for even the most accomplished girls.

There appears to be a contradiction. Would not this single-minded, individualistic pursuit of academic and social success, prefiguring success in the global labour market, be more easily associated with hegemonic masculinity? Are we seeing a reworking of femininities in school? Have traditional, 'girly' femininities given way in classrooms to 'girl power' versions? The reality, as always, is more complicated, and requires us to think about femininities, their history, and their current configurations. Blaise summarizes how Connell's work on masculinities has been used to develop understandings of femininities:

> According to Connell's (1987) understandings of femininity and masculinity, there is no femininity in our present society that is hegemonic. Instead, there is a type of femininity called emphasized femininity, which is defined around the compliance with subordination and is oriented around accommodating the interests and desires of men. In other words, emphasized femininity does not regulate other forms of femininities, but is always constructed in relation to hegemonic masculinity . . . Both hegemonic masculinity and emphasized femininity maintain practices that institutionalize men's dominance over women, or . . . boys' dominance over girls. As a result, the gendered social order is regulated by the children *themselves* as they take an active part in the gendering process. (2005: 21)

A traditional emphasized femininity, then, might be associated with the stereotype of the 'dumb blonde': the passive, intellectually and physically weak, indecisive, heterosexually appealing (and available) girl or woman who invites and submits willingly to another's control. Such a stereotype would seem to have nothing at all to do with the high-achieving girls of the early twenty-first century. And yet *Mizz* magazine, which styles itself the 'BIGGEST fortnightly girls' mag', aimed at the pre-teen market, carried articles in 2008 that would appear to exude emphasized femininity. For instance, in a 2008 edition, 'we get to go aahhhh over cute, fluffy animals' and 'everything we own is pink' were listed as amongst the best things about being a girl. The fortnightly *Mizz Boys* page carries sections on 'Flirting Tips', 'Bag Your Crush', 'What do They [boys] Think?' and 'Problems Answered', where it is clear the problems will relate to securing and retaining the attentions of boys (2008). Firminger's (2006) study of North American girls' magazines would appear to suggest that the objectification of boys as potential 'boyfriend material' constructs a commodified version of emphasized femininity in which girls' opportunities to shop around the boyfriend market are contingent on the extent to which they can produce themselves as both desirable and informed consumers: 'socialised to be purchasers of beauty and fashion products that promise to make them attractive to boys, girls are "in charge" of themselves and the boys they "choose". It's a competitive market, so they better have the right understanding of boys, as well as the right body and outfit to go with it' (Firminger 2006: 306). It might be supposed, then, that emphasized femininity has not so much given way to powerful and high-attaining versions of femininity, but exists alongside them. The gendered social order regulated by today's schoolgirls involves them in consciously producing themselves as successful objects of boys' desires, in order to maximize their 'capital' on the relationship market. Here, the successful girl is bright, sharp and able to make informed choices, and her intellectual capital is an important part of her production of a desirable and desiring self. This version of emphasized femininity, contingent as ever on eventual subordination to boys but reworked in the context of consumerist practices, is not necessarily incompatible with academic success. Academic success is one amongst many markers of successful girlhood: its significance varies across socio-economic and ethnic groups, and is worked into the negotiation of the peer-group cultures that exist in and beyond schools. Depending on local context, academic success might stand for power and status, or might come to signify over-compliance with authority, but is always amenable to being co-opted into traditional versions of femininity. The point here is that emphasized femininity – part of the constellation of practices that maintain boys' dominance over girls – is far from obsolete, and girls' academic success is not necessarily its antithesis.

In these twenty-first-century practices and understandings, we can discern many echoes and influences from the gender regimes of the past. Walkerdine and the Girls Into Mathematics Unit (1989) and

Walkerdine and Lucey (1989) have shown how, in earlier decades, notions of learning and teaching developed from the long-standing association of attributes such as rationality, objectivity and self-confidence with men and boys, and the association of attributes such as emotion, subjectivity and self-doubt with women and girls.[7] They argue, for instance, that the philosophy of child-centred education, which was central to the development of schooling for much of the 1970s and early 1980s, had at its implicit heart the rational, incrementally-developing boy, serviced in his 'natural' learning by caring, intuitive women teachers and by hardworking, compliant girls (Walkerdine 1981; Walkerdine 1988). Where teachers have tended to attribute boys' success to natural brilliance and their failure to inadequate motivation, they have tended to attribute girls' success to hard work and industry, whilst at the same time blaming their failure on an intrinsic lack of intelligence (Benjamin 2002; Benjamin 2003b; Cherland 1994; Walkerdine 1990). In other words, girls have tended to be perceived by teachers as lacking the 'natural' ability possessed by boys, but able to achieve through determined hard work and 'plodding'. Such a perception (which may well be implicit and seldom articulated) draws on the traditional Enlightenment construction of men and boys as inherently rational beings and women and girls as inherently emotional ones. Several things may be happening when girls are recast as the success story of contemporary schooling. There has undoubtedly been a shift in gender relations, and in the expectations of girls and women. With the opening up of multiple femininities, girls can no longer *simply* be associated with the emotional realm. I would, however, argue that this residual discourse is a powerful one, and that it has been reworked rather than overturned. Two important changes in policy and practice have enabled this reworking. First, the increasing emphasis on assessed coursework in place of unseen examinations has allowed the Enlightenment model to be used to explain girls' success. Francis and Skelton (2005: 104) refer to this as a 'discourse of disparagement concerning the 'feminization of assessment'. The

[7]This association dates from the eighteenth-century Enlightenment. One of the core projects of the Enlightenment was for man (or more accurately, white, able-bodied, powerful men) to secure domination over his environment through the exercise of scientific rationality. Women, (and non-white men, disabled people and the poor) were the Other of this project, and were associated with reason's antithesis: emotion, nature and the body.

discourse equates 'sudden-death tests with robustness, assertive confidence, 'hard' curricula' ... in opposition to coursework which is positioned as gentle, easy, nebulous, mediocre, not properly academic and feminine'. Second, the traditional discourse of the diligent, hardworking girl sits comfortably with the meritocratic fantasy that anyone with a modest level of talent can succeed if they work with due diligence and perseverance, set themselves challenging but achievable goals, constantly adapt themselves to the changing conditions of the labour marketplace and want success hard enough (Bauman 2006; Kenway and Bullen 2001; Sennett 1998; Sennett 2003; Sennett 2006). The repositioning of girls as the success story of a quasi-marketized education system does not, therefore, require us to replace the traditional association of boys and men with reason: instead it requires us to set aside the belief that 'natural' talent and intellect will procure success in favour of a neo-liberal belief that each individual is responsible for their own destiny in the globalized marketplace.

'Cleverness', for girls, has therefore tended to be seen as something struggled for, both in the past and today; where the achievements of boys who do well tend to be attributed to 'natural' brilliance, the achievements of girls have been attributed to their capacity for hard work, born out of a desire to please (Rossiter 1994; Walkerdine 1988), and out of physical inability to access, or disinclination towards, heterosexual attractiveness, though this has, arguably, been reworked to some extent. What about those girls who do not do well at school? And in particular, what about girls identified as having SEN? Girls at the margins of SEN[8] can often blend into the normative range of the class by positioning themselves as hardworking and diligent, and their difficulties may escape 'official' detection (Benjamin, 2002). But girls whose difficulties are more severe may find their room for manoeuvre severely constrained by the expectation that they will remain rather endearingly vulnerable.

---

[8]SEN is a broad category, including (amongst other things) intellectual and physical impairments, specific learning impairments such as dyslexia, and behaviour considered to be challenging. In Scotland, the ASN designation goes even wider, encompassing, for example, children who have experienced bereavements. The largest incidence group are children experiencing mild to moderate learning difficulties which affect all aspects of learning; it is primarily, though not exclusively, to this group that I am referring here.

> I sit with the science group. Anna is struggling . . . She asks if I will help her, and to refuse seems inhumane. She doesn't seem to like writing. She wants me to point to each word as she copies it. I get the impression that she doesn't actually need this amount of help, but it's a way of securing and retaining my attention. Every time I turn to Joe and Kofi, who are sitting next to her, she stops work. They, also, are doing very little. I try to help Joe to write a draft of his conclusion. All he then has to do is copy it out, but he doesn't do this. Instead, he starts to tease Anna. He makes fun of her, talking in a voice that is clearly supposed to be an imitation of the younger-than-eight-sounding way in which she speaks. Kofi tells him to leave Anna alone . . . I try to reconnect him with his work, but he is not having this. He calls Anna 'Sabrina the teenage witch' and she retaliates by saying that she really *will* be a witch when she grows up, and will turn him into a frog. She turns to me and asks if this is indeed a possibility – can one realistically hope to become a witch? Her question is transparently coquettish. (Observation, mainstream primary school, England)

Both Anna and Joe have been identified as having SEN, and described further as having moderate learning difficulties (MLD). In the above extract from my fieldnotes, Anna is positioning herself squarely within a discourse of rather charming, ultra-childlike vulnerability, securing the adult help that will enable her to complete her work but also re-inscribing herself as needy of help. There is a tendency for SEN discourses in school to draw upon what has been called the 'charity/tragedy model of disability' (Allan 1999; Barton and Oliver 1997; Thomas and Loxley 2001). The charity/tragedy model, which originated in the nineteenth century but continues to influence perceptions and practices today, positions people with disabilities as the helpless objects of pity, concern and charity, and is used to legitimate their control by non-disabled people. Likewise, SEN discourses can position particular children as the passive recipients of care and control (Tomlinson 1982), though this may not be the explicit intention of the educational professionals who work with them. As Riddell notes, 'there are clear connections between the child-centred approach in special educational needs and the individual tragedy discourse identified by disability theorists' (Riddell 1996: 4).

It is interesting to think about how class and 'race', as well as gender and SEN, are played out in the reported incident. Anna had turned on me such a look of pathetic 'helplessness' when I sat at her table that I could not do anything other than pay attention to what she was saying and doing. She was able to keep my attention focused on her through strategies that made her seem younger and less able to manage than was really the case: a conundrum of independence made to look like dependence, and activity made to look like passivity. Writ large in her production was the classed and raced stereotype of the 'dumb blonde': a version of emphasized femininity made readily available to Anna who happens to be blonde, working class, and small for her age. Joe and Kofi aided and abetted her in this strategy. Kofi took up a 'gentlemanly' role in relation to Joe's teasing, positioning himself as Anna's protector. Joe's teasing worked to distance him from the position of needy, vulnerable child, enabling him to resist the position of recipient of help, and also drew attention to Anna's production of herself as needy and ultra-childlike. In parodying Anna's 'babyish' voice, he made the strategy look ridiculous, and also made me want to protect Anna from him, further inscribing Anna and myself within a helper/helped relationship. When my strategy for putting an end to the teasing was unsuccessful, Anna made use of a very different kind of feminine archetype – that of the witch – that Joe had introduced into the encounter. In momentarily abandoning the dumb blonde in favour of the mysterious and powerful figure of the witch, Anna threatened to strip Joe of his masculine power by turning him into a frog. But this repositioning was short-lived, and she threw herself straight back into neediness and vulnerability, by asking me, with what seemed like deliberate childlike 'charm', whether she could really be a witch.

How does this incident, representative as it is of the everyday negotiations of power taking place in classrooms, articulate with policies and practices on a broader scale? The proportion of girls identified as having SEN (or ASN in Scotland) and being in receipt of extra provision, is far lower than that proportion of boys (Organisation for Economic Co-operation and Development 2000; 2008). We could, from this, infer that girls are intrinsically less likely to encounter problems with schooling or we could, on the other hand, infer that girls' needs are less likely to be recognized. Evidence would seem to indicate the second possibility is more likely (Benjamin 2003a; Daniels et al., 1996; Skarbrevik 2002). Something paradoxical is going on. If girls can be much more readily recognized as vulnerable and needy, and SEN discourses draw on vulnerability and neediness, why is it that girls are less likely to be identified as having SEN? Perhaps the answer to this lies partly in the fact that although SEN discourses draw on the (feminized) notions of care and concern for the helpless they also draw on the masculine notions of imposing control through a technical, managerial apparatus. Girls' expertise seems to lie in securing informal help: which can mean they access the help they need without recourse to the official channels of SEN identification and assessment, but could also mean that their difficulties 'may remain undiagnosed and invisible' (Riddell 1996), and that their access to SEN resources is unduly limited. Once identified as having SEN, however, girls find themselves all-too easily inscribed within traditional discourses of vapid and vulnerable femininities.

All of this takes us a long way from the implicit notion that boys' underachievement must somehow mean all is well with the girls. Yes, there are high-achieving girls progressing through the system, but with potential costs to themselves. Meanwhile, plenty of girls are still struggling to achieve in a system that apparently values girls' supposed capacity for hard work and application and sets it alongside boys' supposed laddishness, resistance to academic work and generally more problematic nature. Perhaps what is missing most of all from (or has perhaps been written out by) the underachieving boys narrative is proper attention to the part played by schooling in producing and reproducing a gender regime: it has all but obliterated the many stories that exist to be told about the production and reproduction of gendered relations of power.

Conclusion

This chapter has largely concentrated on unravelling the popular focus on boys' apparent underachievement in schools. I began by identifying three problems with this focus. First, that it requires and implies an uncritical acceptance of current preoccupations with measuring standards, a preoccupation that I suggested is linked to the marketization of schooling in the wake of globalization. Second, that it posits 'boys' and 'girls' as homogenous, polarized groups, ignoring the fact that differences in attainment within each gender are greater than those between them, drawing attention away from the much more significant and always co-constructed influences of socio-economic background and ethnicity in children's attainment at school, and obscuring the complexities of the ways in which those multiple differences are lived by real children in real schools. And third, that the focus on boys' 'underachievement' would tend to suggest that boys are the problem for school whilst all is well for girls. By considering the foundations of what has been called by some commentators the moral panic around boys' attainment in school, in terms of gender theories and residual, overlapping discourses, I have tried to write back into the picture some of what habitually is left out through a focus on boys' attainment. Paradoxically, this has meant I have returned, over and over again, to that very focus. But such a corrective is necessary, I would argue, given the dominance of the perceived problem of boys and their attainment on the educational landscape.

Before finishing, however, I would like to look to the future. If, as I have argued here, boys and their attainment should not be the preoccupying question for educators, where, then, should we focus? As we move towards and through the second decade of the twenty-first century, what questions do we need to address? For me, one of the answers is to be found amongst the other chapters in this book. There has been a tendency for sociologists of education to concern themselves with schooling, and with schools as institutions, to the exclusion of other institutions and practices that shape children's lives. But now, as practitioners move further towards interagency and collective approaches, the time seems right for sociologists of gender and education to address the conceptual separation of schooling from other aspects of children's lives and to explore the gendered nature of schooling in interaction with home, street and family life. Another priority must surely be the increasingly globalized and mediated world in which children are growing up, and which forms the context for how schools shape children's sense of who they are. There has been time for only the briefest of glances in this direction in this chapter, but there can be little doubt that the field of gender and schooling can and should productively explore the reworkings of gender relations that globalization brings in its wake. Finally, though, a chapter on gender and education would not, in my view, be complete without an acknowledgement of the enduring legacy of feminism, and feminism is deserving of the last word here. It was second-wave feminists who, in the 1970s and 1980s, drew our attention to the reproduction of unequal gender relations in school. Much has changed since then. But at the heart of the engagement with gender and education still lies that imperative to question, spotlight and challenge the ways in which schools can be complicit in reproducing old inequalities, and the desire to help construct more equal and life-enhancing gender relations.

References

Ali, S. (2003) To be a girl: culture and class in schools. *Gender and Education*, 15 (3): 269–83.

Allan, J. (1999) *Actively Seeking Inclusion: Pupils With Special Needs in Mainstream Schools.* London, Falmer Press.

Ball, S. (1990) Discipline and chaos: the New Right and discourses of derision. In S. Ball (ed.), *Politics and Policy-Making in Education: Explorations in Policy Sociology.* London, Routledge.

Barton, L. and Oliver, M. 1997. *Disability Studies: past, present and future.* Leeds: Disability Press.

Bauman, Z. (2006) *Liquid Fear.* Cambridge, Polity Press.

Benjamin, S. (1998) Fantasy football league: boys learning to 'do boy' in a special (SEN) school classroom. In G. Walford and A. Massey (eds.), *Children Learning in Context.* New York, Jai Press Inc.

Benjamin, S. (2001) Challenging masculinities: disability and achievement in testing times. *Gender and Education*, 13 (1): 39–55.

Benjamin, S. (2002) *The micropolitics of inclusive education: an ethnography.* Buckingham, Open University Press.

Benjamin, S. (2003a) Gender and special educational needs. In C. Skelton and B. Francis (eds.), *Boys and Girls in the Primary Classroom.* Maidenhead, Open University Press.

Benjamin, S. (2003b) 'Valuing diversity': a cliche for the 21st century? *International Journal of Inclusive Education*, 6 (4): 309–23.

Blaise, M. (2005) *Playing it Straight: Uncovering Gender Discourses in the Early Childhood Classroom.* Abingdon, Routledge.

Burgess, S., McConnell, B., Propper, C. and Wilson, D. 2008. Girls rock, boys roll: an analysis of the age 14–16 gender gap in English schools *CMPO Working Paper Series.* Bristol: Centre for Market and Public Organisation, University of Bristol.

Cherland, M.R. (1994) *Private Practices: Girls Reading Fiction and Creating Identity*. London, Taylor and Francis.

Connell, R.W. (1987) *Gender and Power*. Cambridge, Polity.

Connell, R. W. (1995) *Masculinities*. Cambridge, Polity.

Connell, R. W. (2002) *Gender*. Cambridge, Polity.

Curtis, P. 2008. SATS results reach plateau as boys struggle with reading. *The Guardian*.

Dalley-Trim, L. (2007) The boys' present . . . hegemonic masculinity: a performance of multiple acts. *Gender and Education*, 19 (2): 199–217.

Daniels, H., Hey, V., Leonard, D. and Smith, M. 1996. *Gender and Special Needs Provision in Mainstream Schooling*. Swindon: Economic and Social Research Council.

Davies, B. (2006) Subjectification: the relevance of Butler's analysis for education. *British Journal of Sociology of Education* 27 (4): 425–38.

Department for Education and Skills 2006. *Ethnicity and Education: The Evidence on Minority Ethnic Pupils Aged 5–16*. Nottingham: Schools Analysis and Research Division, Department for Education and Skills.

Epstein, D., Elwood, J., Hey, V. and Maw, J. (1998) Schoolboy frictions: feminism and 'failing boys'. In D. Epstein, J. Elwood, V. Hey and J. Maw (eds.), *Failing Boys? Issues in Gender and Achievement*. Buckingham, Open University Press.

Epstein, D. and Johnson, R. (1998) *Schooling Sexualities*. Buckingham, Open University Press.

Firminger, K. B. (2006) Is he boyfriend material? Representations of males in teenage girls' magazines. *Men and Masculinities*, 8 (3): 298–308.

Francis, B. (2005) Not know/ing their place: girls' classroom behaviour. In G. Lloyd (ed.), *Problem Girls: Understanding and Supporting Troubled and Troublesome Girls and Young Women*. London, RoutledgeFalmer.

Francis, B. and Skelton, C. (2005) *Reassessing Gender and Achievement*. Abingdon, Routledge.

Gard, M. (2001) 'I like smashing people and I like getting smashed myself': addressing issues of masculinity in physical education and sport. In W. Martino and B. Meyenn (eds.), *What About the Boys? Issues of Masculinity in Schools*. Buckingham, Open University Press.

Hayes, D., Mills, M., Christie, P. and Lingard, B. (2006) 'Teachers and schooling making a difference: productive pedagogies, assessment and performance'. Crows Nest NSW: Allen and Unwin.

Haywood, C. and Mac an Ghaill, M. (1996) Schooling masculinities. In M. Mac an Ghaill (ed.), *Understanding Masculinities*. Buckingham, Open University Press.

Jackson, C. (2006) *Lads and Ladettes in School: Gender and a Fear of Failure*. Maidenhead, Open University Press.

Johnson, R. (1991) My New Right education. In C. S. B. Education group 2 (ed.), *Education Limited: Schooling, Training and the New Right Since 1979*. London, Unwin Hyman.

Jones, C. and Mahony, P. 1989. *Learning Our Lines: Sexuality and Social Control in Education*. London: The Women's Press.

Kenway, J. and Bullen, E. (2001) *Consuming Children: Education, entertainment, advertising*. Buckingham, Open University Press.

Kenway, J., Kraack, A. and Hickey-Moody, A. (2006) *Masculinity beyond the Metropolis*. Basingstoke, Palgrave.

Mac an Ghaill, M. (1994) *The Making of Men: Masculinities, Sexualities and Schooling*. Buckingham, Open University Press.

Martino, W. (2001) 'Powerful people aren't usually real kind, friendly, open people!' Boys interrogating masculinities at school. In W. Martino and B. Meyenn (eds.), *What About the Boys? Issues of Masculinties in Schools*. Buckingham, Open University Press.

Mizz (2008) The BIGGEST fortnightly girls' mag. Panini UK Ltd.

Organisation for Economic Co-operation and Development 2000. Special needs education: statistics and indicators. Paris, OECD: Centre for Educational Research and Innovation.

Organisation for Economic Co-operation and Development 2008. Students with disabilities, learning difficulties and disadvantages: statistics and indicators. Paris, OECD.

Osler, A. and Vincent, K. (2003) *Girls and Exclusion: Rethinking the Agenda*. London, RoutledgeFalmer.

Paechter, C. (2007) *Being Boys, Being Girls: Learning Masculinities and Femininities*. Maidenhead, Open University Press.

Reay, D. and Lucey, H. (2000) Children, School Choice and Social Differences. *Educational Studies*, 26 (1): 83–100.

Renold, E. (1997) 'All they've got on their brains is football': sport, masculinity and the gendered practices of playground relations. *Sport, Education and Society*, 2 (1): 5–23.

Riddell, S. (1996) Gender and special educational needs. In G. Lloyd (ed.), *'Knitting Progress Unsatisfactory': Gender and Special Issues in Education*. Edinburgh, Moray House Institute of Education.

Ringrose, J. (2007) Successful girls? complicating post-feminist, neoliberal discourses of educational achievement and gender equality. *Gender and Education*, 19 (4): 471–90.

Rossiter, A. B. (1994) Chips, coke and rock-'n'-roll: children's mediation of an invitation to a first dance party. *Feminist Review*, 46: 1–20.

Sennett, R. (1998) *The Corrosion of Character: The Personal Consequences of Work in the New Capitalism*. New York and London, WW Norton & Co.

Sennett, R. (2003) *Respect: The Formation of Character in an Age of Inequality.* London, Allen Lane.

Sennett, R. (2006) *Culture of the New Capitalism.* New Haven, Yale University.

Skarbrevik, K. J. (2002) Gender differences among students found eligible for special education. *European Journal of Special Needs Education,* 17 (2): 97–107.

Skelton, C. (2001) *Schooling the Boys: Masculinities and Primary Education.* Buckingham, Open University Press.

Slee, R., Weiner, G. and Tomlinson, S. (1998) Introduction: school effectiveness for whom? In R. Slee, G. Weiner and S. Tomlinson (eds.), *School Effectiveness for Whom? Challenges to the School Effectiveness and School Improvement Movements.* London, Falmer.

Smith, J. (2007) 'Ye've got to 'ave balls to play this game, Sir!' Boys, peers and fears: the negative influence of school-based 'cultural accomplices' in constructing hegemonic masculinties. *Gender and Education,* 19 (2): 179–98.

Thomas, G. and Loxley, A. (2001) *Deconstructing Special Education and Constructing Inclusion.* Buckingham, Open University Press.

Thorne, B. (1993) *Gender Play: Girls and Boys in School.* New Brunswick, Rutgers University Press.

Tomlinson, S. (1982) *A Sociology of Special Education.* London, Routledge and Kegan Paul.

Tomlinson, S. (1994) Educational reform and its consequences. London: Rivers Oram Press.

Walkerdine, V. (1981) Sex, power and pedagogy. *Screen Education,* 38.

Walkerdine, V. (1988) *The Mastery of Reason.* Cambridge, Routledge and Kegan Paul.

Walkerdine, V. (1990) *Schoolgirl Fictions.* Verso.

Walkerdine, V. and Lucey, H. (1989) *Democracy in the Kitchen: Regulating Mothers and Socialising Daughters.* London, The Women's Press.

Walkerdine, V., Lucey, H. and Melody, J. (2001) *Growing Up Girl: Psychosocial Explorations of Gender and Class.* Basingstoke, Palgrave.

Walkerdine, V. and The Girls into Mathematics Unit (1989) *Counting Girls Out.* London, Virago.

Willis, P. (1977) Learning to labour: how working-class kids get working-class jobs. Farnborough, Saxon House.

5

Are Abused Women 'Neglectful' Mothers? A Critical Reflection Based on Women's Experiences

Simon Lapierre

Researcher:	What happened when social services told you that you were an unfit mother?
Denise:	I agreed with them.
Researcher:	Do you think you were an unfit mother?
Denise:	Yeah . . . Because I keep putting my children in that [violent] situation . . . I should have been strong enough to have left the situation years before, but I wasn't. It's that double edged sort of thing; you're not the one who has done the violence, but you are still in the wrong because you haven't protected. A mother's job is to protect.

Gender and Child Welfare in Society Edited by Brid Featherstone, Carol-Ann Hooper, Jonathan Scourfield, and Julie Taylor.

Introduction

For a long time, women have been held responsible for the upbringing of their children, and this has been particularly evident in the child welfare arena (Gordon, 1988; Parker, 1995; Swift, 1995; Krane, 2003; Scourfield, 2003). Changes in our views of children and of the conditions that affect their safety and development therefore modify the social expectations that are placed on women as mothers.

Over the last two decades, there have been growing concerns with the situation of children living with domestic violence (Jaffe, Wolfe and Wilson, 1990; Abrahams, 1994; Brandon and Lewis, 1996; Mullender and Morley, 1994; Edleson, 1999; Graham-Bermann and Edleson, 2001; Wolfe et al., 2003), and the literature in this field has focused on the negative consequences for children of being exposed to the abuse of their mothers:

> The corpus of empirical literature clearly establishes that children who live in maritally violent homes are at risk for a wide variety of problems. Associating marital violence with children's emotional and behavioral problems has been the primary question in most of the research published to date. In studies that are sometimes referred to as 'first generation' research on the topic, numerous investigators have successfully linked children's exposure to family violence with a range of behavior and adjustment problems. (Holden, 1998: 6)

This scholarship has been instrumental in raising awareness in relation to the issue of domestic violence in child welfare (Featherstone and Trinder, 1997; Humphreys and Stanley, 2006), and authors have argued that many children who live with domestic violence 'fulfil the criteria outlined in the legislation, on an impairment of their emotional and social development which amounts to "significant harm"' (Carroll, 1994: 11). As a result, changes have taken place in child welfare policies and practices in order to address the needs of these children better (Humphreys and Stanley, 2006; Rivett and Kelly, 2006; Featherstone and Peckover, 2007). In England and Wales, there has been some recognition of the problem of domestic violence since the implementation of the Children Act 1989, which made no reference to this issue (Hester and Radford, 1996; Harrison, 2006). For instance, the guidance *Working Together to Safeguard Children: A Guide to Inter-Agency Working to Safeguard and Promote the Welfare of Children* states that the 'prolonged and/or regular exposure to domestic violence can have a serious impact on a child's development and emotional well-being, despite the best efforts of the victim parent to protect the child' (Department of Health, 1999: 9) and that 'both the physical assaults and psychological abuse suffered by adult victims who experience domestic violence can have negative impact on their ability to look after their children' (ibid.). More recently, the Adoption and Children Act 2002 extended the definition of harm set out in the Children Act 1989 to include the 'impairment suffered from seeing or hearing the ill treatment of another', which has the potential to make cases of domestic violence more visible in child protection work.

Despite such changes, scholars have criticized child welfare workers for avoiding and minimizing domestic violence (Mullender, 1996; Humphreys, 1999; Saunders, 2003), and for 'letting men get away with it' (Featherstone and Peckover, 2007; see also Farmer and Owen, 1995; Pringle, 1995; Farmer, 2006). Moreover, given the assumption that the care and protection of children constitute women's responsibilities, these changes may have had the pernicious effect of posing women as responsible for their children's exposure to domestic violence and its consequences. In this sense, child protection statistics from Canada and the United States reveal that abused women are routinely accused of 'neglecting' or 'failing to protect' their children (Kantor and Little, 2003; Lavergne, Chamberland and Laporte, 2001; Hartley, 2004). Although data from England are limited, the official definition of child neglect does open the door to such allegations:

> Neglect is the persistent failure to meet a child's basic physical and/or psychological needs, likely to result in the serious impairment of the child's health or development. Neglect may occur during pregnancy as a result of maternal substance abuse. Once a child is born, *neglect may involve a parent or carer failing to*: provide adequate food, clothing and shelter (including exclusion from home or abandonment); *protect a child from physical and emotional harm or danger*; ensure adequate supervision (including the use of inadequate care-givers); ensure access to appropriate medical care or treatment. It may also include neglect of, or unresponsiveness to, a child's basic emotional needs. (HM Government, 2006: 38, emphasis added)

One of the main problems with charging abused women with accusations of 'neglect' or 'failure to protect' is that it shifts the focus away from men's violence onto women and their mothering (Magen, 1999). Moreover, such practices are likely to be experienced by women as punitive, particularly if they are not followed through by more supportive intervention strategies, and may in turn discourage abused women from reaching out for assistance (DeVoe and Smith, 2003; Peckover, 2003).

Nonetheless, limited attention has been paid to the relationship between domestic violence and child neglect, particularly from a critical perspective. In order to initiate a critical reflection on this issue, this chapter draws upon the findings of a participative and qualitative study that investigated the experiences of 26 women in relation to their mothering in the context of domestic violence in contemporary Britain.[1] The first part of the chapter presents the modalities of the study. The following part looks at the experiences of the women who had been in contact with child welfare services and argues that the tendency to charge abused women with accusations of 'neglecting' or 'failing to protect' their children constitutes a manifestation of mother-blaming. The third part argues that this reflects an incomplete and inaccurate view of abused women's mothering; on this basis it proposes a more holistic and complex understanding that takes into account both the difficulties these women face and the strategies they develop in order to protect and care for their children.

The study: investigating women's experiences of mothering in the context of domestic violence

The research that is reported in this chapter drew upon a qualitative and participative methodology combining group and individual interviews. A qualitative methodology provides a space for women's 'voices' to be listened to and articulated (Reinharz, 1992; Maynard,

[1]This research project benefited from the financial support of Fonds québécois de recherche sur la société et la culture (Quebec, Canada), Universities UK and the University of Warwick. For more details on the research, see Lapierre (2007).

1994; Skinner, Hester and Malos, 2005) and has the potential 'to enable silenced women to tell their own stories in their own voices' (Davis and Srinivasan, 1994: 248) and to take into account – and account for – diversity amongst women. In addition, the use of a participative methodology means that the research is conceptualized as a collaborative or collective enterprise, and the 'research subjects' as 'research participants' (Martin, 1994; Renzetti, 1997). Renzetti argues that an important benefit of a participative methodology is that 'the most significant issues – from the perspective not only of the researcher but also of the researched – get identified and studied' (1997: 142). In this regard, the group interviews were primarily seen as a means of involving women in the early stages of the research process and initiating with them a critical discussion, whilst the individual interviews aimed at gathering data on the women's personal experiences of mothering in the context of domestic violence. A short questionnaire was also used to collect socio-demographic data on the participants, and fieldwork notes were recorded in a research diary.

In total, 26 women took part in the study, through five group interviews and twenty individual interviews. The participants were recruited through a small group of women activists (who were primarily interested in issues around child contact and domestic violence) and through support groups for women who have experienced domestic violence (these groups were run in one community centre and two family centres), as well as through a refuge for Asian women. The following two selection criteria were identified: the women needed to have experienced domestic violence (self-defined), which could include physical, sexual, psychological, emotional or financial abuse; and the women needed to have at least one child under 18 years of age at the time they were experiencing violence.

All the participants had experienced psychological and emotional abuse, the majority mentioned experiences of physical abuse and a small number of women also talked about sexual and financial abuse. Most participants had experienced repeated and long-term violence, including post-separation violence, but were no longer in an intimate relationship with their violent partners at the time of the interviews. A number of women had mobility impairments caused by the violence. The women were aged between 21 and 67 years of age and had between one and five children, who were aged between 1 and 44 years – only one participant did not have children, but her sense of belonging to the group and her interest in the research meant that it would have been inappropriate to exclude her from the group interview. In terms of the women's ethnicity, 16 women identified themselves as white-British, two as Irish, one as Scottish, one as black-Caribbean, one as black-other, one as Indian, one as Pakistani and one as white-European. At least two women were in a same-sex relationship at the time of the interviews.

The interviews were conducted in English, but two participants spoke little English and this required the work of an interpreter (Birbili, 2000; Temple and Edwards, 2002). All the interviews were tape-recorded and transcribed (verbatim) and content analysis was conducted using the N*Vivo software. The analysis aimed at making women's experiences visible and developing a feminist standpoint on mothering in the context of domestic violence (Kelly, Burton and Regan, 1994; Thompson, 2001). The following sections present the findings of the research.

Women's experiences of child welfare interventions

Amongst the women who were involved in the research project, 13 had been in direct contact with child welfare services. These women recognized that assistance had been needed whilst they had gone through domestic violence, and some talked in positive terms about the material and practical support that had been provided by social workers in these circumstances. This was particularly significant in Alison's account. She was a mother of five children who had experienced multiple forms of abuse and had faced financial hardship because of her partner's spending on alcohol and drugs:

> While all this was going on, if it wasn't for my social worker and all the people that used to help by looking after my children for a few hours to give me a couple of hours' break or what have you, I don't know how I'd have got through, I really don't . . . There was times, I mean, I had one nappy, one last bottle of milk for my son and my husband had got £140 odd in his pocket, which most of that was for the kids . . . If it wasn't for the [social workers] then, I wouldn't have got, like, bits of

> money to get the electric, food . . . They gave me food parcels, nappies, things like that . . . There was one Christmas, I had nothing and they turned up on the doorstep with a big black bag of toys, as presents for my kids and a food parcel and a turkey, on Christmas Eve. I could not believe my eyes, I could not believe it. And the presents wasn't even cheap presents, they were proper expensive, some of them expensive presents, for all my kids. (Alison)

However, the general picture of social services depicted in the participants' accounts was a more negative one. On the one hand, a number of women highlighted difficulties in accessing professional support, feeling that they had been left on their own to protect and care for their children. This was illustrated in the account given by Lorraine, who had contacted her local authority because of worries about the behaviours that had been displayed by her 7-year-old son in the aftermath of the violence:

> The lady [social worker] came out and she said that there is nothing she can do for me, there was nothing she can do for the kids, because I wasn't threatening my kids, I wasn't beating my kids; my kids are normal kids, they've got nothing to worry about . . . They expect that a women who's gone through domestic violence, she's gonna be aggressive towards her kids, she's insane. That's the only way they're gonna help you, if you end up beating your child, threatening your kids. That's the only way they're gonna help you. But apart from that, they're not helping you. (Lorraine)

It seems that as long as women are judged as 'coping' with the situation and as being 'good enough' mothers it is difficult for them to access professional support for themselves or for their children. This raises questions about the availability and organization of resources, but also about the view of women as being responsible for their children whilst not competent enough to determine what their children's needs are and what is the best way to meet them. This echoes the feminist critique in regard to the 'professionalization' of motherhood, which points out that notions of children's needs and social prescriptions for mothering are established by 'expert' discourses with recourse to 'science', thus undermining women's experiences and related knowledge (Marshall, 1991; Phoenix and Woollett, 1991; Hays, 1996; Nicolson, 1997).

A different issue was that several women who had been in contact with the child welfare system had been offered services that did not correspond to what they had asked for, or had had professional interventions imposed to them. These women reported that they had been described by social workers as 'neglecting' and 'failing to protect' their children as a result of their partners' violence, and had struggled with such views. For instance, Fiona explained that she had been accused of 'neglecting' and 'failing to protect' her two sons because she had not been able to leave their home following incidents of domestic violence, in part because she had no access to housing benefits:

> Children on the Child Protection Register . . . because I failed to protect them, by not leaving my house. I failed to protect them, she [social worker] said, by not leaving the house. But I was in a Catch-22, because I own half the house, the housing will not give me anything . . . She said that I put my house before my children. And I'm thinking hang on a minute, I need a house for these children. Would you let go of your place knowing that you've got no family, nobody to turn to? Where am I suppose to go? (Fiona)

What added to Fiona's confusion in regard to these accusations of 'neglect' was the feeling that she had been successful in looking after her children despite the violence, which seems to have been confirmed by a number of professionals:

> According to the conference when I had the child protection thing, my children passed everything. The doctor said that they are up to date with their immunisations; in fact, he said that if anything I was rather over-protective of my children, because I'm the sort like if they start to cough, 'Off, quick, quick let's go to a doctor in case it gets into a chest infection.' School reports were absolutely immaculate, above average for the both of them. So in that respect I was not neglecting my children at all; they were clean . . . Everyone said how clean and well looked after these children are. But she insisted that I failed to protect them. (Fiona)

Such accusations had been experienced by the participants as blaming, which is hardly surprising given the extent to which women are seen – and see themselves – as being responsible for the care and protection of their children. In addition, some participants stated that these feelings had been exacerbated by the social workers' blaming attitudes. This was the case for Angela, a young woman who had been struck by the social worker's attitude when she had contacted social services for assistance in leaving her abusive partner:

> I can't remember her [social worker's] exact words, but she more or less said that I was a bad mother, because if I was allowing my children to still be in that situation, even though they weren't being physically harmed. Because I was allowing them to be in that situation, then I was a bad parent, which made me feel really crap to be particularly honest. (Angela)

In several cases, child welfare services had become involved in the situation following a diagnosis of 'depression' or 'post-natal depression', and the women's mental health problems had then become the focus of intervention. In this regard, a growing number of empirical studies demonstrate that women may experience mental health problems as an effect of abuse (Humphreys and Thiara, 2003). However, in the context of child protection work such problems can be seen as the causes for women to fall short of the social standards of 'good enough' mothering, therefore obscuring men's violence and its consequences for both women and children. For instance, Sharon explained that the issue of domestic violence had seldom been addressed throughout the years she had been in contact with child welfare services, as the focus had been on her 'mental breakdown', which she saw as being a direct consequence of the abuse:

> Because of my breakdown, they [social services] didn't think I could cope ... I think they mentioned domestic violence when they were preparing to take the children ... and that was the only time they mentioned it. (Sharon)

In two other cases, it is the women's violence towards their partners that had constituted the focus of intervention, despite the fact that they had used violence as a mean of defending themselves and their children after years of severe abuse.

All these examples illustrate how the focus tends to be shifted away from men's violence and its impacts on both women and children, to emphasize women's 'deficiencies' and 'failures' as mothers. This echoes the findings of a study of child protection case files for 32 families, which revealed a dominant pattern of avoidance and minimization of domestic violence (Humphreys, 1999). The findings of this study suggested this had happened because of the failure to treat domestic violence as an issue to be considered, reporting it as 'fighting' or 'marital conflict', naming women's violence as equivalent to or more important than men's violence and naming other issues as the problem and focusing on these issues rather than on men's violence. Moreover, this needs to be understood in relation to the positioning of women as responsible for the care and protection of their children, and the pervasive tendency to blame women for everything that happens to their children.

It seems that once child welfare services are involved in a situation, all aspects of the woman's mothering can come under scrutiny, and the literature suggests that this is even more likely to happen when the woman is perceived as 'neglectful' (Swift, 1995; Appell, 1998: 356–81; Scourfield, 2003). In what is perhaps an extreme example, Fiona recalled a particular incident when the social worker had blamed her for something that had no bearing on the situation that had caused concerns in the first place, and which had no clear incidence on the children's safety and development:

> She [the social worker] came to my house and said, 'Have you got crisps?' And I thought she was hungry, so I said, 'Yes'. And as soon as I gave her this bag of crisps, she started shouting at me like a little child. She said, 'I don't want you having crisps in your house, look your child is overweight'. I said, 'This is not what you come for.' (Fiona)

There was indeed a sense that these women's mothering had come under scrutiny and constant observation from the child welfare system. In the following quotation, Pam explained that she had used to feel under pressure whilst she had been involved with social services:

> Being on social services, I've always felt like somebody is behind me. Everywhere I turn I watch what I am doing, 'I can't do this, I can't do that' . . . I've always felt on edge. (Pam)

In all the participants' accounts, there had been apprehensions regarding the fact that social workers had the legal power to remove their children from their custody in order to place them into foster care, which was perceived as an extremely punitive measure. In some cases, social workers had threatened to remove the children to ensure that the women would comply with their requirements, such as leaving their violent partners or not returning with them. For instance, Denise mentioned that social services had contacted her following an incident of violence, telling her that they would have to take the children into care if she was to return to her abusive partner:

> They [social workers] wanted my children . . . I was black and blue, being told that I was going to lose the most important thing and precious thing in my life . . . I had to fight for three days and prove that I wasn't having my husband back for me to keep my children. (Denise)

In another instance, Angela explained that she had been struck by the social worker's attitude when she had contacted social services for assistance in leaving her abusive partner, but she had also been disturbed by the threat of having her children taken into foster care:

> The social worker I spoke to basically turned around to me and put me in a room and walked in and turned around and said, 'Right, you are going to a hostel' . . . I thought, 'Great, fantastic, give me all the details and I will go home, get a few things packed, get some money, you know, get some nappies and whatever for the baby', to be told, 'No, you don't.' 'Excuse me, what?' 'You're not going back home.' I went, 'Yeah, I know, but I need stuff.' 'If you walk out of here to go back to your house, we're taking your children off you and putting them into care, because you are putting them in a dangerous situation' . . . At the time, I was only in my very early twenties, and been through all of that, and being made to feel absolutely worthless and everything as it was, only to be told by somebody I'm expecting to help me that they were going to take my children away if I didn't do what they said . . . In a way, I may as well have just stayed at home, because that was like my ex-partner, you know, 'Do as you're told, you know, or you get a slap.' So in a way they were saying to me, 'Do as you're told or we'll take your kids away.' So it was just like going from one bad situation to another for me. (Angela)

A number of participants had had their children placed in foster care. The women's accounts of these experiences were emotionally charged. In addition, these participants felt that the social workers had provided them with unsatisfactory contact arrangements throughout the placements, and reported that it had been extremely difficult for them to regain custody of their children. This was the case for Joanne, who had her children placed in foster care for several years following an incident when she had stabbed her partner as a means of defending herself and her children:

> When your children get taken into care, they are there for quite a while. You have to really fight ... There is always review, after review, after review. Issue, after issue, after issue. So they are there for quite a while. (Joanne)

Even the women who initially agreed with the placement expressed disagreements with the way contact arrangements had been managed, and reported difficulties in having their children restored to their custody. For instance, Sharon talked at length about how she had experienced the placement of her children as a punishment and about the long and complicated process she had been through in order to retrieve the custody of all of them:

> The social worker came and I told them everything ... They thought it would be a good idea for me, because I was on anti-depressant, to get my head sorted, to get my life sorted, and for the children to go with family. I agreed to that, but it was a hell of a job to get my children back! ... If I wanted to see my children, I was allowed an hour with them. That was their favour to me to allow me an hour with the children ... I'd go to all these meetings and they would say, 'Well we want you to do this and to do that.' And everybody listened and I had to do everything ... Like basically sort out my life, come off the anti-depressant ... Move from where all the violence had occurred, get a new home, do it up and everything, because they didn't think it would be fair for the children going back to that house where we were after the oldest had seen everything. So I thought okay, basically they want me to make a fresh start. So I'd done that and then little silly things. You know, if you move into a house you're gonna have boxes everywhere, and the one social worker she was so horrible, 'Well that isn't safe there, we want this done and we want them to have these kind of wardrobes and we want you to have this kind of stuff' ... So after a bit I would do everything to make her happy and it still wasn't good enough. (Sharon)

A final issue that emerged from the participants' experiences of contact with child welfare services refers to the fact that the focus on women's 'deficiencies' and 'failures' as mothers does not necessarily mean that these women will be offered support for their mothering. Indeed, there is no guarantee that the blaming practices that have been described above will be followed through by more supportive intervention strategies. This point was explicitly made by a number of participants:

> They [the children] were just on the Register for the sake of it. I've never got help. She [the social worker] never said 'Come to the housing to see if we can get you an emergency housing in some way.' Never. (Fiona)

> The children went onto the Protection List and we didn't seem to get no help . . . Why the hell should these children be on the Protection List when you're not offering them no support? (Pam)

This seems to be particularly problematic when the children are placed into foster care, as the women may receive little or no help in leaving their violent partners and recovering from abuse. This was significant in the account given by Sharon, who explained that she had not received any support from social services throughout the long and complicated process of retrieving the custody of her children.

> They weren't helping, they weren't helping at all! They didn't say to me, 'There is this place where you can go, we are here to support you.' It didn't matter to them . . . They'd done their job apparently and that was it. They got what they wanted, the kids, and your life don't matter, you know, you don't have a life. So when you wanted someone to talk to, there were no one there to talk to. (Sharon)

Throughout the interviews, there was a sense that child welfare workers are primarily concerned with children, and their interest in women and their mothering is instrumental in ensuring that their children are safe and cared for. This is consistent with the findings of an ethnographic study conducted in a child protection agency in the United Kingdom, which revealed that social workers tend to identify children as their clients despite in fact focusing their interventions on women (Scourfield, 2003). It also reflects the more general trend in social work to consider mothering solely in terms of its impacts on children (Featherstone, 1999).

Men's violence can pose a threat to the safety and well-being of both women and children, and child welfare workers frequently have to take difficult decisions in such cases. Child welfare workers are concerned with the situation of children who live with domestic violence, but the focus tends to be shifted away from men's violence to emphasize women's 'deficiencies' and 'failures' as mothers. This is evident when the situations are framed through the notion of child neglect, and it can be seen as constituting an important manifestation of mother-blaming. The notion of mother-blaming does not imply that women should not hold any responsibilities in regard to their children, but highlights the processes by which women are unfairly defined as 'bad' mothers in such circumstances.

The next section of the chapter argues that this definition of abused women as 'neglectful' mothers reflects an incomplete and inaccurate view of women's experiences of mothering in the context of domestic violence. It continues to draw upon the experiences of the women who were involved in the research project and proposes a more holistic and complex understanding of what it is like to raise children in the context of domestic violence.

Towards a more holistic and complex understanding of mothering in the context of domestic violence

The particular context created by men's violence is clearly at odds with the high social expectations that are placed on women as mothers. Indeed, whilst all the women who were involved in the research project expressed a strong desire to be 'good' mothers, and to be seen as such, they also stated that it had been hard to care for their children in these circumstances:

> I mean to be a good mum, but sometimes it's really hard, you know, when you're in a situation to deal with. (Joanne)

> That was hard. I wouldn't say being a mother is easy, by any way, but when you are in an abusive relationship it is harder. (Angela)

Nevertheless, a closer look at women's experiences of mothering in these circumstances challenges the view of these women as 'neglectful' mothers. First, it shows that abused women face important difficulties on account of the fact that their partners specifically target their mothering as part of their general pattern of domestic violence, that they need to respond to their children's greater needs and that there is little support available for their mothering. Second, it highlights the multiple strategies that women develop in order to protect and care for their children.

Abusive men target mothering as part of their violence

Men's violence typically affects all aspects of women's lives, including their physical and mental health (Kelly, 1988; Humphreys and Thiara, 2003; Walby and Allen, 2004). It is therefore more difficult for women who are subjected to male violence to perform the hard and time-consuming work involved in mothering. For instance, Sharon explained that the distress caused by several years of abuse had made it more difficult for her to find the energy required to care for her children:

> It was quite difficult. I couldn't cope, to be honest, I couldn't cope. I was trying, but because I was so weak I just didn't have no energy . . . I had a breakdown and I couldn't cope. (Sharon)

This is often exacerbated by the fact that abusive men routinely target women's mothering as part of their violence. For instance, the participants reported that their partners had used violence towards them in front of their children in order to undermine their authority as mothers, sending the message that these women had not been able to protect themselves let alone their children. In the same vein, the participants reported that their partners had threatened and used violence towards their children in order to affect women and undermine their mothering. These findings are consistent with the work of Kelly (1994) on the interconnectedness of domestic violence and child abuse, and support the importance of understanding the 'double level of intentionality' in men's violence: the fact that an act directed towards either a woman or a child can be at the same time intended to affect the other.

The participants reported that their partners had also used more subtle manipulation strategies in order to undermine their mothering. For instance, Lorraine explained how she had struggled in disciplining her children because her partner constantly challenged her authority:

> It's like he [ex-partner] always tried to . . . manipulate me, with my son. If my son is eating his dinner, he would come in and he's giving his son sweets. And I'm saying, 'Let him eat the sweets after he had his dinner.' And he's like, 'He can eat it now while he's eating.' And I'm like, 'No.' Because of that my son don't want his dinner, he wants the sweets. And I'm saying, 'No.' And this is what it was always like. (Lorraine)

In addition, a number of women mentioned that they had frequently been told by their partners that they were 'bad' mothers. In some cases, their partners had even threatened to make a referral to child welfare services on this basis. Given the women's overall negative views of social services, and their fear of having their children removed from their care, this had constituted a powerful threat.

These findings demonstrate that abusive men use a range of strategies to attack women's mothering as part of their general pattern of violence, but such strategies can only be successful because they take place in a social context that poses women as responsible for their children and places high expectations on women as mothers. As pointed out by Mullender et al. in their work on children's experiences of domestic violence, 'it is not an accident that abusive men attack women's abilities to mother, they know that this represents a source of positive identity, the thing above all else that abused women try to preserve, and also that it is an area of vulnerability' (2002: 158).

Responding to children's greater needs

As mentioned above, there is now a general recognition that domestic violence is likely to affect children who have been exposed to the abuse of their mothers (Jaffe, Wolfe and Wilson, 1990; Abrahams, 1994; Mullender and Morley, 1994; Brandon and Lewis, 1996; Holden, 1998; Edleson, 1999; Graham-Bermann and Edleson, 2001; Wolfe et al., 2003). This was echoed in the participants' accounts, and it had added to the burden of mothering, as the participants were aware that their children had required a greater level of protection in the context of abuse. In this regard, the women's idea of protection was twofold. First, they had been concerned with ensuring that their partners would not be violent towards their children, which referred to the men's use of 'direct' violence and excluded the broader idea of children's exposure to domestic violence. Second, they had wished to ensure that their children would not witness the men's violence towards their mothers and would not be aware of the problem present in their homes. This concept of protection was rooted in the idea that both being directly abused and witnessing domestic violence can have negative consequences for their children.

The participants also reported that their children had greater emotional needs as a result of the abuse, and they had had to constantly reassure their children and to compensate for what they had been through. In addition, the participants expressed worries about their children's actual or potential behaviour problems. For instance, Pam talked at length about her son's violent behaviours, which were perceived as a direct consequence of his exposure to domestic violence:

> My 12-year-old [son], like I said, he can be a very nasty piece of work when he wants to ... He reminds me of his dad ... He's such a bully to his little sister. Do you know what I mean? He is always bullying her and calling her names, 'Bitch' and 'Nit head' and ... (Pam)

For most participants, this has different implications for girls and for boys. In general, the women were concerned with their son's actual or potential violent behaviours and with their daughter's potential victimization, as illustrated in the following quotation:

> To me, it's not nice because, when you've got kids, you're basically saying to your kids 'It's okay, it's okay.' You know, I've got a girl child and I've got a boy child, and I don't want my daughter to think that if she is in a relationship and her boyfriend hits her 'It's okay, put up with it.' It's not. (Lorraine)

Given the women's sense of responsibility in regard to their children, it is hardly surprising that the consequences of abuse on children had in turn impacted on their experiences of mothering. In this regard, Featherstone (1999) argues that it is important to recognize that the relationships between women and children are not unidirectional, and that children's behaviours also impact on their mother's experiences. The multiple strategies that abused women develop in order to protect and care for their children will be presented in detail below.

Lack of support

In the face of such difficulties, the participants had had access to little support for their mothering, which had reinforced their sense of sole responsibility in regard to their children. For instance, Lorraine mentioned that she had generally been on her own to care for her children whilst she had been through domestic violence:

> If I didn't do it, who else would do it? Nobody else. Not their dad. So I had to do it. (Lorraine)

Whilst a number of participants subscribed to a general discourse that emphasizes the potential for men to take more responsibility in relation to children and to support women through their mothering, their own experiences tended to emphasize their partners' general lack of interest in their children:

> He [ex-partner] used to be really lovely, he used to be so loving and protective, but then he just lost interest in them [the children], me and the house. (Sharon)

In several cases, this lack of interest had been compounded by the men's misuse of alcohol and drugs. Indeed, a large number of women talked about their partners' substance misuse and argued that, as a result, their children had been exposed to 'inappropriate' behaviours. They had also perceived their partners' misuse of alcohol and drugs as increasing the risk of the children being 'directly' abused. This means that not only had these women been unable to rely on their partners to support them in performing the work involved in mothering, but that to do so could have been dangerous and damaging for the children. These findings raise questions regarding abusive men's parenting that require further investigation and reflection, but they do challenge the idea that abusive men can be 'good enough' fathers (see also discussion in Eriksson and Hester, 2001; Bancroft and Silverman, 2002; Harne, 2005; Featherstone and Peckover, 2007).

Furthermore, the participants mentioned that they had been isolated from their friends and family members whilst they had gone through domestic violence, which had further limited their opportunities for support. This had been a particularly significant issue for the women who had been in Britain for a relatively short period of time and for the women who had spoken little or no English, as their social networks had been even more limited. For instance, Fiona explained that having left her home country and her family to follow her partner to the United Kingdom meant that she had had no one to help her with the care of her children:

> It was very, very hard for me, because I have no family in this country at all and at the time I had no friends either, because I wasn't allowed to have any friends. (Fiona)

Finally, as has been mentioned above, it is often difficult for abused women to access professional support for themselves or for their children.

Multiple strategies

Notwithstanding the difficulties that have been described above, abused women typically strive to be 'good' mothers and develop a range of strategies in order to meet the high social expectations that are placed on women as mothers. The participants stated that whilst they often had to juggle their children's needs with their partners' demands in the context of domestic violence, they had continuously prioritized the protection of their children:

> You, sort of, try to do everything that is possible to put them [children] out of harm's way. (Angela)

In order to protect their children, the women had developed a range of strategies, and all the participants reported their use of multiple and successive strategies. First, the women had been attentive to what had happened in their homes and had tried to monitor their partners' mood and behaviours, attempting to predict the incidents of violence. In this regard, Angela argued that, over time, she had become able to identify signs indicating an eventual incident of violence:

> I sort of knew. Over time, I got to know the signs when things were going . . . (Angela)

The women had also tried to prevent such incidents, often by behaving in ways that they had thought would not upset their partners. This had included being in the house when their partners had wanted them there, cleaning and cooking at the time their partners had wanted and being quiet and not confronting their partners. This was the case for Razia, a young woman originating from South East Asia who had been in the United Kingdom for a relatively short period of time:

> She [Razia] used just to cook and clean and she used to try to keep him [ex-partner] happy. He never used to allow her to go out, but she wouldn't challenge that or say 'Why am I not allowed to go out?' She just accepted it thinking that will make him happy, so she just stayed in, cooked and cleaned. (Razia's interpreter)

Moreover, behaving in ways that they had thought would not upset their partners had also included asking the children to be quiet and to behave in ways that would not upset their fathers, or the mothers' partners, as illustrated in the following quotation:

> Nine times out of ten you could guarantee he would have a drink at a certain time of the day, he would go pass out on the sofa and he'd wake up usually around four o'clock and the first words out of his mouth was dinner; where the so and so is my dinner? So it was like get the kids in, get them upstairs quiet, you know, 'Don't make a sound. Don't wake Daddy.' Get in the kitchen, get the dinner on, get it done, get it on the table. So, as soon as he woke up, 'Yeah, it's there. It's done.' (Angela)

However, men's violence is often unpredictable and tends to happen regardless of women's and children's behaviours. During incidents of violence the women had tried to keep their children away, either outside the house or in another room inside the house, to ensure that their partners would not be violent towards them and to ensure that they would not witness the violence. The women's concern with ensuring that their children would not witness the violence also meant that they had tried to avoid their children overhearing the violence from another room in the house or seeing the bruises or injuries caused by the violence.

For some women, it had been difficult to prevent the children from witnessing the violence, particularly when their partners had intentionally used violence in front of the children. Some women had also lived in small flats, and therefore had nowhere to send the children during the incidents of violence. In instances where the children had witnessed the violence, the women's main concern had been to ensure that their partners would not also use 'direct' violence towards the children, and several women had put themselves at greater risk of being harmed in order to protect their children. For instance, Joanne explained how threats to her children's safety used to trigger something that had pushed her to protect them, even if she had placed herself at greater risk of being injured:

> I remember their dad lifted his hands to them [the children] and, even though I know he would have beat me up, I'd still jump on him, trying to protect them, if you understand. In other words, 'You can hit me, but you can't touch my kids.' . . . So, no, it's really hard to protect them, because you are so scared. Not scared that you don't protect your children, because it triggers something off in here, inside, so you always protect your children, I think, physically. But, you know, you're gonna end up the worse anyway, because there's nothing me and my little kids could do to stop him. (Joanne)

The participants also reported attempts to challenge their partners' violent behaviours and to get their partners to leave their homes. In some of the more extreme cases, a small number of women had used violence against their partners in order to protect their children.

Although the participants had prioritized the protection of their children, they were aware that their children had a wide range of needs. Again, the women had to develop a range of strategies in order to care for their children, and the women reported that they had generally managed to meet at least their children's 'basic' or physiological needs. The strategies reported varied from one situation to the other and from one woman to the other. For instance, Angela talked about having developed an ability to decode the signs in her children's behaviours that gave her an indication of their needs:

> You have to just sort of gauge the twitchings and the looks and the body language to know what the child wants. I found that, if the children were constantly, like, licking their lips, they need to drink. I could tell if my kids were hungry, needed a drink, tired, wanted the toilet, needed nappies changing or whatever, without them ever opening their mouth, because I learnt their body language and I had to. (Angela)

Alice talked about bringing food home from work and hiding it in the attic, so that her children had been able to eat:

> When I picked myself up and got that job, places that we cleaned sometimes had buffets and whatever. And I used to take up some of the stuff that was meant to go in the bin like sandwiches and biscuits and bring them home and give them the kids. And my kids had to go, it was like a attic house, and they had to go up to the top and eat it so he [ex-partner] would never know. And then we'd still pretend that we was hungry, but I knew my kids got fed through things that was going to be thrown away. (Alice)

Lorraine talked about how she had managed to drive her children to school every morning, despite several severe injuries and her doctor's advice not to drive:

> God's honest truth, at the present moment you're just numb; you don't think about you, you don't think about what's hurting and what's not hurting . . . You don't care, you've just got to do what you have to do; and that's what I've done . . . Stitches at the bottom of my feet, I was told don't drive, don't do nothing, get off your feet. I had to drive my kids to school, so I still had to walk, even though he [partner] was there and he knew that I had an operation. Didn't do nothing to help me. (Lorraine)

The women had also developed strategies in order to meet their children's emotional needs, which included spending time and playing with the children whilst their partners were not at home and doing activities with the children outside the house.

Conclusion

This chapter has examined the experiences of 13 abused women who had been in contact with child welfare services. The overall picture of social services that has been presented in the women's accounts is a negative one, particularly the tendency to charge abused women with accusations of 'neglecting' and 'failing to protect' their children. Women tend to experience such practices as blaming, because those shift the focus away from men's violence to emphasize women's 'deficiencies' and 'failures' as mothers. Furthermore, it seems that such practices are generally not followed through by more positive strategies to support these women through their mothering.

Given that child welfare policies and practices are increasingly concerned with the situation of children living with domestic violence (Featherstone and Trinder, 1997; Humphreys and Stanley, 2006; Rivett and Kelly, 2006), social workers will inevitably exercise judgements about abused women's mothering and will have to take difficult decisions in these circumstances. However, in order to develop less blaming interventions, social workers need to be explicit about men's violence and to acknowledge women's experiences of abuse. In addition, they should be commuted to a more holistic and complex understanding of women's experiences of mothering in the context of domestic violence. As pointed out by Krane and Davies in their work on practice with women and children in refuges, 'an understanding of the emotional complexities and challenges of everyday mothering is a prerequisite for practice with women and children' (2007: 24).

In fact, this chapter has argued that a more holistic and complex understanding of women's experiences of mothering in the context of domestic violence challenges the view of these women as 'neglectful' mothers. It reveals that abused women face important difficulties but can, at the same time, develop multiple strategies in order to protect and care for their children. In being committed to such an understanding, child welfare workers will be able to build on these strategies and thus design more effective interventions. As pointed out by Mullender and Morley, 'women's and children's interests may conflict but, except where this is demonstrably and irresolvably the case, the most effective and cost effective way to help children is to understand what is happening to their mothers and to work in alliance with them' (1994: 10).

References

Abrahams, C. (1994) *The Hidden Victims: Children and Domestic Violence.* London, NCH Action for Children.

Appell, Annette R. (1998) On fixing 'bad' mothers and saving their children. In M. Ladd-Taylor and L. Umansky (eds.), *'Bad' Mothers: The Politics of Blame in Twentieth-Century America.* New York: New York University Press.

Bancroft, L. and Silverman, J. G. (2002) *The Batterer as Parent: Addressing the Impact of Domestic Violence on Family Dynamics.* Thousand Oaks, Sage.

Birbili, M. (2000) Translating from one language to another. *Social Research Update.* <sru.soc.surrey.ac.uk/SRU31.html> accessed 12 March 2007.

Brandon, M. and Lewis, A. (1996) Significant harm and children's experiences of domestic violence. *Child and Family Social Work,* 1 (1): 33–42.

Carroll, J. (1994) The protection of children exposed to marital violence. *Child Abuse Review,* 3: 6–14.

Davis, V. and Srinivasan, M. (1994) Feminist research within a battered women's shelter. In E. Sherman and W. J. Reid (eds.), *Qualitative Research in Social Work.* New York, Columbia University Press.

Department of Health (1999) *Working Together to Safeguard Children: A Guide to Inter-Agency Working to Safeguard and Promote the Welfare of Children,* London, The Stationery Office.

DeVoe, E. R. and Smith, E. L. (2003) Don't take my kids: barriers to service delivery for battered mothers and their young children. *Journal of Emotional Abuse,* 3 (3–4): 277–94.

Edleson, J. L. (1999) Children's witnessing of adult domestic violence. *Journal of Interpersonal Violence,* 14: 839–70.

Eriksson, M. and Hester, M. (2001) Violent men as good-enough fathers? A look at England and Sweden. *Violence Against Women,* 7: 779–98.

Farmer, E. (2006) Using research to develop practice in child protection and child care. In C. Humphreys and N. Stanley (eds.), *Domestic Violence and Child Protection: Directions for Good Practice.* London, Jessica Kingsley Publishers.

Farmer, E. and Owen, M. (1995) *Child Protection Practice: Private Risks and Public Remedies.* London, HMSO.

Featherstone, Brid (1999) Taking mothering seriously: the implications for child protection. *Child and Family Social Work*, 4: 43–53.

Featherstone, B. and Peckover, S. (2007) Letting them get away with it: fathers, domestic violence and child welfare. *Critical Social Policy*, 27 (2): 181–202.

Featherstone, B. and Trinder, L. (1997) Familiar subjects? Domestic violence and child welfare, *Child and Family Social Work*, 7: 147–59.

Gordon, L. (1988) *Heroes of Their Own Lives: The Politics and History of Family Violence, Boston 1880–1960.* New York, Penguin Books.

Graham-Bermann, S. A. and Edleson, J. L. (2001) *Domestic Violence in the Lives of Children. The Future of Research, Intervention, and Social Policy.* Washington DC, American Psychological Association.

Harne, L. (2005) Researching violent fathers. In T. Skinner, M. Hester and E. Malos (eds.), *Researching Gender Violence. Feminist Methodology in Action.* Cullompton, Willan Publishing.

Harrison, C. (2006) Damned if you do and damned if you don't? The contradictions between private and public law. In C. Humphreys and N. Stanley (eds.), *Domestic Violence and Child Protection: Directions for Good Practice*, London, Jessica Kingsley Publishers.

Hartley, C. C. (2004) Severe domestic violence and child maltreatment: considering child physical abuse, neglect, and failure to protect. *Children and Youth Services Review*, 26: 373–92.

Hays, S. (1996) *The Cultural Contradictions of Motherhood.* New Haven, Yale University Press.

Hester, M. and Radford, L. (1996) Contradictions and compromises: the impact of the Children Act on women and children's safety. In M. Hester, L. Kelly and J. Radford (eds.), *Women, Violence and Male Power.* Buckingham, Open University Press.

HM Government (2006) *Working Together to Safeguard Children: A Guide to Inter-Agency Working to Safeguard and Promote the Welfare of Children.* London, The Stationery Office.

Holden, G. W. (1998) Introduction: the development of research into another consequence of family violence. In G. W. Holden, R. A. Geffner and E. N. Jouriles (eds.), *Children Exposed to Marital Violence: Theory, Research, and Applied Issues.* Washington, DC, American Psychological Association.

Humphreys, C. (1999) Avoidance and confrontation: social work practice in relation to domestic violence and child abuse. *Child and Family Social Work*, 4: 77–87.

Humphreys, C. and Stanley, N. (2006) Introduction. In C. Humphreys and N. Stanley (eds.), *Domestic Violence and Child Protection: Directions for Good Practice.* London, Jessica Kingsley Publishers.

Humphreys, C. and Thiara, R. (2003) Domestic violence and mental health: 'I call it symptoms of abuse.' *British Journal of Social Work*, 33 (2): 209–26.

Jaffe, P. G., Wolfe, D. A. and Wilson, S. K. (1990) *Children of Battered Women.* Newbury Park, Sage.

Kantor, G. K. and Little, L. (2003) Defining the boundaries of child neglect. When does domestic violence equate with parental failure to protect? *Journal of Interpersonal Violence*, 18 (4): 338–55.

Kelly, L. (1988) *Surviving Sexual Violence.* Minneapolis, University of Minnesota Press.

Kelly, L. (1994) The interconnectedness of domestic violence and child abuse: challenges for research, policy and practice. In A. Mullender and R. Morley (eds.), *Children Living with Domestic Violence.* London, Whiting and Birch Ltd.

Kelly, L., Burton, S. and Regan, L. (1994) Researching women's lives or studying women's oppression? Reflections on what constitutes feminist research. In M. Maynard and J. Purvis (eds.), *Researching Women's Lives From a Feminist Perspective*, London, Taylor and Francis.

Krane, J. (2003) *What's Mother Got to Do With It? Protecting Children from Sexual Abuse*, Toronto, University of Toronto Press.

Krane, J. and Davies, L. (2007) Mothering under difficult circumstances: challenges to working with battered women, *Affilia: Journal of Women and Social Work*, 22 (1): 23–8.

Lapierre, S. (2007) 'Taking the blame? Women's experiences of mothering in the context of domestic violence.' Unpublished PhD thesis, Coventry, University of Warwick.

Lavergne, C., Chamberland, C. and Laporte, L. (2001) Violence conjugale et mauvais traitements envers les enfants: étude des cas signalés à la direction de la protection de la jeunesse au Québec. *Actes du colloque de l'ACFAS.* Sherbrooke, May.

Magen, R. H. (1999) In the best interest of battered women: reconceptualizing allegations of failure to protect. *Child Maltreatment*, 4 (2): 127–35.

Marshall, H. (1991) The social construction of motherhood: an analysis of childcare and parenting manuals. In A. Phoenix, A. Woollett and A. Lloyd (eds.), *Motherhood: Meanings, Practices and Ideologies*, London, Sage.

Martin, M. (1994) Developing a feminist participative research framework: evaluating the process. In B. Humphries and C. Truman (eds.), *Re-Thinking Social Research*, Aldershot, Avebury.

Maynard, M. (1994) Methods, practice and epistemology: the debate about feminism and research. In M. Maynard and J. Purvis (eds.), *Researching Women's Lives from a Feminist Perspective.* London, Taylor and Francis.

Mullender, A. (1996) *Rethinking Domestic Violence: The Social Work and Probation Response.* London, Routledge.

Mullender, A. and Morley, R. (1994) Context and content of a new agenda. In A. Mullender and R. Morley (eds.), *Children Living with Domestic Violence.* London, Whiting and Birch Ltd.

Mullender, A., Hague, G., Imam, U., Kelly, L., Malos, E. and Regan L. (2002) *Children's Perspectives on Domestic Violence.* London, Sage.

Nicolson, P. (1997) Motherhood and women's lives. In V. Robinson and D. Richardon (eds.), *Introducing Women's Studies*, 2nd edn., Basingstoke, Macmillan.

Parker, R. (1995) A brief history of child protection. In E. Farmer and M. Owen (eds.), *Child Protection Practic : Private Risks and Public Remedies.* London, HMSO.

Peckover, S. (2003) 'I could have just done with a little more help': an analysis of women's help-seeking from health visitors in the context of domestic violence. *Health and Social Care in Community*, 11 (3): 275–82.

Phoenix, A. and Woollett, A. (1991) Motherhood: social construction, politics and psychology. In A. Phoenix, A. Woollett and A. Lloyd (eds.), *Motherhood: Meanings, Practices and Ideologies.* London, Sage.

Pringle, K. (1995) *Men, Masculinities and Social Welfare.* London, UCL Press.

Reinharz, S. (1992) *Feminist Methods in Social Research.* New York, Oxford University Press.

Renzetti, C. M. (1997) Confessions of a reformed positivist: feminist participatory research as good social science. In M. D. Schwartz (ed.), *Researching Sexual Violence Against Women: Methodological and Personal Perspectives.* Thousand Oaks, Sage.

Rivett, M. and Kelly, S. (2006) From awareness to practice: children, domestic violence and child welfare. *Child Abuse Review*, 15: 224–42.

Saunders, H. (2003) *Failure to Protect? Domestic Violence and the Experiences of Abused Women and Children in the Family courts.* Bristol, Women's Aid Federation of England.

Scourfield, J. (2003) *Gender and Child Protection*, New York, Palgrave Macmillan.

Skinner, T., Hester, M. and Malos, E. (2005) Methodology, feminism and gender violence. In T. Skinner, M. Hester and E. Malos (eds.), *Researching*

Gender Violence: Feminist Methodology in Action. Cullompton, Willan Publishing.

Swift, K. J. (1995) *Manufacturing 'Bad Mothers': A Critical Perspective on Child Neglect*, Toronto, University of Toronto Press.

Temple, B. and Edwards, R. (2002) Interpreters/translators and cross-language research: reflexivity and border crossings. *International Journal of Qualitative Methods*, 1 (2): 1–22.

Thompson, D. (2001) *Radical Feminism Today*. London, Sage.

Walby, S. and Allen, J. (2004) *Domestic Violence, Sexual Assault and Stalking: Findings from the British Crime Survey*. London, Home Office.

Wolfe, D. A., Crooks, C. V., Lee, V., McIntyre-Smith, A. and Jaffe, P. G. (2003) The effects of children's exposure to domestic violence: a meta-analysis and critique. *Clinical Child and Family Psychology Review*, 6: 171–87.

6

The Clock Starts Now: Feminism, Mothering and Attachment Theory in Child Protection Practice

Julia Krane, Linda Davies, Rosemary Carlton and Meghan Mulcahy

Introduction

This chapter explores the potential of attachment theory for therapeutic interventions in child protection practice. Whilst attachment theory has spawned an extensive body of research with implications for practice in the arena of child protection, we argue that its therapeutic potential has not been realized.

Our chapter begins with an overview of the central concepts of attachment theory that are called upon to guide child protection practices. Through an appreciation of feminist understandings of mothering we call into question a narrow and uncontested application of attachment theory to child protection practice – a practice that tends to scrutinize the capacities of often single mothers struggling to raise children under adverse circumstances. We then present the

Gender and Child Welfare in Society Edited by Brid Featherstone, Carol-Ann Hooper, Jonathan Scourfield, and Julie Taylor.

legislative framework and practice trends, informed by attachment theory, that characterize child protection in Canada, with specific reference to Quebec. Against this backdrop, we introduce 'Amber's Story', an example derived from our combined clinical and front-line experiences in child protection, to illustrate practice as usual in the Quebec milieu. Here, we draw out the challenges inherent in engaging in mandated/statutory practice with increasingly intense, complicated and often discouraging situations. Concerned that a constricted use of attachment may result in counterproductive interventions, our final section revisits Amber's story. We conclude with our considerations for rethinking the potential of attachment theory for work with mothers and fathers that supports therapeutic engagement in mandated/statutory practice.

Attachment theory: an overview

Attachment theory originated in the works of Bowlby and Ainsworth, offering a 'paradigm shift in the understanding of human behaviour as a biologically based instinctive behavioural system' (Bacon and Richardson, 2001: 377). Bowlby is widely recognized for developing the conceptual basis of attachment by proposing the centrality of providing a secure base for a child's healthy personal and social development and by suggesting that early attachment experiences between a child and caregiver lay the foundation for the child's lifelong attachment pattern (Bowlby, 1969; 1973; 1980).

Bowlby believed that 'observation of how a very young child behaves towards his mother, both in her presence and especially in her absence, can contribute greatly to our understanding of personality development' (1969: 3). He (Bowlby, 1969) notes that infants instinctually adapted to their environments in response to threat by seeking out the security and protection of their primary attachment figure. Their behavioural responses to real or perceived stress revealed their attachment relationships (Cowan and Cowan, 2007; Glaser, 2001). During infancy and toddlerhood, children are thought to manifest patterns of attachment that vary according to the 'mother–child couple' (Bowlby, 1969: 332) and that remain stable across the lifespan.

Bowlby recognized that a securely attached child demonstrated a desire for closeness with the primary attachment figure when distressed and exhibited confidence in venturing away when comforted. He theorized that secure attachment relationships were enabled by a warm and consistent figure, most often the mother, who was attuned to her children and responded to their distress (Barth et al., 2005). As noted by Bretherton, 'how effectively the attachment figure can [offer security and safety] . . . depends on the quality of social interaction, especially the attachment figure's sensitivity to the infant's signals, although child factors also play a role' (1995: 63).

Of particular interest to Bowlby (1969; 1973) were the long-term implications of attachment style. He considered patterns developed in early attachment relationships with the primary caregiver as templates for future relationships, particularly relationships with one's own children or intimate partner (Bowlby, 1969; 1973; Farnfield, 2007). Thus, parents with their own unresolved childhood attachment relationships are thought to risk reproducing insecure attachment relationships with their own children. According to Walker, the intergenerational transmission of insecure attachment patterns might be thwarted by parental efforts to engage in a process of 'working through and [integrating] childhood experiences [of insecure attachment]' (2008: 50).

Ainsworth's research sought to assess the quality of attachment between mother and toddler, children's attachment patterns, their expectations of comfort when distressed, and their perceptions of self-worth, love and support. Based on observations, Ainsworth and associates identified securely attached children as those who expressed distress when their caregiver left, greeted their caregiver upon her return and, once comforted, resumed play (Ainsworth et al., 1978; Cowan and Cowan, 2007). Children identified as 'anxious avoidant' seemed to be distressed during the separation from the mother and avoided proximity to or interaction with her upon her return; their behaviours appeared to be compliant, independent or self-contained, possibly masking fear (Ainsworth et al., 1978; Farnfield, 2007; Walker, 2008). 'Anxious ambivalent' children appeared to simultaneously seek and resist contact and interaction with the mother. Their behaviours seemed particularly angry or conspicuously passive (Ainsworth et al., 1978). These children seemed to display attention seeking behaviours as evidenced by clinging or neediness or using tantrums in an attempt to ameliorate the anxiety caused by their attachment relationships (Cowan and Cowan, 2007; Walker, 2008).

Work with maltreated children led to an identification of 'disorganized attachment' (Crittenden, 1988; Main and Hesse, 1990; Main and Solomon, 1990). In fact over the past 20 years, research has provided evidence that maltreated children are more likely than non-maltreated children to exhibit insecure or disorganized attachment patterns (Bacon and Richardson, 2001; Cicchetti and Toth, 1995; Crittenden and Ainsworth, 1989; Mennen and O'Keefe, 2005). Main and Solomon (1990) proposed an array of behaviours displayed by a child with disorganized attachment: contradictory seeking of and resisting proximity to the parent, freezing, stilling or apparent dissociation, abnormal movements, evidence of apprehension of the parent, or evidence of disorganization or confusion. Main and Hesse (1990) explained that for 'disorganized' children, incomprehensible frightening or frightened parental behaviour meant that these children could not expect a secure base from their primary caregiver and thus their development of an organized strategy for coping in situations of distress was impeded. Unable to resolve their anxiety through the comfort of familiar relationships, these children displayed fear, apprehension and confusion toward the attachment figure.

Feminist reconsideration of attachment theory

A feminist critique of attachment theory begins with an appreciation of the pervasive maternalist and pronatalist ideologies following World War II. At that time, in both Britain and North America, the fluctuating needs of industry impacted on women as mothers and workers (Riley, 1983). Fears about the declining birth rate and the return of predominantly male soldiers to the workforce created pressure on women to return home. Thus the time was ripe for the emergence of Bowlby's maternal deprivation theory (Franzblau, 1999). Bowlby theorized that a child's selective attachment to his/her mother provided emotional security and laid the foundation for healthy social relationships throughout life. These insights gave rise to social policies that encouraged women to 'stay home and concentrate their efforts on child care' (Franzblau, 1999: 28). Throughout the last few decades, feminist activists and scholars have been especially vocal about the exclusive positioning of women as mothers relegated to the private sphere of the family and responsible for children's well-being and development. Feminists exposed the invisible complexities of mothering, bringing to light the ideological, material and emotional facets of mothering and its diversification across culture and class (Collins, 1994; McMahon, 1995; Parker, 1995; 1997). For example, Collins argued dominant conceptions of white, Western, middle-class motherhood rendered the experiences of African American mothers marginal in relation to their labour-force participation and shared childcare arrangements involving kin and non-kin 'othermothers'.

Feminists have also confronted the inextricable interconnection between children's emotional, physical and psychological well-being and maternal care, and have challenged the notion of mothers as the exclusive, best and expected carers of children. In disrupting assumptions about mothering as 'natural' to women, instinctive and effortless, Ruddick (1989; 1994), for example, maintained that mothering is a sophisticated, ethical, skilled, disciplined, difficult and thoughtful work to be learned and shared by mothers and fathers. 'Motherwork', she contended, transcends gender identities. Eyer (1992) and Birns (1999) disputed the idea that children suffer life-long developmental traumas when not cared for by 'all available/all loving' mothers. Exclusive maternal child-rearing arrangements may well leave mothers, fathers and children vulnerable to fantasies that split mothers into 'all good' or 'all bad', 'all powerful' or 'diminished/devalued'. Feminists also looked critically at unrealistic expectations of maternal perfection in relation to the caring and rearing of children. They drew attention to pervasive mother blame internalized not only by mothers but also by professionals with whom they come into contact (Caplan, 2000; Featherstone, 1997; Krane, 2003), suggesting that mothers are simultaneously idealized and demonized. This constrained portrait leaves women little opportunity and permission to explore the emotional and situational complexities that they experience as mothers.

Against this backdrop, feminist theorists have been particularly cautious about attachment theory given the pervasive assumption that attachment bonds are 'natural, self-evident and unequivocal outcomes of mothering and attachment behaviours and traits as fixed and stable properties of separate, autonomous individuals' (Bliwise, 1999: 43). Attachment theory 'has equated the care and protection of infants with mothering, contributed to the reification of maternal sensitivity as the primary agent responsible for childhood and adult social relations, and glorified autonomy as the desirable outcome of development' (ibid.: 49).

In her review of attachment theory research, Bliwise came to appreciate that 'children [can] form meaningful relationships with multiple caregivers' rather than with only the mother, and rather than being fixed in the very early years of an attachment relationship, patterns of attachment are susceptible to change (1999: 44). Recent longitudinal research conducted in Sweden exploring the attachment patterns of children placed in out-of-home care similarly reported that 'new influential attachment relationships can be formed at a later stage in childhood and that early mother–child relationships need not be decisive' (Andersson, 2005: 54).

The social circumstances of caregiving have also been thought to affect the development of attachment patterns. Separate studies of maternal and paternal attachment have suggested 'that the total number of personal, family and social resources (agreeableness, extroversion, low neuroticism, easy infant temperament, high quality marriage, social support and low work–family stress) was a stronger predictor of child attachment security than any single parent, child or social variable' (Bliwise, 1999: 46).

In reference to another study that found an association between economic hardship and maternal emotional distress, low sensitivity in mother–infant interaction, poor quality childcare and insecure child attachment, Bliwise (1999) proposed that environments that support the well-being of caregivers are optimal for the development of secure attachments. Haight, Doner Kagle and Black also pointed to research that suggests attachment relationships are affected by life stressors, specifically 'parents who are preoccupied with job or marital problems, family illness, or other common stressors may be less sensitive in their responses to their infants and young children' (2003: 200). Not surprisingly, these reviews of attachment research studies suggest that attachment is not determined by individual variables alone, that the quality of interaction is centrally important and that children are active versus passive participants in developing and maintaining attachment relationships.

Regarding the influence of class and culture on attachment relationships and patterns, an assumption of the universality of attachment has been challenged. Cowan and Cowan (2007) suggest that caregiver expressions of sensitivity and security have strong cultural components, and they note that attachment theory emerged in an era during which the primacy of the mother was expected. Cultural and socioeconomic factors influencing attachment relationships have now begun to garner attention (Bliwise, 1999; Bolen, 2000; Bretherton, 1995; Haight, Doner Kagle and Black, 2003).

Attachment meets child protection

In the context of child protection it has recently been suggested that 'attachment theory is arguably the most popular theory for explaining parent–child behaviour' (Barth et al. 2005: 257). In their empirical investigation of 100 cases followed by Scottish child protection services, involving children who had been freed by the courts for adoption, Hill et al. (1992) noted that in every case the quality of the parent–child attachment was considered as a rationale in the assessment of risk and ensuing protection decisions.

However, recent research in Canada suggests the necessity of reexamining the forces that bring families to the attention of child protection authorities. These families are typically living in very precarious circumstances. Their housing conditions are often unsafe (Chau et al., 2001) and they are significantly more likely than the general population to be living on social assistance (Trocmé et al., 2005). Characteristic of female caregivers involved with child protection authorities are experiences of domestic violence, few social supports, mental health problems, maltreatment as a child and drug and alcohol use (ibid.). The problems most frequently noted in male caregivers involved with this system are few social supports, drug and alcohol use, mental health issues, maltreatment as a child and criminal activity (ibid.). Not surprisingly neglect, a category of child maltreatment that is inexorably linked to conditions of poverty, is the most common reason for bringing families to the attention of child welfare agencies in Canada (ibid.). These factors call into question the primacy of the parent–child attachment rationale for risk and protection decisions.

The current Canadian child welfare system responsible for investigating, assessing and intervening in situations of risk to children is widely recognized as a residual 'threshold' system. Thus, child welfare authorities are legally sanctioned to intervene with children and their families only when parental care is deemed to have fallen below a minimum standard (Cameron, Coady and Adams, 2007). In theory, such intervention entails investigating allegations of maltreatment or neglect, protecting children from maltreatment, providing guidance, counselling and other services to families with the goal of protecting children, providing alternate care or supervision for children when needed and overseeing adoption placements.

Though many parents might struggle to care for their children, it is only in those situations considered to pose serious risk to a child's wellbeing, safety, or security that warrant intervention in what is assumed to be the private sphere of families. In addition to suspected or actual neglect, physical or sexual abuse, abandonment and psychological maltreatment, 'parental failure to protect', the exposure of a child to domestic violence or a 'serious risk' of being subjected to abuse or neglect is now found in child protection legislation across the country. The cardinal principles delineated in legislation that guide child protection intervention in response to these identified situations of risk centre on promoting the best interests, wellbeing, security or development of a child whilst recognizing that parents are primarily responsible for their children. Currently, across provinces, legislative principles affirm support for the autonomy and integrity families; support intervention on the basis of mutual consent; espouse consideration of the least disruptive course of action; recognize the centrality of providing services that respect a child's need for continuity of care and stable family relationships within a cultural environment; promote early assessment planning and decision making to achieve permanent plans that include participation from children, parents and relatives; and provide services that respect cultural, religious and regional differences (Bala, 2004).

Since the mid-1980s, revisions to child protection legislation in Canada have oscillated between a preoccupation with child safety and a commitment to family preservation and autonomy. Briefly, prior to the 1980s child protection practice centred only on the most obvious cases of abuse and neglect, and intervention consisted primarily of the removal of children from unsafe care or circumstances (ibid.). By the mid-1980s, a swell of concern for the emotional damage caused by separating children from their primary caregivers, with whom they may have formed attachments, gave rise to practices that now made every effort to keep children in their families (ibid.). Coupled with the realization that 'too often decisions to remove children from parental care reflected biases of class or race' (Bala, 1998: 29), family preservation practices were introduced to keep children with their primary caregivers. By the mid-1990s, public outcry over child deaths (Gove, 1995; Sanders, Colton and Roberts, 1999) led to the scrutiny of the family preservation approach, and a shift towards protecting and preserving the safety of the child was once again in evidence. Under this approach, swift reactions to potential child risk were promoted and realized through interventions that prioritized stability, consistency and the opportunity for children to form secure attachments for their healthy development (Bala, 1998).

In practice, this shift resulted in a reduction in the time given to parents to rectify their situation, increased the likelihood that parental rights would eventually be terminated and emphasized planning for alternative permanent placements for children concurrent with planning for family reunification. This trend, informed by attachment theory, is now well entrenched in practice and legislation. With increased awareness of the detrimental impacts on children's development of remaining in circumstances of risk or in temporary care for lengthy periods, and of experiencing multiple moves within care or between care and home, Quebec's Youth Protection Act, for example, now defines the maximum duration of temporary placements to be 12 months for children under 2 years, 18 months for children aged from 2 to 5 years and 24 months for children aged 6 years and over (Articles 53.0.1 and 91.1). These timelines reflect an understanding of the extent to which the first months and years of a child's life are crucial to establishing secure attachment relationships and patterns. Current legislation further dictates that when parents are unable to correct the situation of risk within the official time frames, an alternate plan for permanency must be put into action. Whilst by tradition permanency plans were introduced only once all possibilities for keeping a child with, or returning a child to, his or her parent(s) had been exhausted, the present trend of concurrent planning requires developing an alternative permanency plan at the same time as working with a family to alleviate the risks to the children (Katz, 1999; Schene, 2001).

Simultaneous with the emphasis on permanency planning has been the widespread adoption of standardized tools for risk assessment. As noted in their review of the scholarship on risk assessment, Krane and Davies identified risk assessment systems as being 'meant to enhance the effectiveness of child protective service investigations and procedures related to service provision ... as well as [to] filter out high risk cases from the rest' (2000: 36). 'Advocates of risk assessment have praised these systems for their capacity to reduce worker professional and personal bias, streamline worker decision making, reduce discretion, and generally sharpen professional thinking about the broad range of factors related to assessing risk' (ibid.: 37). However, feminist scholars have cautioned that 'typical items on risk assessment measures promote the rapid scrutiny and classification of parents, largely mothers, through a filter of cultural, class, and gender assumptions. The ideological and material contexts in which the mothering of children takes place are concealed while deviations from the eurocentric, middle-class standard of good mothering are suspect' (ibid.: 42).

Whilst risks to children emanate from a number of sources, Freymond and Cameron argue that such risks are all too often considered to be 'a function of the number and the severity of problems affecting mothers' capacity to parent'(2007: 79). Consequently, the classification of parent problems, the gathering of evidence and the control through surveillance of families has become a common feature of contemporary child welfare practice (Davies and Leonard, 2004; Cameron, Coady and Adams, 2007). As Davies and Collings put it, now 'much of child welfare practice is centred on the science of detection with a focus on searching out and responding to specific observable behaviours' (2004: 46).

These trends have significantly altered the scope of practice for child protection social workers. Lowering the threshold for definitions of child abuse and neglect has led to an increase in referrals and time spent on investigation (Freymond and Cameron, 2007; Krane, 2003; Krane and Davies, 2000; Whittaker and Maluccio, 2002). As reports of abuse continue to rise 'the ability of social welfare services to respond has been greatly curtailed by government spending cutbacks' (Brown, 2006: 354). Child welfare work has come increasingly to be comprised of the documentation and assessment of risk and of ensuring parental compliance (Cameron, Coady and Adams, 2007). Today's workers are granted less discretionary power and less time for direct engagement with mothers and fathers. At the same time, they experience less clinical supervision in their work and yet remain responsible for life-altering decisions and liable for managing risk (Davies and Collings, 2004; Krane and Davies, 2000).

To think through how attachment theory emerges in the everyday mandated practice of child protection we turn to Amber's story and how we imagine it might unfold.

Amber's story

Amber came to the attention of child protection services in Quebec after a call from her neighbour with a complaint that Amber's partying was getting out of hand. Amber, 24 years of age, is the mother of three young children. Not having completed high school and unemployed, Amber relied on social assistance. The neighbour reported that Amber's apartment was like a revolving door. Knowing that Amber's boyfriend had been in and out of jail, she worried about the kind of people the two of them were letting into the building. She suspected Amber was using alcohol and cocaine, and worried about the effects on Amber's children, Ashley aged 7 years, 4-year-old Carley, and 2-year-old Nicolas. When the neighbour confronted her, Amber blew up and told the neighbour to mind her own damn business.

An investigation was launched, as it was sure to be, with a protection worker going unannounced to Amber's two-bedroom apartment in a subsidized housing unit in a poor district of the city. Appearing dishevelled, tired and possibly hung over, Amber let the worker into her apartment. They walked past the three children sitting on the floor watching TV and munching on cereal. Remnants of the previous night's party were evident and the place smelled strongly of stale alcohol and cigarette smoke. Whilst Amber shuffled about the kitchen making attempts to clean up, Brandon, age 38 years and father of the two youngest children, entered the room. Amber acknowledged having had a party the night before but vehemently denied having a substance abuse problem. Brandon seemed to become increasingly agitated as the investigation progressed. Roughly pushing back his chair, Brandon raised his voice and objected to the social worker's questions. He stomped out of the kitchen and left the apartment moments later. Amber explained that the partying happens when Brandon is around but that Brandon has been in and out of jail for drug related charges and is only sporadically present.

When asked about the children, Amber was proud to report that Ashley does well in school and is quite helpful at home, making meals and getting her siblings ready for bed. Amber does worry that Ashley has few friends and is often bullied by classmates. According to Amber, Ashley refuses to consider Brandon as a father. Amber reported that Carley attends a half-day pre-kindergarten program. Described by Amber as a handful, she is easily frustrated by a speech delay that challenges her abilities to communicate and be understood. Amber confided that she had been removed from home herself between the ages of 6 and 8. Over that time, she was in and out of care. She said she would do whatever it takes to keep her children.

Undoubtedly, this situation would be deemed urgent and Amber's children in need of protection. Guided by Quebec's *Youth Protection Act* (2007) the worker would consider Amber and Brandon seemingly unable to meet the children's basic needs as both are 'failing to provide the [children] with the appropriate supervision or support' (Article 38(b)). Specifically, concerns would arise in relation to Amber's current and past use of substances whilst responsible for the care and supervision of the children and to the children's exposure to an atmosphere of partying, of excessive use of drugs and alcohol and of possible domestic violence. Brandon's inconsistent involvement and the intermittent presence of indiscriminate people in the home exacerbate the risks to the children. Added to this nexus of factors are the children's young ages, Carley's speech delay and its impact on her relationship with Amber, Ashley's difficulties with peers, signs of parentification and school absenteeism. Whilst one might imagine these factors to be obvious indicators of risk, in everyday practice a worker would rely on clinical judgement to ascribe meaning to these observations to determine risk. Practicing in an arena inspired by attachment theory, a skilled worker would pay particular attention to the nature and extent of both Amber and Brandon's sensitivity to and capacity for recognizing and responding to the needs, desires and distresses of the children. As well she or he would take notice of the children's behaviours and how they sought contact with and the attention of Amber and/or Brandon. The unpredictability of Brandon's presence and his possible aggression and impulsivity as evidenced by his behaviour during the initial investigation might heighten the worker's awareness of a lack of security, stability and consistency in the home environment. Bearing in mind that decisions about the children's safety must be made quickly, the opportunity for the worker to explore in depth the meaning attributed to these kinds of observations is likely curtailed.

We imagine that as a result of the investigation giving rise to the determination that the children are at risk and in need of protection, and in keeping with the legislative framework and practice trends, every effort would be made to engage both Amber and Brandon voluntarily. An agreement outlining the specific concerns warranting action would be drawn up. Assuming Brandon's commitment as a father, both parents would be required to undergo a drug and alcohol evaluation, which might include random drug testing and which would specify that they refrain from substance use in the presence of the children. Amber and Brandon would be expected to follow through with any recommendations arising from the evaluation, which might include attending a residential treatment programme. They would be asked to ensure an assessment of Carley's development, especially her speech, and would be directed to participate in a parenting group. They would also be required to assure school attendance. The agreement would stipulate that support and guidance be provided to the family by a child protection authority. If Brandon refused to comply with the conditions of the agreement he would be excluded from the above set of expectations and instead limits would be specified regarding his contact with the children – that is, no entry to the home whilst under the influence, and only supervised contact with the children. The agreement would be set for one year with ongoing monitoring. It would conclude with a clear statement that failure to comply in any of the conditions that had been set to address the circumstances of risk would result in court involvement and the possible removal of the children.

Despite sensitivity to the struggles Amber faces in parenting virtually alone without any consistent support and in far less than optimal emotional and material conditions, Amber's worker would be faced with determining whether or not she or he may have to remove the children. The worker would be expected to put into place an intervention plan for the family, all the whilst being aware of the strict timelines for decision-making and permanency planning. Aware that time is of the essence, the worker would let Amber know that if she does not follow through with treatment recommendations related to drug and alcohol use she risks losing her children for a period of time. Depending on the assessment of the degree of risk to the children, especially young Nicholas, Amber's worker would develop a concurrent permanency plan for alternate care of the children. Whilst it is unlikely that Amber's children would be removed immediately the notion of long-term stability and consistency of care would weigh heavily on the social worker. As Gauthier, Fortin and Jéliu observed, a '"child's time" in the crucial early years is much shorter than the "adult's time": A young child cannot wait for the parents to solve their persistent personality problems, childhood traumas, drug abuse, and violence. A child cannot be put "on hold"' (2004: 394).

We would anticipate that in the present child protection context Amber is set up to fail. In the real world of child protection practice, the clock starts ticking when the initial complaint is received and at no point is time frozen. Time and temporality feature centrally in contemporary child protection organizations (Holland, 2004; White, 1998). 'Organizational practices of case planning and review, with their respective anticipation of the future and scrutiny of the past are essentially temporal activities' that drive child protection decisions (White, 1998: 56). It would be next to impossible for Amber to incorporate all of the identified changes in her life in the time allowed and with the limited resources available to workers and families. Child protection interventions are often incongruent with the daily adversities experienced by child protection-involved mothers such as Amber, and, in a legislative climate focused on expediency, the needed time to achieve meaningful change is rarely available (Freymond and Cameron, 2007: 98)

In our discussion of typical practice, it is likely that the influence of attachment theory is reduced to a narrow focus on time frames whilst its therapeutic potential to guide work with clients of child protection is lost. In the section that follows, we return to Amber's situation to explore how a richer, more complex understanding of attachment theory might enrich child protection practice and lessen the harmful consequences of its limited application. Admittedly, any efforts to bridge a protection mandate with therapeutic practice is rife with challenges. In closing our chapter, we suggest not only slowing down the clock but rethinking what we do with the time that we have to work with already often disenfranchised women and their children.

Rethinking attachment in work with mothers and other carers

What does it mean to take concepts from attachment theory seriously in the context of statutory practice? Although child protection practice has tended to render mothers little more than 'servicers of children' (Featherstone, 1997: 9) feminist scholars have come to identify the complex, contradictory and often invisible emotional experiences and labour of mothering. Incorporating feminist understandings of mothering into the framework of attachment theory might benefit both the care of children and enhance women's relationships with child protection workers.

As we have elaborated elsewhere (Davies et al., 2007; Krane and Davies, 2000), eliciting women's experiences as mothers is of primary importance in child protection. Engaging women in development of a 'mothering narrative' may enable women to express the actual daily physical and emotional experiences of caring for their children, including the stresses, emotional intensity, challenges and pleasures they face. This narrative aims to deepen an appreciation of the conditions that shape mothering practices and allows protection workers a more accurate evaluation of a given child's situation. Pursuing a woman's account of her mothering experiences ought to begin at the onset of intervention. Amber, for example, could be provided with the opportunity to explore her account of how and why her family has now come to the attention of child protection services and to reflect on her experiences of mothering through a detailed examination of a typical day with her three children, paying particular attention to the support, if any, that she receives from Brandon or other people in her life. 'Throughout this conversation, the worker purposefully listens for the emotional and material contexts within which the woman mothers and the impact these contexts may have on her daily experience of care giving, including the tensions or hardships she faces' (Davies et al., 2007: 29).

Guided by central concepts from attachment theory, a mothering narrative ought also to explore a mother's attachment history and the subsequent development of her own internal working model. By walking Amber through a chronology of her experiences of being cared for as a child, especially in relation to her placement history, we might explore her memories, emotions and thoughts with particular sensitivity to any articulation of trauma and loss. This conversation allows us to consider how Amber's experiences of trauma and loss have shaped her internal working model or sense of self as well as her relationships with her children and her partner. This narrative might also offer an opportunity for the worker to gain insights into how the children's needs might provoke powerful but unresolved feelings of suffering and powerlessness in Amber, given her own history of care and, maybe, feelings of rejection. Rather than risking attachment theory becoming yet another framework within which mothers are blamed and their deficits are seen as evidence of risk to their children, embarking upon this kind of narrative is meant to generate a more thorough understanding of Amber and her needs. As Walker suggested, 'traumatic experiences in childhood are not in themselves problematic in terms of parenting ability; what becomes crucial is whether the individual has been able to resolve the issues' (2007: 77). The mothering narrative, embracing attachment history, provides a forum in which Amber might begin to work towards a resolution of her traumatic experiences, thereby preventing the intergenerational transmission of insecure or disorganized attachment patterns and relationships.

Work with Amber should also focus on her interactions with her children and on her sensitivity and responsiveness (Howe, 2005) to her children's needs. Workers need adequate institutional support for assessing and working through attachment relationships and patterns. With its disproportionate allocation of time and resources to forensic investigations and determinations of risk, this is no easy task. In order to establish a therapeutic practice guided by attachment theory, Featherstone, amongst others, has advocated providing clinical space and material resources for workers to enable parents 'to think about themselves and their practices as [mothers and] fathers', noting that this opportunity is especially important for those economically and socially marginalized parents who come into contact with child protection authorities (2003: 247). As Turney and Tanner suggest, with support and training, social work professionals are 'hungry to do what they still see as "real" social work' (2001: 200). Clinical supervision provides the necessary support and a safe environment for workers to process their encounters with families in distress and the resultant feelings that arise (Davies and Collings, 2004). Supervision which focuses on clinical work with attachments between parents and children rather than the administrative duties of child protection practice can help workers to develop relationships with parents. Institutional support might also include training for workers on the broad range of factors that come into play in interactions and relationships between parent and child and understandings of the varying styles of childrearing and attitudes to the subject both in birth families and foster families in order for them 'to recognize secure and insecure attachments and the parenting behaviours that help create secure attachments. For example, in cultures where interdependence is more valued than individual autonomy, parents are likely to show more control over children including more physical discipline without negatively affecting the quality of attachment' (Mennen and O'Keefe, 2005: 583).

Should Amber's children require placement at any point during the child protection intervention, attachment theory suggests the importance of respecting and nurturing any existing healthy attachments whilst simultaneously fostering new positive caregiver–child interactions. Palmer's (1995) study of children's experiences of placement found insufficient emotional preparation of children prior to placement in foster care. Social workers were reluctant to address the painful feelings evoked in children, as well as in them, in response to the placement process. Attachment-based practice calls for mothers' involvement in the placement of children both to help prepare the children and to maintain existing attachments. One might forecast Amber's pain at these crossroads as she tries to mediate the impact of placement on her children whilst suffering their loss. Attachment theory might also compel workers to consider a shared parenting model of intervention which 'includes broader groupings of service providers and family and community members as partners in caring for children' (Freymond and Cameron, 2007: 110). Shared parenting may involve expanding voluntary placement options, providing respite care, encouraging relationships between foster and biological carers or open adoptions.

In the illustration provided in this chapter, as is often the case with families coming to the attention of child protection authorities, a father figure is potentially available to participate in establishing a secure caregiving relationship within which the children might flourish. Child protection practice has a long history of focusing almost exclusively on mothers and reproducing constructions of women as solely responsible for the care and protection of children (Krane, 2003; Krane and Davies, 2000) whilst fathers have remained at the periphery of encounters with families. The tendency has been to regard fathers as dangerous (Guterman and Lee, 2005), thus silencing discussions around the ways in which they may enrich family life. 'There is little discussion of fathers as resources or assets' (Featherstone, 2002: 123), although there is now a growing international conversation about the changing family and the role of fathers. From an attachment theory perspective, the significance of fathering is now being recognized as important to the development of children. Whilst maternal attachment has been promoted as essential for children's well-being since its resurgence, attachment to both parents is now regarded as beneficial for children. Though few studies have explored fathering through the lens of attachment theory, fathers might similarly benefit from the opportunity to negotiate their own caregiving narratives and attachment histories (Daniel and Taylor, 2001).

All talk of attachment falls by the wayside without the creation of a therapeutic relationship with mothers and other carers. Howe reminds us that 'professionals working with parents ... have to remember that the supportive nature of their involvement will activate old unconscious childhood experiences of being cared for. This will affect how parents behave with professionals' (2005: 261). Hill et al. (2004: 28) observed that mothers who have experienced 'low care in childhood', as one might imagine would have been Amber's experience, tend 'to expect or elicit low support, or to have a reduced capacity to make use of the support that is provided' when they are placed in a 'vulnerable situation'. It is unlikely that the involvement of child protection authorities would evoke anything less than feelings of vulnerability for mothers. This vulnerability may influence a mother's interactions with her children and have an impact on the therapeutic relationship with her child protection worker.

Entering into a therapeutic relationship with Amber thus requires a worker, for example, not only be highly attuned to his or her position of power with the authority to apprehend her children but also to be sensitive and responsive to Amber's unresolved losses and traumas as well as the strategies she uses for coping with low expectations of care or support activated by the intervention. Lyons-Ruth et al. suggest that therapeutic relationships evolve from the practitioner's ability to provide a client with a 'secure base' characterized by safety and trust in order to explore her historical and current attachment relationships and patterns. Establishing a secure base is said to be facilitated by listening, expressing approval and providing positive feedback, encouraging discussion of emotions, accepting and engaging with anger, explicitly acknowledging the complexities of parenting whilst taking a problem solving approach and by maintaining a collaborative dialogue (Lyons-Ruth et al. 2004). What is needed to establish and maintain a secure base stands in contrast to the organizational structure of child protection services in that families are regularly transferred from worker to worker. These disruptions jeopardize the potential for developing a consistent, collaborative and ultimately therapeutic worker–client relationship.

In addition to the emotional support crucial to enhancing parental capacity, material support is necessary to develop a secure base. 'Research highlights the powerful role that support plays in people's ability to cope with the stresses and strains of everyday life' (Howe, 2005: 229), and there is accumulating evidence 'noting the positive impact on children's long-term development of providing both *practical* and *emotional* support to at-risk parents and families' (ibid.: 230 original emphasis). Having someone to babysit or to help with shopping or other daily tasks, receiving financial or housing assistance, having a confidant(e), a reliable person to turn to when in need or someone who validates parenting are all key supports for parents in forming secure attachment relationships with their children (Howe 2005). Alongside explorations of Amber's experiences of mothering and attachment history, then, particular attention should be paid to the social supports and resources available to her – lest she be held responsible for ameliorating risks to her children's safety that are beyond her control. In other words, the continued absence of supports may well undermine the benefits of engaging in a therapeutic process with Amber.

In closing, we suggest that the therapeutic potential of attachment theory in child protection can only emerge with a deep appreciation of the context within which children and parents are living. Families involved with child protection have depleted emotional and material resources and they face multiple changes which defy quick remedy. In sharp contrast, child protection interventions are driven by expedient screenings of risk, a stress on parental compliance in reducing risk to children and simultaneous alternative permanency planning for children. In child protection practice, the view of the child as the primary client to the relative exclusion of the parents and their needs means that attachment theory translates into strict time frames for parental change so as to halt the damage caused by insecure attachments and presumably allow the child to develop more secure attachments. In this chapter, we have suggested a more profound understanding of attachment is possible when we engage in conversations about mothering, fathering and attachment histories and simultaneously attend to the actual daily life stresses faced by families. This therapeutic approach opens up the possibility of nurturing healthier attachments between parents and children whilst intervening in the cyclical intergenerational transmission of attachment patterns.

References

Ainsworth, M. D. S., Blehar, M., Waters, E. and Wall, S. (1978) *Patterns of Attachment.* Hillsdale, Erlbaum.

Andersson, G. (2005) Family relations, adjustment and well-being in a longitudinal study of children in care. *Child and Family Social Work,* 10 (1): 43–56.

Bacon, H. and Richardson, S. (2001) Attachment theory and child abuse: an overview of the literature for practitioners. *Child Abuse Review,* 10 (6): 377–97.

Bala, N. (1998) Reforming child welfare policies: don't throw the baby out with the bathwater. *Policy Options/Options Politiques,* September: 28–32.

Bala, N. (2004) Child welfare law in Canada. In N. Bala, M. K. Zapf, R. J. Williams, R. Vogland and J. Hornick (eds.), *Canadian Child Welfare Law: Children, Families and the State.* Toronto: Thompson Educational Publishing.

Barth, R. P., Crea, T. M., John, K., Thoburn, J. and Quinton, D. (2005) Beyond attachment theory and therapy: toward sensitive and evidence-based interventions with foster and adoptive families in distress. *Child and Family Social Work*, 10 (4): 257–68.

Birns, B. (1999) Attachment theory revisited: challenging conceptual and methodological sacred cows. *Feminism & Psychology*, 9 (1): 10–21.

Bliwise, N. G., (1999) Securing attachment theory's potential. *Feminism & Psychology*, 9 (1): 43–52.

Bolen, R. (2000) Validity of attachment theory. *Trauma, Violence, & Abuse*, 1 (2): 128–53.

Bowlby, J. (1969) *Attachment and Loss: Vol. 1. Attachment.* New York: Basic Books.

Bowlby, J. (1973) *Attachment and Loss: Vol. 2. Separation: Anger and Anxiety.* New York: Basic Books.

Bowlby, J. (1980) *Attachment and Loss: Vol. 3. Loss: Sadness and Depression.* New York: Basic Books.

Bretherton, I. (1995) The origins of attachment theory: John Bowlby and Mary Ainsworth. In S. Goldberg, R. Muir and J. Kerr (eds.), *Attachment Theory: Social, Developmental and Clinical Perspectives.* Hillsdale: Analytic Press.

Brown, D. J. (2006) Working the system: re-thinking the institutionally organized role of mothers and the reduction of "risk" in child protection work. *Social Problems*, 53 (3): 352–70.

Cameron, G., Coady, N. and Adams, G. R. (2007) Introduction: finding a fit: family realities and service responses. In G. Cameron, N. Coady, and G. R. Adams (eds.), *Moving Toward Positive Systems of Child and Family Welfare: Current Issues and Future Directions.* Waterloo: Wilfred Laurier University Press.

Caplan, P. (2000) *The New Don't Blame Mother: Mending the Mother–Daughter Relationship.* New York, Routledge.

Cicchetti, D. and Toth, S. L. (1995) Child maltreatment and attachment organization: implications for intervention. In S. Goldberg, R. Muir and J. Kerr (eds.), *Attachment Theory: Social, Developmental and Clinical Perspectives.* Hillsdale: Analytic Press.

Chau, S., Fitzpatrick, A., Hulchanski, D., Leslie, B. and Schatia, D. (2001) *One in Five: Housing as a Factor in the Admission of Children in Temporary Care.* Toronto: Centre for Urban and Community Studies, University of Toronto. <www.urbancentre.utoronto.ca/pdfs/researchbulletins/05.pdf> accessed August 22, 2008.

Collins, P. H. (1994) Shifting the center: race, class, and feminist theorizing about motherhood. In D. Bassin, M. Honey and M. M. Kaplan (eds.), *Representations of Motherhood.* New Haven and London: Yale University Press.

Cowan, P. A. and Cowan, C. P. (2007) Attachment theory: seven unresolved issues and questions for future research. *Research in Human Development*, 4 (3): 181–201.

Crittenden, P. M. (1988) Distorted patterns of relationship in maltreating families: the role of internal representational models. *Journal of Reproductive and Infant Psychology*, 6 (3): 183–99.

Crittenden, P. M. and Ainsworth M. (1989) Child maltreatment and attachment theory. In D. Cicchetti and V. Carlson (eds.), *Child Maltreatment, Theory and Research on the Causes and Consequences of Child Abuse and Neglect.* New York: Cambridge University Press.

Daniel, B. and Taylor, J. (2001) *Engaging Fathers: Practice Issues for Health and Social Care.* London: Jessica Kingsley.

Davies, L. and Collings, S. (2004) Subject-to-subject: reclaiming the emotional terrain for practice. In L. Davies and P. Leonard (eds.), *Social Work in a Corporate Era: Practices of Resistance and Power*, Aldershot: Ashgate.

Davies, L., Krane, J., Collings, S. and Wexler, S. (2007) Developing mothering narratives in child protection practice. *Journal of Social Work Practice*, 21 (1): 23–34.

Davies, L. and Leonard, P. (2004) Introduction. In L. Davies and P. Leonard (eds.), *Social Work in a Corporate Era: Practices of Power and Resistance.* Aldershot: Ashgate.

Eyer, D. E. (1992) *Mother Infant Bonding: A Scientific Fiction*, New Haven: Yale University Press.

Farnfield, S. (2007). A theoretical model for the comprehensive assessment of parenting. *British Journal of Social Work*, 38 (6): 1076–99.

Featherstone, B. (1997) 'I wouldn't do your job!': Women, social work and child abuse. In W. Holloway and B. Featherstone (eds.), *Mothering and Ambivalence*, London: Routledge.

Featherstone, B. (2002) Gender and child abuse. In K. J. Wilson and A. L. James (eds.), *The Child Protection Handbook.* Edinburgh: Baillière Tindall.

Featherstone, B. (2003) Taking fathers seriously. *British Journal of Social Work*, 33 (2): 239–54.

Franzblau, S. H. (1999) Historicizing attachment theory: binding the ties that bind. *Feminism & Psychology*, 9 (1): 22–31.

Freymond, N. and Cameron, C. (2007) Mothers and child welfare placements. In G. Cameron, N. Coady and G. R. Adams (eds.), *Moving Toward Positive Systems of Child and Family Welfare: Current Issues and Future Directions*, Waterloo, Ontario: Wilfred Laurier University Press.

Gauthier, Y., Fortin, G. and Jéliu, G. (2004) Clinical application of attachment theory in permanency planning for children in foster care: the importance of continuity of care. *Infant Mental Health Journal*, 25 (4): 379–96.

Glaser, D. (2001) Attachment and child protection. *Child Abuse Review*, 10 (6): 371–5.

Gove, T. J. (1995) *Executive Summary: Report of the Gove Inquiry into Child Protection in British Columbia.* Victoria: BC Government. <www.qp.gov.bc.ca/gove/gove.htm> accessed March 8, 2007.

Guterman, N. and Lee, Y. (2005) The role of fathers in risk for physical child abuse and neglect: possible pathways and unanswered questions. *Child Maltreatment*, 10 (2): 136–49.

Haight, W. L., Doner Kagle, J. and Black, J. E. (2003) Understanding and supporting parent child relationships during foster care visits: attachment theory and research. *Social Work*, 48 (2): 195–207.

Hill, M., Lambert, L., Triseliotis, J. and Buist, M. (1992) Making judgments about parenting: the example of freeing for adoption. *British Journal of Social Work*, 22 (4): 373–89.

Hill, J., Murray, L., Woodall, P., Parmar, B. and Hentges, F. (2004). Recalled relationships with parents and perceptions of professional support in mothers of infants treated for 'cleft lip'. *Attachment & Human Development*, 6 (1): 21–30.

Holland, S. (2004) *Child and Family Assessment in Social Work Practice.* Thousand Oaks: Sage.

Howe, D. (1998) Relationship-Based Thinking and Practice in Social Work. *Journal of Social Work Practice*, 12 (1): 45–56.

Howe, D. (2005) *Child Abuse and Neglect: Attachment, Development and Intervention.* New York: Palgave MacMillan.

Katz, L. (1999) Concurrent planning: benefits and pitfalls. *Child Welfare*, 78 (1): 71–87.

Krane, J. (2003) *What's Mother Got To Do With It?* Toronto: University of Toronto Press.

Krane, J. and Davies, L. (2000) Mothering and child protection practice: rethinking risk assessment. *Child and Family Social Work*, 5 (1), 35–45.

Lyons-Ruth, K., Melnick, S., Bronfman, E., Sherry, S. and Llanas, L. (2004) Hostile–helpless relational models and disorganized attachment patterns between parents and their young children: review of research and implications for clinical work. In L. Atkinson and S. Goldberg (eds.), *Attachment Issues in Psychopathology and Interventions.* Mahwah, NJ: Lawrence Erlbaum Associates.

Main, M. and Hesse, E. (1990) Parents' unresolved traumatic experiences are related to infant disorganized attachment status: is frightened/frightening parental behavior the linking mechanism? In M. T. Greenberg, D. Cicchetti and E. M. Cummings (eds.), *Attachment in the Preschool Years: Theory, Research and Intervention*, Chicago: University of Chicago Press.

Main, M. and Solomon, J. (1990) Procedures for identifying infants as disorganized/ disoriented during the Ainsworth strange situation. In M. T.

Greenberg, D. Cicchetti, and E. M. Cummings (eds.), *Attachment in the Preschool: Theory, Research and Intervention years.* Chicago: University of Chicago Press.

McMahon, M. (1995) *Engendering Motherhood: Identity and Self-Transformation in Women's Lives.* New York: Guilford.

Mennen, F. E. and O'Keefe, M. (2005) Informed decisions in child welfare: the use of attachment theory. *Children and Youth Services Review*, 27 (6): 577–93.

Palmer, S. (1995) *Maintaining Family Ties: Inclusive Practice in Foster Care.* Washington: Child Welfare League of America.

Parker, R. (1995) *Torn in Two: The Experience of Maternal Ambivalence.* Virago: London.

Parker, R. (1997) The production and purposes of maternal ambivalence. In W. Holloway and B. Featherstone (eds.), *Mothering and Ambivalence.* London: Routledge.

Quebec (2007) *Youth Protection Act*. R.S.Q. c. P-34.1

Riley, D. (1983) *War in the Nursery.* London: Routledge.

Ruddick, S. (1989) *Maternal Thinking: Towards a Politics of Peace.* Boston: Beacon.

Ruddick, S. (1994) Thinking mothers/conceiving birth. In D. Bassin, M. Honey and M. Kaplan (eds.), *Representations of Motherhood.* New Haven: Yale University Press.

Sanders, R., Colton, M. and Roberts, S. (1999) Child abuse fatalities and cases of extreme concern: lessons from reviews. *Child Abuse and Neglect*, 23 (3): 257–68.

Schene, P. (2001) *Implementing Concurrent Planning. A Handbook for Child Welfare Administrators.* Portland, ME: National Child Welfare Resource Center for Organizational Improvement.

Trocmé, N., Fallon, B., MacLaurin, B., Daciuk, J., Felstiner, C., Black, T., *et al.* (2005) *Canadian Incidence Study of Reported Child Abuse and Neglect – 2003: Major Findings.* Ottawa: National Clearinghouse on Family Violence.

Turney, D., and Tanner, K. (2001) Working with neglected children and their families. *Journal of Social Work Practice*, 15 (2): 193–204.

Walker, J. (2007) Unresolved trauma in parents and the implications in terms of child protection. *The Journal of Social Work Practice*, 21 (1): 77–87.

Walker, J. (2008) The use of attachment theory in adoption and fostering. *Adoption and Fostering Journal*, 32 (1): 49–57.

White, S. (1998) Time, temporality and child welfare: notes on the materiality and malleability of time(s). *Time & Society*, 7 (1): 55–74.

Whittaker, J. K. and Maluccio, A. N. (2002) Rethinking 'child placement': a reflective essay. *Social Service Review*, (March): 108–34.

7

Engaging Fathers – Promoting Gender Equality?

Brid Featherstone

Introduction

Over the last two decades successive governments in the United Kingdom have introduced initiatives to mandate or encourage specific fathering practices. The initial emphasis on the provision of economic maintenance by non-resident birth fathers has continued but co-exists with broader imperatives, all of which encapsulate a shift from rights to responsibilities. These concern post-divorce parenting, work/care responsibilities and an unprecedented expansion of the role of child welfare services (Collier and Sheldon, 2008). This chapter offers an overview of developments but the specific focus is on policy and practice in the arena of children's services.[1]

[1]This term refers to the restructuring of services that occurred in England from 2004 onwards (see Parton, 2006).

Gender and Child Welfare in Society Edited by Brid Featherstone, Carol-Ann Hooper, Jonathan Scourfield, and Julie Taylor.

There is a well-developed scholarship exploring the impact of policies, such as those in relation to employment or post-divorce parenting, on gender relations and the prospects for gender equality. However, policies encouraging services to 'engage' fathers in the arena of children's services have not received comparable scrutiny. This chapter is a tentative contribution to this project. It argues that the policies being developed in relation to children's services do not locate themselves within a gender-equality frame. Whether they should or not remains an open question. It is of concern, however, that such policies are being developed within an overall context which has failed to offer genuine policy choices to men and women in relation to the sharing of work and care.

Interrogating gender equality

Fraser (1994) identified two approaches by feminists towards reforming the welfare state in gender-egalitarian directions – the 'universal breadwinner' and 'caregiver parity' approaches (see Orloff, 2007). The universal breadwinner approach encourages women to act as men do in the economy, as breadwinners with care work left to others. This approach falls within a liberal equality paradigm.

By contrast, the 'caregiver parity' model does not neglect care, or women's work as caregivers, but tries to compensate women for the disadvantages this work creates. Thus, women and men continue to be different but women are protected from the consequences. Fraser outlined the problems with both approaches and advanced an influential synthesis of them – the 'universal caregiver' model in which men are made the focus of efforts to change rather than women (see Lister, 2006).

Orloff (2007)[2] argues that this was an important analytic innovation on the part of Fraser, decentring the masculine and valorizing care whilst not leaving it solely to women. Fraser does note that a precondition for this kind of gender equity would be to end gender as we know it which, as Orloff notes, is a revolutionary demand. But a more

[2] I am grateful to Ann Orloff for permission to draw on the paper cited here.

reformist version is to attempt to make men more like women by finding ways to encourage their participation in care with policies such as individual leave entitlements. However, Orloff argues that Fraser's position does not engage adequately with the deep investments men and women have in gender and the ways in which subjectivity and knowledge are grounded in gender categories. She argues that taking account of these investments matters insofar as it points not only to men's investments in preserving the power that current social arrangements give them but also to women's concerns to preserve their power in the domain of the private, caregiving realm: identities are formed in relation to whether men and women see themselves as caregivers or not.

Doucet (2006a) notes, however, the consensus amongst scholars that, in certain theoretical and historical contexts, the concepts of gender equality and gender differences are highly interdependent. She argues that in order to move out of the equality–difference gridlock, the following is of use. She shifts her analytic lens from equality to difference and disadvantage. Difference does not always lead to disadvantage and does not always mean unequal. Doucet suggests that gender difference can co-exist with equality and she, further, suggests the elaboration of a concept of gender symmetry rather than equality.

The idea that equality can co-exist with difference is very important, although it is more complex than Doucet allows for. For example, it is desirable to argue that a key demand today should be for gender equality to be an objective of government policies in relation to the balancing of work and care. The concept of equality being used here is based upon the work of Lewis and Campbell (2007). Their approach to defining gender equality is derived from Sen's (1999) capabilities approach which focuses not on equality of outcome but rather on the importance of agency and the possibility of making a real choice. They argue that such an approach eschews prescription and instrumentalism and allows the reframing of the current policy debates over choice that have become increasingly dominant in a number of European welfare states. The idea of 'real' or 'genuine' choice goes beyond seeing choice as a simple expression of preferences and acknowledges the important role of policy in addressing the constraints on choice. If care is a universal human need then, arguably, it should be possible for anyone to choose to do it. They argue that genuine choice can only exist in a universe of fair and adequate wages, generous family policies, and secure work. They argue that the policies developed in the United Kingdom compromise such a notion of gender equality.

Basically, the argument is for the importance of establishing a framework within which individual men and women can feel genuinely able to decide what kinds of arrangements they want in order to balance work and care without being constrained by gendered inequalities in pay or the low levels of financial support attached to paternity leave, for example. However, there is no attempt to specify what individual men and women might decide is the right thing for them to do in the home on an everyday basis based upon their constructions of good fatherhood or motherhood, although the adoption of compulsory leaves for men, such as 'daddy months', would be necessary according to some feminists (see Lister, 2006). So equality and difference could co-exist if desired, certainly at the level of everyday practices as Doucet suggests. This might be considered problematic by others, however, if it means that low-paid workers from economically deprived sectors of society or other countries are being employed to do the care work (Featherstone, 2009).

An interesting and unprecedented aspect of current developments in relation to policies in children's services is that there appears to be more of an attempt to re-order what actually happens at the level of everyday practices, as is explored further below (for example, fathers are being encouraged to read to children). Is this an appropriate role for the state? Even if desirable what are the implications? Does it reinforce a particular model of father involvement which could provide the building blocks for gender equality or is it antithetical to gender equality? These issues are returned to. First an overview is offered of contemporary developments in a number of key arenas.

Balancing work and care

A range of developments have ensued since 1997 in relation to balancing work and care responsibilities. For example, paid paternity leave for two weeks has been introduced as well as plans for mothers to transfer six months of their leave to fathers. The right to request flexible working has also been introduced.

According to Lewis and Campbell (2007), securing gender equality has not been an explicit priority of the policies that have been developed. Furthermore, they render the possibility of achieving equality more problematic. For example, there is evidence to suggest that for women gender equality is best achieved by short leaves for mothers with paid support for fathers to take leave. The system instituted by the government in the United Kingdom is almost the direct opposite of this, with the longest leave for mothers in the European Union and little paid support for men.

Lewis and Campbell argue that there is considerable evidence from cross-national research on what parental leave should look like if fathers are to take it. It must be an individual entitlement, paid at a high rate of compensation, and be flexible, making possible shorter and longer blocks of leave either full- or part-time. New Labour, by contrast, has instituted a low flat rate of compensation for its two weeks of paternity leave. Additional leave is not an individual right (it is a transfer from the mother's leave), and is not well compensated and flexible. Indeed, the government's own regulatory impact assessment makes it clear that it does not expect many fathers to take up this leave. Such proposals entrench the belief that mothers are the primary care-takers and fathers can take on such roles at mothers' discretion (O'Brien, 2005).

Overall, a telling point made by Lewis and Campbell is that rather than entrenching concrete entitlements, there is a reliance on exhortation. For example, British fathers work the longest hours in Europe, and the UK government negotiated an opt-out from the Working Time Directive which mandated a maximum 48-hour working week throughout the rest of the European Union. In December 2008 the EU commission voted to end such opt-outs and, as yet, it is unclear what the response of the government will be to this. Certainly, over the last decade there appeared to be a hardening of attitudes within the government in support of retaining it. Different policy developments in other countries, such as 'daddy quotas', have not been adopted. Moreover calls to increase two-week paternity leave have been explicitly ruled out on the grounds of cost (Curtis, 2009).

Regulating the 'absent' father

Throughout the 1980s and 1990s an array of constituencies emerged to express concern about the behaviours of particular groups of fathers and/or the adequacy of the supports and controls that were in place in relation to influencing fathers' behaviour (see Williams, 1998).[3] The initial focus was on the responsibilities of fathers to maintain their children financially following separation/divorce; this was a focus evident across a range of countries. As Lewis (2002) notes, whilst the debates in many northern European countries and the United States looked superficially similar, revolving mainly around the responsibilities of fathers to maintain their children financially on separation/divorce, there were real differences in the drivers and nature of debates and policies. She suggests that this is linked to the differing balances drawn between fathers as providers of care and cash in different welfare regimes. In Scandinavia,[4] where the dual-earner model is firmly established and where adult citizenship is tied to participation in the labour market, the focus has been more on the care provided by fathers and has been part of the debate about achieving greater equality in the division of unpaid as well as paid work. Historically, Britain has adhered to a strong male-breadwinner model and placed more emphasis, therefore, on the ability of fathers to maintain their children financially.

The growth in divorce and cohabitation rates had resulted in a separation of marriage and parenthood and a key concern became the need to tie men to families and, crucially, to reduce the social security budget. Child support legislation was introduced but was to face a range of problems in relation to implementation. As Wilkeley (2007) notes, although the British Social Attitudes Survey in 1990 found that 90 per cent of men and 95 per cent of women thought that a father should pay for his children after divorce, the new legislation met with considerable resistance. Over the last decades, there have been

---

[3] As Lewis (2002) notes, there had been periods of concern historically but after World War II these were not in evidence for a number of decades.

[4] 'Scandinavia', strictly speaking, refers to Denmark, Norway and Sweden whilst the Finland and Iceland are often included as members of 'the Nordic countries'. The terms, however, are used interchangeably in the literature (see Ellingsaeter and Leira, 2006).

a number of attempts at revision and the current system includes both strong enforcement measures for those considered the most recalcitrant alongside a clear preference for private arrangements (see Featherstone, 2009).

Developments in relation to child support were top down and did not emerge from demands by fathers; indeed, they were often resisted by fathers' organizations and by individual fathers. Whilst designed to control men's behaviour, they have clearly had implications for women and children. They can be understood within a context of reordering men's and women's relationships such that a 'clean break' after divorce or separation is no longer possible where a couple have children, which has implications for all concerned but does signal that the limited room for establishing 'autonomy' fought for by feminists in the last decades continues to be eroded. I am using the notion of autonomy here to signpost the possibility for women of living independently of men with whom they have had children. This trend is most apparent in relation to developments around contact.

Contact

Collier and Sheldon (2008) note the centrality of the father to a new paradigm of post-divorce family life. A model of the responsible divorce has emerged in which law is seen as having a central and distinctive role in encouraging behaviour modification. Men and women should behave responsibly and cooperate for the sake of their children. Such prescriptions have entered the vocabularies of both parents and are interpreted in ways that reflect gendered lives and rationalities. Contact is increasingly seen not only as a child's right but also as essential to their welfare, although it is important to point out that the evidence base in relation to the latter is considered by eminent researchers to be shaky (Eekelaar, 2006).

A pro-contact philosophy is now almost hegemonic. This is in contrast with earlier beliefs that a clean break was best for all concerned (see Collier, 1995). Campaigners on domestic violence continue to express considerable concern about the implications of this emphasis and point to the worryingly low levels of refusal of contact given the statistics on the prevalence of domestic violence (Harrison, 2006).

However, Reece (2006) contests the hegemonic position that domestic violence has attained in campaigns around contact and points to the almost complete erosion of a language around women's autonomy. Whilst she does not offer a definition of autonomy she refers to a range of literature which has pointed out that the gendered division of labour exists in most families and that this is continued post-separation with serious implications for women's ability to construct 'new' lives. Basically, divorce and separation do not allow women to leave inequitable settlements behind but may indeed reinforce or intensify such settlements.

Wallbank (2007) suggests that the developments in relation to contact can render women obstructive even if their concerns are about fathers' unreliability or poor parenting, and there is little space to raise issues such as the amount of work women may need to do to ensure contact enhances their children's welfare.

Fathers' demands in relation to contact may be seen to reflect important desires in relation to 'good fatherhood'. Good fathers fight to stay involved with their children (Collier and Sheldon, 2008). Such desires need to be located within understandings of the influence of gendered inequalities. For example, they may be pursued in a context which allows pronouncing on what children need whilst failing to share the work required to meet those needs. Moreover, it is argued by some feminists that demands in relation to contact by some fathers are concerned primarily with controlling women in a context where marriage is no longer reliable and, therefore, such demands are not really about children at all. Others argue that the demands are about recognition rather than the desire to actually share the work of caring for children and have a symbolic purpose in a society where it is believed that the mother–child bond is accorded priority (Featherstone, 2009).

Most of the contemporary fathers' groups construct themselves primarily as wanting to advance child welfare. Mothers who are living apart from their children are called upon as allies by organizations such as Families Need Fathers, but what about other mothers? Some are seen as endangering their children by unsafe partnerships, and there is a clear ideological bifurcation between the safe birth father and the dangerous step-father evident in many of the statements by fathers' organizations in this area (see Featherstone, 2009). Others are seen as making false allegations and using domestic violence in particular. Anti-women rhetoric is not common amongst the more established groups, though it is a feature of others. But the focus is on children, with the needs and desires of women either effaced or constructed as illegitimate.

Overall, the principle that parenthood, including fatherhood, is for life has been enshrined and can be seen within an increasing legislative trend to support fathers having a direct and unmediated relationship with children (that is, unmediated by marriage). Indeed Collier and Sheldon (2008) note that the legal focus more broadly has shifted from a concentration on horizontal relationships (between adult partners) towards vertical relationships (between adult and child).

Alongside these developments, a range of unprecedented developments have emerged which directly concern practitioners delivering services in an array of arenas from education, health and preventive services. These are now explored.

Engaging fathers

In November, 2008 the Minister for Children, Beverley Hughes, announced a 'Think Fathers' campaign, in order 'to dispel the myth that dads are the "invisible parent"'. She argued that there should be an expectation by services of fathers' involvement – from birth, through early years and in schools.

Further calls in 2009 from the minister ordered government departments to 'dad-proof' services amidst concerns that schools, hospitals and other services were preventing fathers from taking a more active role in their children's lives. 'Everything is so mother- dominated in public services and we're trying to change that. The benefits for children of fathers being involved in their early lives are considerable: not just for boys, but there is a particular effect with sons. The relationship with the father is important for a boy's attainment, behaviour and emotional resilience' (Hughes, quoted in Curtis, 2009). Hughes announced the following as being amongst the policies being developed:

- plans for schools to send children's reports to fathers who live elsewhere;
- encouragment for hospitals to make it possible for fathers to stay the night after their partner has given birth;

- a new government-run website for dads;
- a dad's version of a baby handbook;
- a drive to encourage fathers to read to their children;
- training for all professionals who work with children on how to communicate with dads;
- promotion of childcare services to black and minority ethnic fathers;
- developing activities at children's centres for fathers.

Although welcoming the above, a prominent campaigner, Duncan Fisher, noted that whilst the current system in relation to paternity leave remained there would continue to be significant obstacles to fathers engaging with their children. However, others such as Bristow (2009) argue that

> Thinking [*sic*] Fathers means ignoring the importance of a father's wage-earning role and castigating him for not changing enough nappies ... It also means turning the (positive) fact that many fathers do not feel they need parenting advice from the authorities into a problem to be tackled by getting employers, children's services, practitioners and voluntary organisations to look at what more can be done to give dads the support they need.

The origin of the focus on services rather than concrete entitlements can, to a certain extent, be located in developments in the 1990s. An influential report by Burgess and Ruxton (1996) highlighted the role of services in promoting a culture which increased fathers' marginalization in their children's lives (Williams, 1998). A further set of contemporaneous developments highlighted the importance for children, particularly boys, of having male role models. Social unrest in different areas in the 1990s supported calls from Left and Right about the undesirable social consequences of children, especially boys, growing up in lone mother families. In 1998 the first ever consultation document on supporting families to be issued by a government contained the following statement:

> 6.5 The Ministerial Group on the Family will carry on its work and during the course of next year reports will be published, and further measures will be taken to improve public policy. In particular, the Ministerial Group will be focusing on the needs of young men

> and the support available to fathers. 6.6 Increasingly, boys and young men seem to have difficulty maturing into responsible citizens and fathers. Declining educational performance, loss of traditional 'male jobs', the growth of a 'laddish' antisocial culture, greater use of drugs, irresponsible teenage fatherhood, and the rising suicide rate may all show rising insecurity and uncertainty among young men. This has worrying implications for the stability of family life and wider society. For example, recent research suggests that young men may not grow out of crime in their late teens, as they were once assumed to do. 6.7 Fathers have a crucial role to play in their children's upbringing, and their involvement can be particularly important to their sons. Most voluntary and professional organisations currently working with parents acknowledge that it is much more difficult to encourage fathers to participate in parenting support than mothers. Some organisations have already developed programmes which specifically target fathers. The Ministerial Group for the Family will be looking at ways of encouraging the development of more widespread support for fathers (Home Office, 1998 quoted in Featherstone 2009: 139–40).

A range of projects directed at fathers received funding (see Featherstone 2004). These were time limited and were located in a variety of agency settings. Interestingly, despite the emphasis on fathers providing role models for sons and on dealing with troublesome behaviour, very few initiatives were funded directed solely at fathers and sons.

Over the intervening decade such developments have moved into the mainstream. A consultation commissioned by the government in 2008 found nine government documents that the consultants considered to contain 'the most sustained and detailed recognition of fathers' (Page, Whitting and McLean, 2008: 4). An exploration of a number of these would suggest that the documents reproduce to varying degrees the argument that there is a clear evidence base with regards to the importance of involvement of fathers in promoting good outcomes for children. The following discussion interrogates this and also considers the following questions: Who is being called upon as a father? What is meant by involvement? What are the difficulties with assigning services such a central role? What role, if any, are mothers being called upon to play? How are children being constructed in these documents? It will be argued that the lack of an explicit engagement with gender equality evident in developments in relation to the balancing of work and care is also evident in such documents and contributes to some of the other difficulties which are highlighted.

Is there a clear evidence base? Many of the documents repeat each other so this section takes *Every Parent Matters* (Department for Education and Skills, 2007: 6) as typical in exemplifying some of the difficulties with contemporary policy injunctions for services.

> Fathers matter to children's development. Father–child relationships – be they positive, negative or lacking – have profound and wide-ranging impacts on children that last a lifetime, particularly for children from the most disadvantaged backgrounds. Research shows that where fathers have early involvement in a child's life there is a positive relationship to early educational achievement; there is an association with good parent–child relationships in adolescence; and children in separated families are protected from mental health problems.

Whilst the above statements capture important elements of the research, they are also misleading. A systematic review of studies in which maternal involvement had been controlled for, and for which data had been gathered from different independent sources, found a beneficial impact of *positive* father involvement in children's lives (Pleck and Masciardrelli, 2004). What counts as positive depends to some extent on the theoretical models of the psychologists and sociologists and the age of the child but there are certain commonalities: activities likely to promote an emotionally secure environment and well-being in its broadest sense, such as warm, responsive and sensitive interaction, the monitoring and guiding of behaviour to set limits, time spent listening to and talking about the child's concerns, the encouragment of age-appropriate independent action, care for the child's physical welfare. A key point made by many researchers is that 'father involvement cannot be separated from the network of family relationships within which it is embedded. The couple relationship is a key one, setting the scene against which parents negotiate and balance their family and employment roles and responsibilities. Research suggests that high paternal involvement is 'grounded in harmonious couple relationships' (O'Brien, 2005: 9).

This is important, alerting us to the dangers of abstracting father involvement or activities from the overall relationship context in which they operate.

In relation to educational outcomes, the evidence suggests the importance of locating father involvement contextually. For example,

Goldman (2005) points out that fathers are more likely to be involved if the child's mother is involved in the child's learning and education, if they have good relations with the mother, if they or the child's mother have relatively high educational qualifications, if they become involved early on, if their child is in primary school rather than secondary school and if the school welcomes involvement.

Who is counted as a father and what is meant by involvement? These questions are not usually interrogated. However, the plans as they were announced suggest that it is the birth-father who is being called upon by the policies. Moreover, whilst involvement is not spelled out, it can be pretty minimal, such as reading to children. Certainly no documents suggest that involvement should include taking responsibility for making medical appointments or lunch boxes and keeping the house clean.

Every Parent Matters outlines the barriers to father involvement with services as insensitive services and their overly female focus and culture. There is a lack of confidence about explaining to female service users why it is important to engage fathers. Furthermore, services are considered to underestimate the significance of a father's involvement if he is not visible or living with the child. All these factors are located in a deficit approach which locates the 'failures' to engage fathers solely in the hands of services. Thus there is no engagement with the complexities of gender and help-seeking or, indeed, some men's resistance to becoming involved with their children. Furthermore, there is no consideration of whether fathers are available to be involved, and indeed there is an explicit rejection of doing more at the policy level to provide a well-resourced framework to facilitate such involvement.

Mothers, or 'female service users', are portrayed in a rather problematic way. For example, they need to have the importance of the involvement of fathers explained to them. Moreover, women workers lack the confidence to explain it to them. Indeed, in many documents, the father–child relationship is constructed as a dyad from which mothers have disappeared. For example, the Children's Plan (2007) argues for engagement with both mothers and fathers except where there is a clear risk to the child in doing so. Whilst this may be intended to encompass a range of possibilities in relation to risk it avoids any discussion of gendered inequalities in relation to violent behaviour and produces children as the only legitimate objects of concern. However, whilst children are invoked as the reason for policies they are often silent or invisible in the documents. The focus on child outcomes means that inadequate attention is paid to individual journeys and to children's own views about what matters to them.

The literature drawn upon is limited and there is little engagement, for example, with that which interrogates both paternal and maternal identities. Bristow (2009) argues that 'policy interventions that attempt to "engage" fathers in parenting services threaten to have a destabilizing impact upon both fathers' and mothers' sense of their own role and identity'. However, it could also be argued that they are a very unwelcome attempt to reinforce a particular model of identity which reinforces fathers' importance without actually asking them to rethink very much the nature of their actual contribution. Crucially, the absence of any emphasis on engaging with mothers' identities signals that the following problematic assumptions may be at work: mothers are not to be relied upon to socialize children appropriately; mothers can be taken for granted in supporting whatever is considered to be necessary for the advancement of children's welfare; mothers will block the involvement of fathers and thus a project is necessary which calls upon workers (in these services these are often poorly paid women) to reorder practices.

Bristow argues that policy makers and regulators are attempting to impose their own rigid ideas about fatherhood on a far messier reality. There is a possibility, however, that this project is a very timid aspect of wider developments which are essentially concerned with securing desirable outcomes for children. It is important to note, for example, that developments such as 'Think Fathers' have no financial incentives attached to them in relation to encouraging services to change their practices and are not mandated by statute.

Bristow is correct, however, to signpost the messy nature of contemporary investments and identities as identified in a range of literature which is turned to now.

Contemporary fathering

The literature on fathers, spanning a range of disciplines, does not lend itself to easy summary. The research, which mainly relies on data from two-parent couple households, would suggest that there has been a change in practices, although there are considerable debates about what should be measured and what counts. For example, men's involvement in taking care of children seems to have increased but their involvement in housework has not. According to Dermott (2008: 143) contemporary fatherhood is centred on a personal connection at the expense of participation in the work of childcare; because caring activities flow from an emotional connection rather than in themselves constituting the fathering role the practicalities of 'intimate fatherhood' are fluid and open to negotiation. She argues that this helps to understand the apparent, and often very irritating, gulf between conduct and culture whereby men continue to do less care whilst professing a strong commitment to being 'involved' with their children.

In terms of those who are engaging in paid work, Dermott suggests that the relationship between paid work and employment is very different for mothers and fathers in the United Kingdom. There is no evidence that fathers as a whole or a significant sub-group are adopting a 'female model' by taking on part-time and reduced hours. She notes that whilst this does not necessarily undermine arguments for the existence of a different discourse around fathering behaviour (emphasizing the emotional and nurturing elements), it does make it clear that this is not translated into alterations to working hours.

Fathers' behaviour will need to be thought about in ways that do not assume female models. According to Dermott, fatherhood has changed, but it has not become motherhood and does not provide the backdoor route to gender equality. She argues that, as intimacy involves a focus on creative personal relationships, conceptualizing contemporary fatherhood as an intimate relationship allows for an emphasis on the aspects of male parenting that fathers themselves view as most significant: emotions, the expression of affection and the exclusivity of the reciprocal father–child dyad.

Dermott's findings leave us with the important question raised by Gatrell (2007). Are men 'cherry picking' the nice bits, and leaving women with the mundane housekeeping roles? However, where does earning come into this? Is economic provision not also a form of care? (O'Brien, 2005).

Collier and Sheldon (2008) argue that fatherhood today is open-ended, fluid and fragmented. The lives of men cannot be comprehended through the deployment of binaries such as good and bad, new and traditional. It's a picture of complexity, change, inconsistency and contradiction.

Research by Doucet (2006a and 2006b) with fathers who identified themselves as primary caregivers for their children in Canada offers insights into the current diversity of fathering practices and is of interest. She found that most fathers believed that fathers and mothers have a different connection to their children and that the one held by the mother is stronger, vaster and more profound. Yet there was also evidence of significant movement and flow, which disrupted this binary picture. The overwhelming picture painted by both mothers and fathers was that mothering and fathering have much in common, but gender differences play out in several ways. Doucet employs the concept of 'borderwork' to capture the emphasis on gender differences. Two recurring instances of borderwork emerged. First, there was a deeply held belief in the intimate connection between mother and child, which was connected with the bodily connection the mother had through pregnancy and breast feeding. Second, there was a strong tendency to identify differing responses by mothers and fathers to children's distress.

A further point relates to maternal gatekeeping and highlights its complexities. Women can range from actively obstructing men's involvement to positively embracing it for a variety of very complex reasons linked to their investment in gendered identities and their understandings of children's needs. These are interrogated in the context of their own particular experiences of real men and children.

> Finally, what emerges as particularly interesting in this study is the idea of women moving over and creating spaces for men. Metaphorically, the image of borders (borderwork) and gates (gatekeeping) can be joined here. It is women, however, who lead in taking down this gender border, or opening the gate, so that men can also participate fully in parenting. This idea of opening and closing borders or gates provides for a more dynamic concept of maternal gatekeeping, and the recognition that whilst it may occur in particular spaces and times, *it does shift and change and even disappear* (Doucet, 2006a: 232, my emphasis).

This raises important questions in relation to the different possibilities open to women to 'make' men into fathers or to 'stop' men from fathering, which are explored further below.

Doucet (2006b) was interested to recover what she considers largely invisible links between theoretical and empirical understandings of fatherhood, caring and embodiment. She makes three key arguments: fathers speak as embodied subjects in caregiving; the care of children is social and occurs not only between carer and cared-for but within larger sets of social relations within which it is perceived and judged, and these social venues draw attention to how space and embodiment constantly intersect. Fathers speak about themselves as embodied agents with their emphasis on play with infants and young children, most highlight their active and outdoor approach to caregiving, and they point to how their experiences as fathers are fundamentally different from those of mothers because of perceived embodied experiences. The overwhelming majority of fathers spoke about having felt a watchful eye on them at least once because of issues around risk and danger. They highlight an area which is of considerable relevance for social care practices: the implications of men moving through women-centred spaces, going for coffee in women's homes and having children to sleep over at their house. There were factors that might minimize the visibility of embodiment. For example, one man, a doctor, reflected that his professional status appeared to render him less threatening, so that class seems to matter. Having a woman act as a bridge and vouch for the man to other women helped. Being known over time and in the community (for example, a gay bookshop owner who adopted a child) also helped.

Doucet (2006b) concludes that whilst many studies on gender and domestic labour assume that men and women are interchangeable disembodied subjects within and between households, her research emphasizes how mothers and fathers are embodied subjects who move through domestic and community spaces with intersubjective, relational, moral and normative dimensions framing this movement. These dimensions are not fixed but contextually negotiated and renegotiated.

Doucet argues that a key finding was that fathers relied on mothers to define their fathering. Some of the men were caring full-time in a context of loss of the relationship with the mother; 'interviews were haunted by the unseen presence of the child's mother. Perhaps most notable is how the majority of fathers' interviews open with a remark about the child's mother' (Doucet, 2006a: 216).

Moreover, the relational losses felt by men when their marriage broke down were stronger than she expected: 'It is as though hegemonic masculinity, with its emphasis on autonomy and self reliance, collapses in those moments of crisis to reveal the hidden influences of connection, relationship and interdependence' (ibid. 217).

Discussion

It is possible to see the kinds of measures that are being developed within children's services as promoting a form of father-involvement which leaves gendered inequality in care-taking more or less intact, and this could chime with the 'preferences' identified by Dermott (2008). Moreover, when located in a context as outlined above, where the social policies developed are unlikely to encourage equality, it would appear that this has not been an issue of concern to government. Indeed, it could be argued that government policies in relation to the balancing of work and care are going with the grain of such preferences.

It is unlikely, even if it were desirable, that practitioners might want to be involved in a project which was highly prescriptive about how mothers and fathers should act in families (for example, in terms of sharing the housework!). However, practitioners are obliged to proscribe certain kinds of practices, and there is a degree of societal consensus about this. For example violent and abusive behaviours are the subject of a great deal of legislation. Indeed, feminists have a long history of campaigning for state involvement in family life in relation to such matters.

Moreover, the exact nature of such involvement continues to be the subject of considerable debate. For example, Scourfield's (2003) findings, from his study of gender and occupational culture in child protection services, suggested that the dominance of practices that ignored men and concentrated on mothers to secure children's welfare reinforced oppressive assumptions about women's responsibility for securing such welfare. A key aspect of support for women and children, he argued, should be direct engagement with men in order to effect behaviour change. The absence of such engagement has resulted, it is argued, in injustices such as women being considered to be failing to protect their children from men by whom they are being beaten (see Featherstone and Peckover, 2007). For example, the recognition that violence by men to women harms children has led to the increased 'mainstreaming' of domestic violence as a child protection issue. Dominant approaches put the onus on women to leave such men or be considered as 'failing to protect' their children.

Not only does this reinforce oppressive gendered constructions in relation to responsibility, it is argued by Ferguson and Hogan (2004) that services' failure to engage young fathers constitutes a lost opportunity for men who are socially and economically excluded. They suggest that a key challenge for professionals is to see beyond young men's enactment of a protest masculinity and to recognize that in a context of overwhelming failure, vulnerable young men can see fatherhood as an opportunity to succeed in a meaningful way in their lives.

It is important for services to recognize not just the messy realities of fathers' identities and investments but also those of mothers. As Doucet (2006a and 2006b) notes, mothers, whether absent or present, play a range of roles in opening up and closing down possibilities for particular kinds of fathering practices, and these are complexly linked to identities which shift and change. The research on post-divorce parenting suggests that mothers may agree that it is desirable for fathers to be involved but that they worry about their own situations and, in particular, the reliability of their own children's father. Some research with mothers attending children's services identified a yearning for birth-fathers to back up mothers in issues of discipline and provide play opportunities for their children. It was also felt that services should provide opportunities for fathers to learn how to manage their anger (Roskill et al., 2008). These mothers, when offered the opportunity to evaluate current service provision, were clear that contemporary practices were lacking. More research is needed, however, in this area. This could test out Gatrell's (2007) finding that in some families children have become the site of gendered power battles. For example, she found that in families where both parents were working, fathers were asserting their 'rights' to children in a context of perceived loss of power in relation to the mothers of their children. Harne (2005) provides an antidote to undue optimism about fathers' motives with her finding that some, who were being violent to mothers, pursued their involvement with children in order to further undermine the mothers.

Conclusion

This chapter is offered as a very tentative contribution to exploring developments in children's services from a perspective which considers gender equality as an important and legitimate societal goal. However, it recognizes the complexities of translating this into practice and highlights the need to delineate the different levels at which it should be pursued in a context of messy and transitional everyday lives. It raises more questions than it answers in relation to what equality might look like in particular contexts and, indeed, what the limits of state involvement in such a project might or should be.

References

Bristow, J (2009) 'Deconstructing Dads'. <www.spiked-online.com/index.php?/site/reviewofbooks_printable6306> accessed 23 March 2009.

Burgess, A. and Ruxton, S. (1996) *Men and their Children: Proposals for Public Policy*. London, IPPR.

Collier, R. (1995) *Masculinity, Law and the Family*. London, Routledge.

Collier, R. and Sheldon, S. (2008) *Fragmenting Fatherhood: A Socio-legal study*. Oxford and Portland, Oregon, Hart Publishing.

Curtis, (2009) Family policies 'dad-proofed' to give fathers bigger role – but no extra paternity leave. *Guardian*, 21 February 2009.

Department for Children, Schools and Families (2007) *The Children's Plan: Building Brighter Futures*. London, The Stationery Office.

Department for Education and Skills (2007) *Every Parent Matters*. London, The Stationery Office.

Dermott, E. (2008) *Intimate Fatherhood*. London, Routledge.

Doucet, A. (2006a) *Do Men Mother?* Toronto, University of Toronto Press.

Doucet, A. (2006b) "Estrogen-filled worlds": fathers as primary caregivers and embodiment. *The Sociological Review*, 54 (4): 696–716.

Eekelaar, J. (2006) *Family Law and Personal life*. Oxford. Oxford University Press.

Ellingsæter, A. L. and Leira, A. (2006) Introduction: politicising parenthood in Scandinavia. In A. L. Ellingsæter and A. Leira (eds.) *Politicising Parenthood in Scandinavia: Gender relations in welfare states*, Bristol, Policy Press.

Featherstone, B. (2004) *Family Life and Family Support: A Feminist Analysis.* Basingstoke and London, Palgrave.

Featherstone, B. (2009) *Contemporary Fathering: Theory, Policy and Practice.* Bristol, Policy Press.

Featherstone, B. and Peckover, S. (2007) "Letting them get away with it": fathers, domestic violence and child protection. *Critical Social Policy*, 27 (2): 181–203.

Ferguson, H. and Hogan, F. (2004) *Strengthening Families through Fathers.* Dublin: Family Affairs Unit, Department of Social and Family Affairs.

Fraser, N. (1994) After the family wage: gender equality and the welfare state. *Political Theory*, 22 (4): 591–618.

Gatrell, C. (2007) Whose child is it anyway? The negotiation of paternal entitlements within marriage. *The Sociological Review*, 55 (2): 352–72.

Goldman, R. (2005) *Fathers' Involvement in their Children's Education.* London, National Family and Parenting Institute.

Harne, L. (2005) Researching violent fathers. In T. Skinner, M. Hester and E. Malos (eds.) *Researching Gender Violence: Feminist Methodology in Action.* Cullompton: Willan Publishing.

Harrison, C. (2006) Damned if you do and damned if you don't? The contradictions between public and private law. In C. Humphreys and N. Stanley (eds.) *Domestic Violence and Child Protection: Directions for Good Practice*, London: Jessica Kingsley.

Hughes, B. (2008) Keynote speech, Family and Parenting Institute Conference, London. November.

Lewis, J. (2002) The problem of fathers: policy and behaviour in Britain. In B. Hobson (ed.), *Making Men into Fathers: Men, Masculinities and the Social Politics of Fatherhood.* Cambridge: Cambridge University Press.

Lewis, J. and Campbell, M. (2007) UK work/family balance policies and gender equality. *Social Politics*, 14 (1): 4–30.

Lister, R. (2006) Children (but not women) first: New Labour, child welfare and gender. *Critical Social Policy*, 26 (2): 315–36.

O'Brien M. (2005) *Shared Caring: Bringing Fathers into the Frame.* University of East Anglia, Norwich, Equal Opportunities Working Paper Series.

Orloff. A (2007) Should feminists aim for gender symmetry? Why a dual-earner/dual-carer society is not every feminist's utopia. <www.ssc.wisc.edu/~mscaglio/2006documents/Orloff_2007_Gender_ Symmetry.pdf > accessed 18 August 2008.

Page, J., Whitting. G. and McLean, C. (2008) *How Fathers Can Be Better Recognised and Supported through DCSF Policy.* London, The Stationery Office.

Parton, N. (2006) *Safeguarding Childhood: Early Intervention and Surveillance in a Late Modern Society.* Basingstoke, Palgrave Macmillan.

Pleck, J. H. and Masciadrelli, B. (2004) Paternal involvement by US residential fathers: levels, sources and consequences. In M.E. Lamb (ed.), *The Role of the Father in Child Development* (4th edn.). Chichester. Wiley.

Reece, H. (2006) UK women's groups' child contact campaign: 'so long as it is safe'. *Child and Family Quarterly,* 18 (4): 538–61.

Roskill, C., Featherstone, B., Ashley, C. and Haresnape, S. (2008) *Fathers Matter Volume 2: Further Findings on Fathers and Their Involvement with Social Care Services.* London, Family Rights Group.

Scourfield, J. (2003*) Gender and Child Protection.* Basingstoke and London, Palgrave Macmillan.

Sen, A. (1999) *Development as Freedom.* London, Knopf.

Wallbank, J. (2007) Getting tough on mothers: regulating contact and residence. *Feminist Legal Studies,* 15 : 189–222.

Wikeley, N. (2007) Child support reform – throwing the baby out with the bathwater. *Child and Family Law Quarterly,* 19 (4): 434–57.

Williams, F. (1998) Troubled masculinities in social policy discourses: fatherhood. In J. Popay, J. Hearn and J. Edwards (eds.), *Men, Gender Divisions and Welfare,* London, Routledge.

8

Working with Violent Male Carers (Fathers and Stepfathers)

Mark Rivett

Introduction

It is not difficult to appreciate the relevance of work with violent male carers in the contemporary climate of child welfare. One recent example of the urgency of this topic is the case of Baby P (Ofsted, Health Care Commission, HM Inspectorate 2008). This 17-month-old child died in August 2007 whilst in the care of his mother, her boyfriend and a male lodger. These two men were convicted in November 2008 of having caused or allowing Baby P to die. The subsequent investigations and Parliamentary questions largely focused upon the procedural failures of Haringey Children's Services (ibid.). The national media on the other hand, placed the blame for Baby P's death *both* on the social services department *and* upon the male carers who were alleged to have perpetrated various forms of violence upon the child.

Gender and Child Welfare in Society Edited by Brid Featherstone, Carol-Ann Hooper, Jonathan Scourfield, and Julie Taylor.

In the detailed description of the interventions used by Haringey staff much was made of the work with Baby P's mother to improve her parenting skills, but little effort was made to engage the men in the household either in treatment or in assessment of the risk to Baby P. No clearer example is needed to emphasize that child welfare workers, from all professions, need to have a greater understanding of the assessment and treatment of violent male carers, whether they are fathers, stepfathers or partners.*

These issues are as complex as many others in the gendered analysis of welfare practice. Therefore, the terms used in this chapter need to be clarified. First, I have chosen the broad phrase 'male carers', although predominantly much of the literature and debate assumes that it is fathers and stepfathers who are being discussed. Even though I will also predominantly refer to the literature about fathers and stepfathers it is important to acknowledge that work with violent and abusive men may also include gay men and boyfriends. Welfare practice that does not encompass such relationships will miss significant relationships in the lives of children. Second, although the terms 'violence' and 'abuse' contain subtle differences, this chapter will assume that when we are talking about the experience of children they are more similar than different. Lastly, because work with those violent male carers who are not sexually abusive is a rare phenomenon, this chapter will predominantly refer to the research and literature on domestic violence. This is because it is in this sphere that treatment, assessment and debate about work with violent male carers is most sophisticated and developed (Featherstone, Rivett and Scourfield, 2007).

The first dichotomy: 'carer/father' or 'violent individual'?

It is hard to disagree with the view that is prevalent in the field of domestic violence that a violent or abusive male carer is per se a poor

---

*I should like to thank Rebecca Barns, Bristol University for contributions to the literature review and for discussions about the place of the father–child relationship in the lives of children who witness domestic violence.

parent. This perspective holds valuable insights and has functioned as a corrective to systems, especially child welfare and court systems, which often seem to operate on the assumption that *any* fathering is better than *none* (Williams, Boggess and Carter, 2004). Jaffe and Geffner write that: 'one parent abusing the other [is] a presumption of poor parenting' (1998: 384). They proceed to argue for a thorough assessment of violent male carers before they are allowed to see their children in an unsupervised setting.

Eriksson and Hester (2001) argue that because most agencies value the involvement of fathers they ignore the risks that these men pose both to women and children. Specifically they say that the category of 'father' obscures the violence committed by these men. Saunders (2004) provided stark evidence that this was the case in custody disputes in the United Kingdom. She reviewed court decisions and the outcomes for children and found that 29 children had been killed by their fathers following a court decision that gave these men unsupervised access to those children. If this is the prevalent view within domestic violence services, then it is also prevalent when the abuse or violence is inflicted directly upon children. Crooks et al. (2006) note that a high proportion of alleged perpetrators of child abuse are men whilst men predominate in the perpetration of sexual abuse. Not surprisingly, Crooks et al. (2006) and Kelly and Wolfe (2004) note that few services have been created for work with these men because it is assumed that work should continue with the *non*-abusing parent (for example, the mother). Paradoxically, the assumption that men are not going to be 'safe parents' leads to an emphasis on women's parenting which once more reinforces patriarchal assumptions and an essentialist description of gender roles (Featherstone, Rivett and Scourfield, 2007).

There are a number of consequences of this emphasis upon the 'violent' category within the phrase 'violent male carers'. First, most interventions will be targeted at such men within settings where the facts of the violence dominate the context. Here, the assumption made by welfare agencies is that the men need to be taught to be non-violent before they can be helped to be better fathers (and arguably better partners). Not surprisingly, these contexts are often prisons and probation services, which deliver interventions for sex abusers and domestic violence perpetrators (Featherstone, Rivett and Scourfield, 2007; Rivett and Rees, 2008). This context carries its own consequences. It is marked by an attention to standards which can be achieved by all its practitioners; accountability to the 'public'; and a firm concentration on a definition of the man as a 'perpetrator' rather than both a perpetrator *and* a father/carer. A second consequence of the targeting of the 'violent' within the term 'violent male carer' is that services to such men will tend to be placed within 'tertiary' specialist services rather than at the primary level (schools, family centres, GP surgeries) where the vast majority of such men are likely to go for help (Hester et al., 2006; Fagan and Hawkins, 2001; Frost, Lloyd and Jeffery, 2003; Westmarland, Hester and Reid, 2004). This last point reminds us that there are many more violent men than enter the criminal justice or safeguarding/child welfare systems. Current estimates suggest that there are 635,000 domestic violence incidents alone in one year in England (British Crime Survey, 2003). The Department of Constitutional Affairs (2004) estimated that 16,000 male perpetrators of domestic violence had contact with the civil court system each year. Whilst researchers suggest that only a small minority (perhaps only 2 per cent) of domestic violence assaults are reported to the police (Kaufman, Kantor and Strauss, 1990). These figures highlight one disadvantage of an approach to violent male carers which privileges the 'violent' label at the expense of the 'carer' label: it may fail to consider the possibility of intervening with many men whose behaviour negatively affects children.

The disadvantages of such an emphasis have been noted by various commentators. Featherstone and Peckover write that 'it is necessary to take violent men seriously as fathers and father figures' (2007: 181). They suggest that emphasizing the 'perpetrator' label for violent male carers has obscured the fact that they have an identity beyond this label. Indeed, some of them will be important male figures to their children. They continue, 'The construction within contemporary policy discourses of violent men as offenders is not only problematic for criminal justice agencies . . . but it also blurs and distorts understandings of and responses to violent men's involvement in the everyday lives of their families' (ibid.: 187).

Some authors (Ferguson and Hogan, 2004; Perel and Peled, 2008) point out that emphasizing the abusive elements of fatherhood gives no incentive to engaging men in child centred work. Collectively these authors make a utilitarian argument for designing approaches that work with violent male carers *beyond the violent label*. These men will continue to be carers for their children and their relationship with those children will outlast most of the interventions provided, *therefore* their role as carers must also be addressed. Crooks et al. (2006) make a practical case for a both/and approach. They comment that violent fathers need a new approach to their violence which is not accounted for in traditional parenting programmes. Such programmes fail to address the gender issues of masculinity; address the behavioural aspects of parenting at the expense of the emotional aspects (hypothesized to be deficient in violent fathers); and do not account for the subtle abuse that men may use against partner, child, child through partner or partner through child.

What emerges from this discussion is a *both/and* perspective. This supports a kind of work with violent male carers which addresses both the violence and the caring role. However, most current services for these men tend to cluster into one or other of these polarities. On the one hand, there has been a burgeoning of services which work with the 'violent' aspects of men especially in the field of domestic violence (Pence and Paymar, 1993). On the other hand, there have been services that cater for the 'man behind the label' (Jenkins 1990) from the therapeutic world and services that promote active and child focused fatherhood (Biddulph, 1995; Burgess, 1997). In contemporary practice, there is also a debate about how to transport the valuable experience learnt from domestic violence services into contexts which have another (often family) focus (Featherstone, Rivett and Scourfield, 2007). For instance, workers within family centres who are engaging fathers will frequently discover that their clients want help with domestic violence (Ferguson and Hogan, 2004). But such men will not want to attend a 'perpetrator programme' and will cease attending if they feel that are being seen as 'criminals' (Collett, 2001; Crooks et al., 2006). Later, the various treatment approaches available for such men will be explored.

The second dichotomy: violence and men

The second dichotomy to be addressed within work with violent male carers is that between understandings of how men's gender influences their violence. Although at first such a question may sound theoretical, it has a number of important practical consequences.

Clearly, the connection between maleness and violence has been the subject of numerous studies, discussions and public debates (Featherstone, Rivett and Scourfield, 2007). These might be characterized as being divided between those which hypothesize biological connections and those that hypothesize socially constructed connections (see Harway and O'Neil, 1999 for an application of these theories to domestic violence). A few such descriptions are relevant for child welfare professionals. One (Chodorow, 1978) suggests that because in patriarchal societies 'mothering' is equated with 'parenting' a child's gender identity is centred upon identifying or not identifying with the mothering role. This theory is a 'social' version of the Oedipal conflict proposed by Freud which proposed a similar intra-familial process of gender identification. The theory suggests that boys must reject the 'mother' in order to become a man. This rejection, it is argued, entails the rejection of all that is defined as 'feminine', especially feelings of dependency and emotional warmth. In a further elaboration, some psychological theorists have proposed that male sexuality is intimately connected to this rejection, and hence men's sexuality is also frequently harnessed to the desire to dominate and oppress (Benjamin 1988; Jukes, 1994).

Alternative descriptions of masculinities place more emphasis upon the social rather than the psychological. Thus, authors such as Connell (1995) and Whitehead (2002) describe a number of different social constructions which act upon different men's understandings of how they 'do maleness'. Various studies have examined some of these processes and largely confirm that some social processes seem to encourage a connection between selfishness, maleness and aggression (Beynon, 2002). It is interesting that none of these theories are particularly positive about men and masculinity. Most imply a 'deficit' model of maleness, and one moreover that implies that men are uniquely available to 'act out violence' *because of how their gender is constructed*. This has profound practical consequences because these stereotypes suffuse the everyday practice of child welfare workers.

There is ample evidence, from a number of sources, to confirm that many practitioners, and indeed whole welfare agencies, have a view that maleness and violence are intimately connected. Scourfield (2003), for instance, in an ethnographic study of statutory social workers, found that the predominant discourses about men were that they were a threat, absent or 'no use'. Featherstone, Rivett and Scourfield (2007) characterize the discourses about young males as being equally ones that are dominated by a 'threat' perspective which again connect maleness with violence and risk. Similarly, Ferguson and Hogan's (2004) study reveals services which label fathers as 'demonic' and which presume that the male carers are unavailable to their children, partners or welfare workers. Even more stark are the findings from child protection research which confirm that social workers rarely engage fathers and that few are invited to case conferences (Buckley, 1998; O'Hagan, 1997; Scourfield, 2006).

What this evidence suggests is that, regardless of a more balanced view of masculinity within their personal lives (Christie 2006), many child welfare practitioners assume that the male carers in the lives of their child clients are not a resource to those children but a threat or a deficit. Such a view is remarkably consonant with the socially constructed view that men are *by definition* less competent parents than women. Much has been written about this 'deficit' model of masculinity (Connell, 1995; Jukes, 1994; Stoltenberg, 1993; Whitehead, 2002). There are, of course, significant alternative views to this description of maleness. The 'anti-sexist' men's movement has continued to assert that caring masculinities are possible, and many of the people quoted above have built fatherhood literature upon this premise (Biddulph, 1995; Dienhart, 1998; McLean, Carey and White, 1996; Pease, 2000; Seidler, 1997; Stoltenberg, 1993). The 'mytho-poetic men's movement' has also developed strategies for eliciting emotional and respectful qualities in men (Bly, 1991; Meade, 1993).

What emerges from this and the previous section is that child welfare practice is riven with a dichotomy in the gender practice undertaken with violent carers/fathers. On the one hand, the 'fathering role' of such men is seen as irrelevant in the face of their violence. This process is further compounded by a societal construction of masculinity which often privileges a deficit model of male parenting. This process perpetuates a lack of engagement with such men *and may contribute to* tragedies such as that of Baby P. These aspects of practice also lead practitioners into being suspicious of violent male carers and, owing to totally appropriate risk assessment, avoiding work with such men. Before I look at models of working with such men, therefore, we need to interrogate the reasons for doing so from the child's perspective.

Are violent male carers (still) important to their children?

Clearly, this question contains contentious implications. For some practitioners and researchers even asking the question implies that violent carers should have access to their children. Not surprisingly, the empirical evidence is not without its contradictions either. The usual starting place for such a review is to look at that literature that supports the value of fathers in their children's lives. The growing research in developmental psychology strongly supports the value of fathers as a resource to their children (Lamb, 1997; 2004). This research has a number of nuances in terms of its results which consider levels of father involvement, father–child interactions and the impacts of fathers on child development (Guille, 2004; Videon, 2005). It needs to be acknowledged that there are significant theoretical and methodological issues with some of this research (Featherstone, 2004), but the findings do seem remarkably consistent. Moreover, although some aspects of policy in the United Kingdom perpetuate a 'deficit' model of fathering (for example, the philosophy of the Child Support Agency) there are other aspects of policy which seem to have adopted the 'pro-father' research with gusto (Featherstone and Peckover, 2007; Featherstone, Rivett and Scourfield, 2007).

Against this backdrop we must also recognize the overwhelming evidence that being subject to, or witness of, violence has significant negative consequences for children's well-being. Most studies have confirmed that at least a third of children who are living with domestic violence are also being directly abused (Edleson, 1999; Humphreys, 2006) either physically, emotionally or, in significant numbers, sexually. The psychological consequences of child abuse are well known and as such these figures confirm the view that violent male carers are a danger to children. Even when children are not directly abused, they suffer significant consequences as a result of the abuse of others within the domestic setting. These consequences have again been well documented (Geffner, Spurling-Igelman and Zellner, 2003; Hester et al., 2007; Jaffe, Baker and Cunningham, 2004; McGee, 2000; Mullender and Morley, 1994; Mullender et al., 2002; Rossman, Hughes and Rosenberg, 2000). Within these consequences are various *indirect* ones which result from family instability as well as impairments in the mother's capacity to be child-focused in the face of threats, violence and intimidation. Holden (1998) summarized the research when he stated that 40 per cent of children who had been exposed to domestic violence exhibited clinically significant psychological difficulties. These studies also confirm that such difficulties are often long-term and affect children into adulthood.

This literature therefore questions any presumption that contact with violent or abusive men is necessarily in the child's interest. One complicating factor, however, is that not all children exposed to violence do have difficulties. Hughes and Luke (1998) estimated that up to a third of children would exhibit such resilience in the face of violence. Harold et al. (2002) have argued that this may be mediated by the child's *appraisal* of the violence within the context of its relationship between father and mother (or stepfather and mother). Unfortunately, as yet, the quality of the father–child relationship has not been examined as an element of this resilience, although Marshall, English and Stewart (2001) did find that the father–child relationship had some interactional significance in terms of outcomes for children in the child protection system.

There is, however, some evidence to confirm a deficit model of parenting by violent male carers. Two such studies (Fox and Benson, 2004; Francis and Wolfe, 2008) sought to compare the parenting (fathering) practices of abusive and non-abusive men. Both found that on a range of measures, men who had a history of abusive behaviour were more likely to be angry around and with their children, more likely to suffer from mental health difficulties and, crucially, less likely to be empathetic to the children. On the other hand, these authors also recognized that these men had a number of difficulties which contributed to their struggles to be 'good' parents. Lamb (2001) also points out that the complexity of child developmental trajectories makes it very hard to ascertain clear 'impacts' between abusive male figures and children's outcomes. Harne (2008) carried out a qualitative study on men who were involved in domestic violence perpetrator groups and found that they lacked an ability to prioritize their child's needs. Predominantly, these men saw children as a way of experiencing 'unconditional love': perhaps reflecting their own emotional needs not those of the children. What Harne highlighted was that these men spent considerable time with their children but this did not mean that they were any less violent or abusive. This finding confirms the view of domestic violence advocates, that men, even after separation, will use the children to harm the mother.

Young people who have witnessed violence also confirm this picture. They rarely respond with positive statements about the violent male carer whether this is their father or their stepfather. Mullender et al. argue that, in their sample, children were very critical of their fathers. For instance, one child said that violent fathers should 'go and die in a gutter' (2002: 188). However, other children in their sample preferred not to refer to the man at all but kept their comments to the violence and their feelings about it. This might suggest that children work hard to distinguish the *behaviour* from the *man*. McGee also carried out a qualitative study of children and found that they predominantly expressed anger at what the father figure had done. Again, however, she detected some ambivalence about the children's views of their father. She states that this 'conflict appeared to arise from the fact that they liked and loved their father but detested his violence' (McGee, 2000: 86).

This ambivalence has been found in a number of other studies. In a sample of 14 children, Peled (1998) found that the children sought to find positive things about their father even though they also held negative views about the violence. This research suggests that although children are indeed traumatized by experiencing fathers and male carers as violent they do not necessarily reject the father/male carer completely, and it appears as if most continue to value a relationship with that violent man *after the violence has ceased*, and if they are not also being directly abused by that man.

However, the experience of young people needs to be balanced by the overwhelming clinical literature which confirms the view that violent male carers lack the appropriate parenting capacity. Bancroft and Silverman (2002; 2004) explain that domestic violence abusers may pose risks to children both before and after separation. These authors provide a checklist which contains the patterns they have observed in their work with abusers. They talk about men who have rigid and authoritarian parenting styles, who are neglectful and irresponsible parents, who may expose children to assaults on mothers or new partners, who might teach children to abuse/criticize mothers and who provide a poor role model for the child. Eriksson and Hester (2001) comment that once a violent man has separated from his partner he can only continue to exert control over ex-partner through his children. Hence, child welfare practitioners should be wary of such men's stated wish to be good fathers.

However, not all researchers confer with this view. Guille, for instance, points out that 'men who batter . . . are a very heterogeneous group' (2004: 157) and that multiple factors affect their parenting abilities. Thus, blanket views about the parenting capacity for this group of male carers, is unwise. Perel and Peled (2008) certainly identified some of the traits described by other researchers with a sample of 14 men who were involved with domestic violence services in Israel. They confirmed that many of the fathers struggled to understand the emotional turmoil that their violence had caused their children. But, equally, they all had an inner model of a 'good father' and wanted quite desperately to reach this goal. The fathers recognized that they suffered constraints in achieving this goal: constraints caused by both internal and external processes (a similar view to Francis and Wolfe, 2008). Most importantly, Perel and Peled comment that the men yearned 'for a close and warm relationship with the children' (ibid.: 471). They conclude that 'fathering was perceived as being of the utmost importance, the men devoted considerable efforts to being a "good father" as they perceived it and they felt that they were indeed good fathers' (ibid.: 473). The authors therefore argue that any approach to violent male carers should see them 'as simultaneously harmful and vulnerable' (ibid.: 478) and that such approaches should avoid 'one-dimensional' descriptions.

What the violent men told Perel and Peled has been the experience of a number of practitioners who work with this population (Skyner and Waters, 1999). Violent men can frequently empathize with the experiences of their children (often because of their own experiences as children), and the wish to be better fathers can become a motivating factor in change (Rivett and Rees, 2004; Crooks et al., 2006). It is also clear, that violent men will continue to father and stepfather despite the evident deficits in their parenting capacity; therefore, in the interests of children, attempts must be made to work with them.

This is one of the reasons why children's charities in the United Kingdom have shown an interest in working with such men (Rivett and Rees, 2004; Skyner and Waters, 1999). If the previous sections have confirmed that violent male carers must be approached from multiple perspectives then it is important to distinguish between such men in terms of who can be worked with most effectively. This issue provides the substance of the next discussion.

The assessment of violent male carers

There are a multitude of ways in which child welfare practitioners will assess both the risk to children of male violence and the value of contact between a violent male carer and the child. Within these assessments primary focus is given to the safety of the child and frequently forensic/mental health assessments of the man will be sought. Within domestic violence interventions, however, these assessment tools have been slow to develop and their implementation has been even slower. Rivett and Kelly (2006) argue that the slow development of such tools could be understood as a response to the universal assumption that domestically violent men should not have contact with their children despite the ambiguous evidence cited above. Moreover, Rivett and Kelly contend, like many other commentators, that the child protection system has struggled to understand the pervasive, repetitious quality of domestic violence as opposed to the incident focused processes involved in child protection. Rivett (2006) also notes that there had been an historical animosity between domestic violence services and mental health services, which are most likely to be able to assess mental health and forensic risks. This animosity might have its roots in the view that mental health services seek 'explanatory factors' in men's abusive behaviour whereas domestic violence services emphasize responsibility for violent behaviour (Mankowski, Haaken and Silvergleid, 2002). This process echoes that described earlier in which one set of services looks exclusively at the man's role as a 'carer' whilst the other looks exclusively at his 'violent' identity.

Within child-focused practice there are a number of models for assessing the risk to the child of witnessing violence which complement the forensic assessment of the man. Most of these child-focused models are designed to orientate the practitioner to both what form of contact with the violent man is safe and what intervention is needed to help the child recover from what he or she has witnessed. Magen, Conroy and Tufo (2000), for instance, developed a tool for child welfare workers to assess the effects upon children of witnessing or experiencing violence. Bell and McGoren (2003), Calder (2004) and Radford, Blacklock and Iwi (2006) constructed risk assessment tools which seek to differentiate between 'thresholds' of risk and levels of intervention. Rivett and Kelly (2006) express concern that these models of assessment will be deemed as too complex for busy child welfare practitioners to implement. They recognize that at their core they seek to differentiate between children (and male carers) who require significant intervention and those who do not. In other words, they act as a filter to further resources. Unfortunately, since few resources exist either for violent men or child witnesses of violence, they are unlikely to provide clarity or standards for the future.

Bancroft and Silverman (2002; 2004) provide a thorough description of the processes needed to assess the risk that the violent man poses and, more crucially, describe what must be in place for the man to help the child recover from the experience of witnessing violence or from direct abuse. It is clear that child welfare practitioners must indeed take such assessments seriously and must retain scepticism about the fathering of violent male carers. Unfortunately, there are few services designed to work either with violent male carers or with children affected by such violence. In such circumstances, assessment may lead to little substantial intervention. Moreover, as Rivett and Kelly comment (2006), these assessment systems may rarely be implemented by child welfare practitioners who continue to assume that children should be kept away from violent male carers. The varieties of working with these men will now be addressed.

The hegemonic intervention for violent male carers: Duluth

It is not surprising to note that intervention programmes that work with male violence in intimate relationships grew out of *both* the therapeutic, anti-sexist men's movement *and* the women's refuge movement (La Violette, 2001). Historically, however, it is the latter that has emerged to set standards of treatment and safety (Pence and Paymar, 1993). Indeed, the predominant model of intervention with abusive and violent men is that of the Duluth programme (ibid.). This model is now supported by UK governmental guidance, it is the preferred model for voluntary domestic perpetrator programmes and it is the regulated programme for criminal justice settings (Rivett and Rees, 2008). There are a number of fundamental aspects to this model of work. First, intervention with violent men where the target of men's violence is their intimate partners and their children is not meant to be a 'stand alone' process. Rather, such treatment was conceived by the Duluth founders to be a part (and only a minor part) of a whole *coordinated community response* to intimate violence (Shepard and Pence, 1999). Such a response included changing the way all professionals, and, ideally, the community at large, responded to such violence.

Second, the model made some assumptions about *why* men were abusive in the home and why up to the present day, such violence had been socially *sanctioned*. Pence and Paymar express these assumptions in the following way: 'Men are culturally prepared for their role of master of the home even though they must often physically enforce the "right" to exercise this role. They are socialised to be dominant and women to be subordinate' (Pence and Paymar, 1993: 5). The Duluth programme therefore assumes that men are violent to women (and inferentially to children) because society is patriarchal and they have been socialized into believing they have entitlement over women (and children). The Duluth model assumes that these cognitions are socially constructed:

> At the core of the curriculum is the attempt to structure a process by which each man can examine his actions in the light of his concept of himself as a man. That examination demands a reflective process that distinguishes between what is in his nature and what is socially constructed. The things that are socially constructed can be changed. (ibid.: 15)

The third aspect of the Duluth model is that the form of intervention used in 'batterer education programmes' is one in which men's cognitions are challenged and they are taught new, more respectful behaviours. Thus the Duluth model can be termed 'pro-feminist, cognitive behavioural'.

A typical Duluth programme is 24 weeks long and has the format of an open 'modular' group: men can join at any time and continue for the 24 weeks until they have covered everything on the curriculum. This curriculum centres around two teaching tools: the Power and Control and Equality Wheels (Rivett and Rees, 2008). These wheels describe, on the one hand, abusive behaviours and, on the other, respectful, non-violent behaviours. Each wheel has eight sections and the 24-week programme addresses each section over the course of three weeks. Fundamental to each section is the cognitive framework that 'excuses' abusive behaviour. An example would be the section entitled 'Using Male Privilege'. Here abusive men are encouraged to reflect upon why they expect their partners to cook for them, do as they want and satisfy their needs. By the use of role plays, exercises and homework diaries, these underlying sexist assumptions are explored and challenged and then alternative beliefs and behaviours are promoted. In this way, it could be said that the whole of the Duluth intervention is one focused upon how violent men experience masculinity: gender constructs are continually being de-constructed.

From a child welfare perspective, the 'classic' Duluth programme has a number of deficits. Within the Power and Control Wheel there is a section dealing with 'Using Children'. The Wheel's description of this aspect of abuse reads: 'making her feel guilty about the children, using the children to relay messages, using visitation to harass her, threatening to take the children away' (Pence and Paymar 1993: 3). On the Equality Wheel, the opposite behaviour is itemized as: 'sharing parental responsibilities, being a positive non-violent role model for the children' (ibid.: 8). What is evident from these descriptions is that the focus of Duluth group work is on how men use the children against their partners rather than on developing a child-focused intervention.

Child focused intervention with violent male carers

Various responses have been made to this lack of a child-focus within Duluth. Duluth practitioners themselves established alternative interventions to address the 'harm done to children by domestic violence' (McMahon, Neville-Sorvilles and Schubert, 1999). Most Duluth programmes in the United Kingdom increased the amount of time devoted to children within their programmes, and some contracted various children's charities to provide a space in the work for the 'children's voice' (Skyner and Waters, 1999; Rees and Rivett, 2005). Others partially integrated 'fatherhood' issues into the standard Duluth model (Fall, Howard and Ford, 1999). Indeed these developments led to child-focused 'Abuse of Children' and 'Nurturing Children' wheels. However, a more radical departure from the programme is the 'Caring Dads' programme established in Ontario, Canada, and also currently in practice in parts of the United Kingdom. Scott and Crooks argue that 'the treatment needs of maltreating and at risk fathers are unique . . . based on the integration of parenting, child abuse, change promotion and batterer treatment' (2004: 95).

Accordingly, Scott and Crooks have designed a programme which combines a 'fatherhood agenda' and a perpetrator focus. This programme is called the 'Caring Dads' programme. It is 17 weeks long and has four goals. These are to develop trust and engage men in the process of examining their fathering; to increase men's awareness of child-centred parenting; to increase men's awareness of, and responsibility for, abusive and neglectful fathering, which includes the abuse of the children's mother; and to rebuild trust with their children. Although originally created in response to the needs of domestically violent fathers, the programme is increasingly being run through child welfare agencies and has become less 'perpetrator' focused than Duluth style programmes. Indeed, the programme has a very *both/and* philosophy: it relates to men as fathers and as abusers; it contains gender reflections and assumes men can change; and it applies to domestic violence perpetrators as well as men who have hurt only their children. A similar programme is one based in Norway. The Alternative to Violence (ATV) targets fathers who are violent but combines a fatherhood agenda and a perpetrator agenda. This programme has a therapeutic approach and has specific targets for work around the father and the child. Rakil states that the following must be addressed in treatment:

Man's perceptions of themselves as fathers;
How the violence is affecting the father–child relationship;

How the violence is affecting the mother–child relationship;
How the child is affected on both a short- and long-term basis;
The basic psychological needs of the child from a developmental perspective and how these are violated by the presence of violence. (Rakil, 2006: 199)

Since most child welfare agencies will be seeking to work with the violent male carer both to increase the safety of the child and to repair the relationship that the child has with that carer it is likely that these more child- and father-focused interventions will be more 'fit for purpose' for such agencies. Unfortunately, they share with the Duluth programmes a number of issues which may contribute to them failing to engage many violent male carers. Moreover, they may not suit all settings, especially those where the primary focus of intervention is not 'violence' per se.

Some limitations of Duluth

The Duluth programmes could be described as 'doctrinaire', which means they emphasize the philosophy outlined above and do not accept deviations from it. For instance, the leading organization for perpetrator programmes in the United Kingdom, Respect, states in its *Statement of Principles* that 'the use of violence is a choice for which each man is responsible and for which he should be held accountable'. Moreover, 'couples work, anger management, mediation and restorative justice are not appropriate responses to men's abusive behaviour to women' (2004: 16). In the same document, 'minimum standards' for such work are outlined: 'Behavioural change is a long term process ... the duration of the programmes ... should be at least 75 hours over a minimum of 30 weeks' (ibid.: 26).

A number of commentators have noted that such an approach disqualifies the experience of many violent male carers who do not feel powerful and whose use of violence does not fit this description. Neither does the model apply to gay men. (Gadd, 2004; Gelles, 2001). Nor does this model recognize the heterogeneity of violent male carers. Current research confirms that *not all violent men are the same*

(Dutton, 1995; Gondolf, 2002; Gilchrist et al., 2003; Jacobson and Gottman, 1998). There has also been controversy about *kinds* of violence. Johnson (1995) has argued that not all *violence* is the same. His view is that there are two predominant kinds of violence between intimate partners: common couple violence and patriarchal terrorism. He believes that most domestic violence services have equated these forms of violence rather than distinguishing between them. This has significance to the topic of this chapter because men who are violent within 'common couple violence' may need to be worked with differently from patriarchally violent men. Johnson's ideas have been hotly debated and disputed, although some research on couples has promoted the distinction he proposed (Simpson et al., 2007; Simpson et al., 2008). Mankowski, Haaken and Silvergleid (2002) also point out that there are 'unintended consequences' of the discourse predominant in the domestic violence world. One of these is to exclude the value of the insights from psychology and mental health services. Dutton and Corvo (2006) strongly argue for services to violent men to move beyond the 'gender analysis'. They maintain that Duluth-style programmes make the wrong assumption about the cause of male violence and about how to resolve it. They assert that most abusive men are primarily abusive because of the traumas they have experienced as children (Dutton, 2003), rather than being the witting agents of patriarchy. Moreover, they argue that rejecting a therapeutic understanding of these men leads to unskilful methods of engaging them in change. This view is increasingly common. Various practitioners have talked about Duluth interventions being built upon shaming and dominating perpetrators of abuse (Gadd, 2004; Milner, 2004). This criticism of Duluth also echoes the initial dichotomy described at the start of this chapter. Critics claim that Duluth programmes neglect the person of the violent male carer. This therefore leads to challenge and confrontational strategies which contribute to drop out and recidivism (Dutton and Corvo, 2006). One small piece of research may confirm this view. Garfield (2006) conducted a study of three perpetrator programmes with reference to the ability of the facilitators to build a strong therapeutic alliance (Friedlander, Escudero and Heatherington, 2006) with the men on the programme. She found some evidence that the better outcomes and lower drop-out rates were connected to the programmes that had a more therapeutic approach rather than the more standard Duluth programme.

What these controversies appear to suggest is that *one size will not fit all.* It may also suggest that certainty in the field of working with violent male carers is too easily found. Unfortunately, the doctrinaire assertions of the Duluth practitioners *disqualify* any other approach. Indeed, there is a tendency to label any alternative approach as dangerous and pandering to the male abuser's excuses. Yet there is a long tradition of alternative approaches, which have their roots in various therapeutic traditions (Dutton, 2003; Geffner and Mantooth, 2000; Jenkins, 1990; Lee, Sebold and Uken, 2003; Milner and Jessop, 2003; Milner and Singleton, 2008; Murphy and Eckhardt, 2005; Rivett and Rees, 2004; Saunders, 1996; Stith, Rosen and McCollum, 2003; Wexler, 2000). Moreover, the research evidence does not, as yet, prove that any one approach is more successful than any other (Babcock, Green and Robie, 2004; Gondolf, 2002). The other significant finding from research is that although such programmes are generally successful with men who complete, the drop-out rate is very high (Babcock, Green and Robie, 2004; Burton, Regan and Kelly, 1998; Dobash et al., 2000; Gondolf, 2002). The reasons for this high drop-out rate are clearly multiple. However, one factor might be that a long-term treatment programme is simply not suited to many men whose help-seeking behaviour may be constrained by a belief that they should not ask for help and should 'sort the problem out as soon as possible and get on with life' (Featherstone, Rivett and Scourfield, 2007).

Towards variety in work with violent male carers

In this chapter, I have highlighted the dichotomy involved in work with violent male carers: the dichotomy between focusing on the violence versus focusing on the qualities of caring. The above discussion demonstrates that most of the programmes designed to help men change their violence so they can be better fathers/stepfathers tend to concentrate upon the violence rather than the caring. The exceptions to this are the 'Caring Dads' and ATV programmes. However, these also retain some of the disadvantages of the Duluth programmes. They are long-term treatment programmes undertaken in specialist centres by specialist staff. Such programmes ignore the large number of men who may accept help for their violence in more local settings by more local child welfare/mental health service staff but would resist attending a more stigmatizing, group setting. Indeed, research by Westmarland, Hester and Reid (2004) confirms that men do ask for help for their behaviour at local levels: with GPs, Relate, Samaritans etc. Unfortunately, the construction of services for these men is hampered by many of the dichotomies outlined in this chapter. Critics of 'local' services for violent male carers view them as dangerous because they would not be staffed by sufficiently well-trained practitioners; they would fail to have a community context to plan for the safety of the woman and child; they would offer insufficient challenge to the men's behaviour; and they would emphasize the caring role to the detriment of the violent role. Much has been made of the 'mainstreaming' (Hester et al., 2007) of domestic violence services, but it seems that when it comes to working with violent male carers the mainstreaming has been halted by a road sign marked 'no entry'.

This impasse is not as great as it may seem. There are crucial lessons from the Duluth approach which can be integrated into a *both/and* more local intervention for violent male carers. These lessons would include:

- an assessment that takes into account the risks, causes and complications of the violence including the role of substance misuse and mental health issues;
- an agreement that the violence has got to stop and, on this basis, help as well as protective services will be put in place;
- a strong commitment to safety, which would include a community approach to assessment and child/victim support;
- the naming of violence as unacceptable whatever its causes and histories;
- an exploration of the consequences of violence for children, women and men;
- a focused, planned intervention on the violence, whether this be in groups or with individuals and probably lasting less time than the 24-week hegemonic model;
- concomitant intervention for substance misuse, mental health or emotional problems;
- respect for the man who wants to change;
- a holding to account of the man who does not want to change.

From the perspective of encouraging men to identify as fathers/carers would come the following lessons:

- a commitment to help men become better fathers/carers;
- an emphasis on parenting as well as partnering;
- a focus on the needs of children;
- a willingness to work with violent men however they present, in whatever context they present;
- a flexibility allowing for the use of the usual settings in which men present for help, for example, family centres, GP surgeries, health visitors' visits.

Conclusion

This chapter has explored the dilemmas and dichotomies involved in working with violent male carers/fathers. It has established that this is a contested practice and that there are many views about what should be done and by whom. At every step in the discussion there have been uncertainties and controversies. What we have argued is that these complexities point to the embracing of a *both/and* perspective which is informed by a careful understanding of the risks and opportunities available in work with violent men. Such men are often *both* violent *and* also fathers/stepfathers; they are often *both* abusive *and* keen to be better fathers/partners; they can be *both* dangerous *and* open to change; they are violent *both* because of the social construction of masculinity *and* because of individual psychological processes. As such, services for violent male carers must *both* adapt to a specialism engendered by practice with such men *and* be local to the services these men connect with. Practitioners working with violent male carers must *both* be able to engage the men in change *and* be critical of the risks of the work. These practitioners must inhabit *both* a safeguarding/child welfare world *and* a world where risks are shared between adult-focused services. Moreover, these practitioners must *both* be rigorous in their intervention *and* be able to adapt to work with the men in a time frame and context that will engage them.

Clearly, such a proposal for working with violent male carers will require a change in the targeted and doctrinaire models of intervention currently available. It will also require an investment in training and service provision. But, with the burgeoning of interest in working with men (Featherstone, Rivett and Scourfield, 2007) and with the mainstreaming of domestic violence services, such a union of the two fields seems like the next step in a truly coordinated community response to the violence experienced by children. Baby P probably died because little attention was given to engaging and working with the male carers in his life. Tragically, he is not alone. For all these children, work with violent male carers needs to become a more accepted part of child welfare practice, despite the difficulties practitioners and policy makers alike have in reconciling the dichotomies involved in this work.

References

Babcock, J., Green, C. and Robie, C. (2004) Does batterers' treatment work? A meta-analytic review of domestic violence treatment. *Clinical Psychology Review*, 23: 1023–53.

Bancroft, L. and Silverman, J. (2002) *The Batterer as Parent: Addressing the Impact of Domestic Violence on Family Dynamics.* Thousand Oaks, Sage.

Bancroft, L. and Silverman, J. (2004) Assessing abusers' risks to children. In P. Jaffe, L. Baker and A. Cunningham (2004) *Protecting Children from Domestic Violence.* New York: Guilford Press.

Bell, M. and McGoren, J. (2003) *Domestic Violence Risk Assessment Model.* Ulster, Northern Ireland, Barnardos.

Benjamin, J. (1988) *Bonds of Love.* New York, Pantheon.

Beynon, J. (2002) *Masculinities and Culture.* Buckingham, Open University Press.

Biddulph, S. (1995) *Manhood.* Lane Cove NSW, Finch Publishing.

Bly, R. (1991) *Iron John.* Shaftesbury, Element Books.

British Crime Survey (2003) *British Crime Survey Interpersonal Violence Module.* London, Home Office.

Buckley, H. (1998) Filtering out fathers: the gendered nature of social work in child protection. *Irish Social Worker*, 16 (3): 7–11.

Burgess, A. (1997) *Fatherhood Reclaimed.* London, Vermillion.

Burton, S., Regan, L. and Kelly, L. (1998) *Supporting Women and Challenging Men.* Bristol, Policy Press.

Calder, M. (2004) *Children Living with Domestic Violence: Towards a Framework for Assessment and Intervention.* Lyme Regis, Russell House Publishing.

Chodorow, N. (1978) *The Reproduction of Mothering.* Berkeley, CA, University of California Press.

Christie, A. (2006) Negotiating the uncomfortable intersections between gender and professional identities in social work. *Critical Social Policy*, 26: 390–411.

Collett, P. (2001) Working with men in family centres. In L. McMahon and A. Ward, (eds.), *Helping Families in Family Centres.* London: Jessica Kingsley Publishers.

Connell, R. (1995) *Masculinities.* Cambridge, Polity.

Crooks, C., Scott, K., Francis, K., Kelly, T. and Reid, M. (2006) Eliciting change in maltreating fathers: goals, processes and desired outcomes. *Cognitive and Behavioral Practice*, 13: 71–81.

Department of Constitutional Affairs (2004) *Consumer Strategy: Domestic Violence Phase 1 Report.* London, HMSO.

Dienhart, A. (1998) *Reshaping Fatherhood.* Thousand Oaks, Sage.

Dobash, R., Dobash, P. Cavanagh, K. and Lewis, R. (2000) *Changing Violent Men.* London, Sage.

Dutton, D. (1995) *The Batterer: A Psychological Profile.* New York, Basic Books.

Dutton, D. (2003) Treatment of assaultiveness. *Journal of Aggression, Maltreatment and Trauma*, 7: 7–28.

Dutton, D. and Corvo, K. (2006) Transforming a flawed policy: a call to revive psychology and science in domestic violence research and practice. *Aggression and Violent Behavour*, 11: 457–83.

Edleson, J. (1999) Children witnessing adult domestic violence. *Journal of Interpersonal Violence*, 14: 839–70.

Eriksson, M. and Hester, M. (2001) Violent men as good enough fathers? A look at England and Sweden. *Violence against Women*, 7: 779–98.

Fagan, J. and Hawkins, A. (2001) *Clinical and Educational Interventions with Fathers.* New York, Haworth Press.

Fall, K. Howard, S. and Ford, J. (1999) *Alternatives to Domestic Violence.* Philadelphia, Taylor and Francis.

Featherstone, B. (2004) *Family Life and Family Support.* London, Palgrave Macmillan.

Featherstone, B. and Peckover, S. (2007) Letting them get away with it: fathers, domestic violence and child welfare. *Critical Social Policy*, 27: 181–202.

Featherstone, B., Rivett, M. and Scourfield, J. (2007) *Working with Men in Health and Social Care.* London, Sage.

Ferguson, H. and Hogan, F. (2004) *Strengthening Families through Fathers.* Waterford, Centre for Social and Family Relations.

Fox, G. and Benson, M. (2004) Violent men, bad dads? Fathering profiles of men involved in intimate partner violence. In R. Day and M. Lamb (eds.), *Conceptualising and Measuring Father Involvement.* Mahwah, NJ, Lawrence Erlbaum Assoc.

Francis, K. and Wolfe, D. (2008) Cognitive and emotional differences between abusive and non-abusive fathers. *Child Abuse and Neglect*, 32: 1127–37.

Friedlander, M., Escudero, V. and Heatherington, L. (2006) *Therapeutic Alliance in Couple and Family Therapy.* Washington DC, American Psychological Association.

Frost, N., Lloyd, A. and Jeffery, L. (2003) *The RHP Companion to Family Support.* Lyme Regis, Russell House Publishing.

Gadd, D. (2004) Evidence led or policy led evidence? Cognitive behavioural programmes for men who are violent towards women. *Criminal Justice*, 4: 173–97.

Garfield, S. (2006) 'Minding the gap': the therapeutic alliance in domestic abuse intervention groups' PhD thesis, University College London.

Geffner, R., Spurling-Igelman, R. and Zellner, J. (eds.) (2003) *The Effects of Intimate Partner Violence on Children.* New York, Haworth Press.

Gelles, R. (2001) Standards for men who batter? Not yet. In R. Geffner and A. Rosenbaum. (eds.), *Domestic Violence Offenders: Current Interventions, Research, and Implications for Policies and Standards.* New York, Haworth Press.

Gilchrist, E., Johnson, R., Takriti, R., Weston, S., Beech, A. and Kebbell, M. (2003) *Domestic Violence Offenders: Characteristics and Offending Related Needs.* Home Office Findings 217. London, Home Office.

Gondolf, E. (2002) *Batterer Intervention Systems.* Thousand Oaks, Sage.

Guille L. (2004) Men who batter and their children: an integrated review. *Aggression and Violent Behaviour*, 9: 129–63.

Harne, L. (2008) Violent fathering and the risks to children. *Respect Newsletter* (October): 20–6.

Harold, G., Shelton, K., Goeke-Morey, M. and Cummings, E. (2002) Relations between interparental conflict, child emotional security and adjustment in the context of cognitive appraisals. In P. Davies, G. Harold, M. Goeke-Morey and E. Cummings. (eds.), *Child Emotional Security and Interparental Conflict. Monographs of the Society for Research in Child Development*, 67: 41–62.

Harway, M. and O'Neil, J. (1999) *What Causes Men's Violence to Women?* Thousand Oaks, Sage.

Hester, M., Pearson, C., Harwin, N. and Abrahams, H. (2007) *Making an Impact: Children and Domestic Violence.* London, Jessica Kingsley Publishers.

Hester, M., Westmarland, N., Gangoli, G. and Wilkinson, M. (2006) *Domestic Violence Perpetrators: Identifying Needs to Inform Early Intervention.* Newcastle, Northern Rock Foundation and Bristol University.

Holden, G. (1998) Introduction: the development of research into another consequence of domestic violence. In G. Holden, R. Geffner and E. Jouriles. (eds.), *Children Exposed to Marital Violence.* Washington, DC, American Psychological Association.

Hughes, H. and Luke, D. (1998) Heterogeneity in adjustment among children of battered women. In G. Holden, R. Geffner and E. Jouriles. (eds.), *Children Exposed to Marital Violence.* Washington, DC: American Psychological Association.

Humphreys, C. (2006) Relevant evidence for practice. In C. Humphreys and N. Stanley. (eds.), *Domestic Violence and Child Protection.* London: Jessica Kingsley Publishers.

Jacobson, N. and Gottman, J. (1998) *When Men Batter Women: New Insights into Ending Abusive Relationships.* New York, Simon and Schuster.

Jaffe, P., Baker, L. and Cunningham, A. (2004) *Protecting Children from Domestic Violence.* New York, Guilford Press.

Jaffe, P. and Geffner, R. (1998) Child custody and domestic violence: critical issues for mental health, social service and legal professionals. In G. Holden and A. Jenkins, *Invitations to Responsibility.* Adelaide, Dulwich Centre Publications.

Jenkins, A. and Holden G. (1990) *Invitations to Responsibility.* Adelaide: Dulwich Centre Publications.

Johnson, M. (1995) Patriarchal terrorism and common couple violence: two forms of violence against women. *Journal of Marriage and the Family*, 57: 283–94.

Jukes, A. (1994) *Why Men Hate Women.* London, Free Association Books.

Kaufman, M., Kantor, G. and Strauss, M. (1990) Responses of victims and the police to assaults on wives. In M. Strauss and R. Gelles (eds.), *Physical Violence in American Families.* New Brunswick, Transaction Books.

Kelly, T. and Wolfe, A. (2004) Advancing change with maltreating fathers. *Clinical Psychology: Science and Practice*, 11: 116–19.

La Violette, A. (2001) Batterers' treatment: observations from the trenches. In R. Geffner and A. Rosenbaum (eds.), *Domestic Violence Offenders: Current Interventions, Research, and Implications for Policies and Standards.* New York: Haworth Press.

Lamb, M. (ed.) (1997) *The Role of the Father in Child Development*, 3rd edn. Hoboken, NJ, Wiley & Sons.

Lamb, M. (2001) Male roles in families 'at risk': the ecology of child maltreatment. *Child Maltreatment*, 6: 310–13.

Lamb, M. (ed.) (2004) *The Role of the Father in Child Development*, 4th edn. Hoboken, NJ, Wiley & Sons.

Lee, M., Sebold, J. and Uken, A. (2003) *Solution Focused Treatment of Domestic Violence Offenders*. New York, Oxford University Press.

McGee, C. (2000) *Childhood Experiences of Domestic Violence*. London, Jessica Kingsley Publishers.

McLean, C., Carey, M. and White, C. (1996) *Men's Ways of Being*. Boulder, CO, Westview Press.

McMahon, M., Neville-Sorvilles, J. and Schubert, L. (1999) Undoing harm to children. In M. Shepard and E. Pence (1999) (eds.), *Co-ordinating Community Responses to Domestic Violence: Lessons from Duluth and Beyond*. Thousand Oaks, Sage.

Magen, R., Conroy, K. and Tufo, A. (2000) Domestic violence in child welfare preventative services: results from an intake screening questionnaire. *Children and Youth Services Review*, 22: 151–74.

Mankowski, E., Haaken, J. and Silvergleid, C. (2002) Collateral damage: an analysis of the achievements and unintended consequences of batterer intervention programs and discourse. *Journal of Family Violence*, 17: 167–84.

Marshall, D., English, D. and Stewart, A. (2001) The effects of father or father figures on child behavioral problems in families referred to child protective services. *Child Maltreatment*, 6: 290–9.

Meade, M. (1993) *Men and the Water of Life*. San Francisco, Harper.

Milner, J. (2004) From 'disappearing' to 'demonized': the effects on men and women of professional interventions based on challenging men who are violent. *Critical Social Policy*, 24: 79–101.

Milner, J. and Jessop, D. (2003) Domestic violence: narrative and solutions. *Probation Journal*, 50: 127–41.

Milner, J. and Singleton, T. (2008) Domestic violence: solution focused practice with men and women who are violent. *Journal of Family Therapy*, 30: 29–53.

Mullender, A., Hague, G., Imam, U., Kelly, L., Malos, E. and Regan, L. (2002) *Children's Perspectives on Domestic Violence*. London, Sage.

Mullender, A. and Morley, R. (1994) *Children Living with Domestic Violence*. London, Whiting and Birch Ltd.

Murphy, C. and Eckhardt, C. (2005) *Treating the Abusive Partner*. New York, Guilford Press.

Ofsted, Healthcare Commission, HM Inspectorate of Constabulary (2008) *Joint Area Review: Haringey Children's Services Authority Area.* London, HM Stationers.

O'Hagan, K. (1997) The problem of engaging men in child protection. *British Journal of Social Work,* 27: 25–42.

Pease, B. (2000) *Recreating Men.* London, Sage.

Peled, E. (1998) The experience of living with violence for preadolescent children of battered women. *Youth and Society,* 29: 396–430.

Pence, E. and Paymar, M. (1993) *Education Groups for Men who Batter.* New York, Springer.

Perel, G. and Peled, E. (2008) The fathering of violent men: constriction and yearning. *Violence against Women,* 14: 457–82.

Radford, L., Blacklock, N. and Iwi, K. (2006) Domestic abuse risk assessment and safety planning in child protection-assessing perpetrators. In C. Humphreys and N. Stanley (eds.), *Domestic Violence and Child Protection.* London, Jessica Kingsley Publishers.

Rakil, M. (2006) Are men who use violence against their partners and children good enough fathers? The need for an integrated child perspective in treatment work with men. In C. Humphreys and N. Stanley (eds.), *Domestic Violence and Child Protection.* London: Jessica Kingsley Publishers.

Rees, A. and Rivett, M. (2005) 'Let a hundred flowers bloom, let a hundred schools of thought contend': towards a variety in programmes for perpetrators of domestic violence. *Probation Journal,* 52: 277–88.

Respect (2004) *Statement of Principles and Minimum Standards of Practice for Domestic Violence Perpetrator Programmes and Associated Women's Services.* London, Respect.

Rivett, M. (2006) Treatment for perpetrators of domestic violence: controversy in policy and practice. *Criminal Behaviour and Mental Health,* 16: 205–10.

Rivett, M. and Kelly, S. (2006) 'From awareness to practice': children, domestic violence and child welfare. *Child Abuse Review,* 15: 224–42.

Rivett, M. and Rees, A. (2004) Dancing on a razor's edge. *Journal of Family Therapy,* 26: 142–62.

Rivett, M. and Rees, A. (2008) Working with perpetrators of domestic violence. In S. Green, E. Lancaster and S. Feasey (eds.), *Addressing Offending Behaviour.* Cullompton, Wilan Publishing.

Rossman, R., Hughes, H. and Rosenberg, M. (2000) *Children and Interparental Violence.* Philadelphia, Brunner/Mazel.

Saunders, D. (1996) Feminist-cognitive-behavioural and process-psychodynamic treatments for men who batter: interaction of abuser traits and treatment models. *Violence and Victims,* 11: 393–413.

Saunders, H. (2004) *Twenty Nine Child Homicides: Lessons Still To Be Learnt on Domestic Violence and Child Protection.* London, Women's Aid.

Scott, K. and Crooks, C (2004) Effecting change in maltreating fathers: critical principles for intervention planning. *Clinical Psychology: Science and Practice,* 11: 95–111.

Scourfield, J. (2003) *Gender and Child Protection.* London, Palgrave Macmillan.

Scourfield, J. (2006) The challenge of engaging fathers in the child protection process. *Critical Social Policy,* 26: 440–9.

Seidler, V. (1997) *Man Enough.* London, Sage.

Shepard, M. and Pence, E. (1999) *Co-ordinating Community Responses to Domestic Violence: Lessons from Duluth and Beyond.* Thousand Oaks, Sage.

Simpson, L., Atkins, D., Gattis, K. and Christensen, A. (2008) Low level relationship aggression and couple therapy outcomes. *Journal of Family Psychology,* 22: 102–11.

Simpson, L., Doss, B., Wheeler, J. and Christensen, A. (2007) Relationship violence among couples seeking therapy: common couple violence or battering? *Journal of Marital and Family Therapy,* 33: 270–83.

Skyner, D. and Waters, J. (1999) Working with perpetrators of domestic violence to protect women and children. *Child Abuse Review,* 8: 46–54.

Stith, S., Rosen, K. and McCollum, E. (2003) Effectiveness of couples treatment for spouse abuse. *Journal of Marital and Family Therapy,* 29: 407–26.

Stoltenberg, J. (1993) *The End of Manhood.* London, UCL Press.

Videon, T. (2005) Parent–child relations and children's psychological well-being: do dads matter? *Journal of Family Issues,* 26: 55–78.

Westmarland, N., Hester, M. and Reid, P. (2004) *Routine Enquiry about Domestic Violence in General Practices: A Pilot Project.* Bristol, School for Policy Studies, University of Bristol.

Wexler, D. (2000) *Domestic Violence 2000: An Integrated Skills Program for Men.* New York, Norton.

Whitehead, S. (2002) *Men and Masculinities.* Cambridge, Polity.

Williams, O., Boggess, J. and Carter, J. (2004) Fatherhood and domestic violence: exploring the role of abusive men in the lives of their children. In P. Jaffe, L. Baker and A. Cunningham (2004) *Protecting Children from Domestic Violence.* New York: Guilford Press.

9

The Family Group Conference in Child Welfare: A View from New Zealand

Margaret McKenzie

Introduction

At the same time as we recognize the increasing diversity and complexity of family form and life there has been a shift within child welfare practice towards family-focused practice. In particular, the Family Group Conference (FGC) approach is recognized as a significant step forward in the incorporation of family members and groups into child protection and welfare decision-making whilst at the same time reducing the power of professionals and state welfare systems. Whilst undoubtedly this approach has shifted the balance of power between state and family, and as such must be welcomed, the intricacies of gendered, generational and cultural power differentials within and amongst family members, within the FGC practice itself, and within state welfare systems, needs further exploration if the project

Gender and Child Welfare in Society Edited by Brid Featherstone, Carol-Ann Hooper, Jonathan Scourfield, and Julie Taylor.

of family inclusion in child protection is to be fully realized. This chapter will identify and explore a range of potential and practical issues that arise in the implementation of the FGC model where gendered power relations intersect with the potentiality of empowered family decision-making and responsibility.

There is little dispute that family is a gendered concept. It is a core site and microcosm of gender-power relations. Additionally there is little dispute that child protection is a gendered site of interaction between state and family (Parton, 1991; Scourfield, 2003; Featherstone, 2004). Despite this recognition of the complexities of gender-power relations between family and state and their intersection with the dynamics of the family itself, the intervention which is widely lauded as the most promising concept to move forward child welfare protection social work, the FGC, is located firmly within the family.

The FGC is a statutory process at the core of child welfare legislation in New Zealand. It explicitly incorporates family participation into the child protection decision-making process with the aim of increasing family autonomy and sustaining and strengthening family relationships for children in need of care and protection. Essentially, it brings together extended family members with professionals in a formal three-phase meeting: information-sharing, then private family deliberation time and a final phase where, together, plans made by family members are confirmed.

The FGC model grew out of a need to address a range of difficulties existing in the provision of child protection in New Zealand. These included the necessity to respond to challenges from indigenous Maori regarding the over representation of Maori children in out-of-home care and in the care of Pakeha strangers, as well as their concerns about drift in care, abuse within state-sanctioned care and mono-cultural, Eurocentric practice.[1] There were also Maori challenges to over-professionalism, too much social work interference in the family and increasing self doubt in social work itself as to the successful outcomes of its practices.

Whilst these concerns were specific to New Zealand, there were parallels across the 'Western' world, and the FGC has been widely adopted as a best practice model in child welfare. However, despite this interest in, and introduction of, the model in parts of the United Kingdom,

[1] Pakeha: white European.

Scandinavia, Canada and Australia, New Zealand remains the only country to make the practice mandatory. Central to this adoption is the recognition that the core concept of the FGC is empowerment; it is seen as a means of empowering the family, of readjusting the balance between family and state, between professional and state, between Western and indigenous concepts of decision-making and between care provision and protection. These indigenous concepts centre on including the responsibilities of the family and its wider extended net, and indeed those not part of family by blood or kin but because of emotional and psychological relational connection, in formulating decisions and planning for futures of children who come to notice in the child welfare system.

Paradoxically, though the FGC is widely promoted as an empowering process, at the same time we understand that the family is a place of unequal power and that this inequality is centred on differences of gender, of age and sometimes culture. Also, 'family' itself is a contested and arbitrary notion and there is an ever-increasing diversity of form and function which stands in opposition to a unified and uniform conceptualization of 'the family'. How do these complexities intersect in the provision of FGCs and what are the issues that are specifically gender-based?

This chapter is concerned with child protection practice within the broader field of child welfare. A largely feminist critique has identified twin aspects of the gendered nature of child protection. These are, firstly, its overemphasis on the dominant Western ideology of mothering and the consequent emphasis on the scrutiny of adequacies of mothering rather than parenting and, secondly, the fact that most child protection workers are themselves women, especially those in front-line case work roles, although they tend to come from very different social class backgrounds from those of the mothers they work with as 'clients' or 'service users' (Scourfield, 2003: 26). Scourfield's (2003) work on gender and child protection practices firmly locates child protection work within a continuum of gendered social control. Whilst others (Ferguson, 2003; Parton, 2006) dispute or take issue with the singularity of the social control argument and place emphasis on the emancipatory, reflexive life-planning and transformative agency potentials (Ferguson, 2003) also driving current child welfare policy, they nevertheless (Parton, 2006) acknowledge that tensions exist in the child welfare system and that a concurrent broadening of the net of concern in child welfare means control is still central to consideration of child protection at the site of everyday practice. Scourfield provides an excellent analysis of previous research and theorizing on child protection as a specific form of the social control arm of social work's disciplining of populations for the state via the family (Scourfield, 2003); he also highlights the centrality of gender relations to child protection work suggesting that these 'impact on every aspect of the job of child protection' (Scourfield, 2003: 168). He ends his book with a challenge: 'The complexity of social work role and the complexity of gender relations suggest the need for a sophisticated conceptual framework for understanding men and women as clients in child protection', and he cogently states that 'neither a liberal theory of anti-discrimination as equal treatment, nor anti-oppressive theory based on a monolithic notion of men's oppression of woman can capture the subtleties of gender identities and power at the micro level' (ibid.: 182).

It is at this level of micro-practice that I want to focus my discussion. The family group conference is a micro-level decision-making practice intervention for child protection, specifically designed, through its embeddedness in empowerment practices, to address power imbalances. How well does it succeed, especially in the subtleties and complexities of gender relations between and within families and between families and the social work professionals involved in their lives? And how sophisticated a conceptual framework is the FGC?

I will argue in this chapter that whilst FGCs are widely recognized as an innovative policy and practice concept, this should not be seen as an end point in the development of child protection and that after an extensive period (some 18 years) of practice with the FGC process in New Zealand a set of critical issues has emerged that need addressing to move the intervention forward. These are located within the central concern of the child welfare/child protection discourse, namely balancing power and control between state and family, and within families. Gender, generation and cultural considerations are central to these issues.

Firstly, what is the FGC? How and why did it originate? Whilst the development of FGC has been well documented I nevertheless provide a summary here. I do this to highlight the unique mix of circumstances in Aotearoa New Zealand that have lead to the construction of the legislation, of which the FGC is the cornerstone. Whilst aspects or threads of the development can be found in other sites and situations, the initial establishment of FGCs as an invention is unique and specific in response to contextual issues of time, place and history in Aotearoa New Zealand in the 1980s. This brief documenting of some key aspects sets the scene to ask the question where does gender fit in this?

The origins of the FGC in New Zealand

Family group conferences became widely known as a result of their appearance in New Zealand law with the Children, Young Persons and their Families Act 1989. International interest has been strong then and since in FGCs and the New Zealand experience of child protection and child welfare practice. At the time of its inception, the Children, Young Persons and their Families Act 1989 (CYP&F Act), with its inclusion of the FGC process, was seen as a radical shift and paradigmatic advance in the provision of child welfare policy and child protection practice, advancing family decision-making and participatory practice to the foreground as a mechanism of formal incorporation of family members into child welfare/protection decision-making.

Improving child welfare services has long been an unquestioned aim in many countries. But what has been questioned continuously is the form and extent these services should take, with debate focused around the balance between government, community and family obligation as a matter for negotiation and reassessment. Ongoing discussion about reform of New Zealand's child welfare services eventually culminated in 'legislation which captured a fundamental rethinking of the entire framework of child welfare, in enabling families to take the central role in making decisions about children's welfare and in emphasising the importance of cultural heritage and cultural practice, [and] has brought New Zealand to the forefront internationally' (Dalley, 1998: 9).

FGCs are recognized in many countries as being synonymous with innovative, participatory child protection practice and policy, and many countries have adopted forms of this practice into their own local processes. These include Australia, the United Kingdom, the United States and the Scandinavian countries. Whilst none of these jurisdictions has taken the fully mandated legislative approach of New Zealand, underpinning each and all of these adaptations are the key drivers of rebalancing the power differentials between family and state, and incorporating family members into decision-making. The FGC has become synonymous with notions of partnership practice, empowerment and family-centred practice.

Hassall, writing on the origins of the New Zealand legislation, identifies four core contributory philosophical strands which shaped the emergence of the New Zealand legislation and are also common to the international discourse: family responsibility, children's rights, cultural acknowledgement and partnership between the state and community. Importantly, he links these to the larger socio-political context or, as he expresses it, 'eddies in the larger socio-political currents of civilisation', namely consumerism, the market economy, minimal state intervention, the decline of organized religion, the rise of interest groups and their empowerment through rights (Hassall, 1996: 19).

Barbour, an early commentator on the development of FGCs, wrote that their advent in New Zealand was probably inevitable given the climate of the times. They were 'a predictable, if not virtually inescapable outcome of a set of converging effects of history, political struggle and developments in social work practice' (1991: 16). This view reinforces the notion of timeliness but also inevitability.

Complexity arises when we begin to unravel and describe these strands or pathways and recognize that whilst links and parallels to the wider international discourse of child welfare can be made, the eventual conceptualization of the Act and the FGC process within it as a new form of child welfare process focused on empowerment was primarily the result of a unique interplay of a range of influences and factors which were distinctive to New Zealand at that time (Connolly and McKenzie, 1999). Further complexity arises when, in the untangling of the influencing factors, some inherent paradoxes become apparent, including the lack of a philosophical consistency in the underpinning influences, and the fact that despite the widely accepted view that the influence of Maori cultural imperatives was a dominant force other factors were also significant.

Key to an understanding of how the legislation developed with the FGC as its keystone is therefore an understanding of the New Zealand context and the influencing factors. Whilst the legislation was passed in late 1989 and can be seen as a central force in child welfare and protection practice worldwide from the 1990s onwards, it is little recognized beyond New Zealand that there was a long period of gestation and vigorous debate on proposals and counterproposals preceding this. These debates were complicated by a succession of government changes, with fundamental philosophical shifts occurring at the levels of government and child welfare theory, philosophy and practice.

Extensive and public debate had occurred and the FGC did not arise simply because of the ascendancy of one view over others, as might be assumed from the frequent commentaries which foreground the cultural imperatives argument as central to the creation of the FGC process. The development was in fact much more complex and occurred progressively through concerted professional and public debate and consultation over an approximately 13-year period (1976–89). Recommendations in a series of successive reports and draft legislations that can be tracked through this period point not only to the challenge by indigenous Maori to modify mono-cultural social work practice but also to a refining of a view of the family as central to children and young persons' well-being, both in the role of decision-maker and also through a focus on maintenance of kinship links and care as imperative for successful outcomes for children and young people at risk. Hassall (1996: 26) simply but effectively sums up this culminating positioning or argument as one that was 'more likely to be effective, was more just and was simply right'.

This view was certainly underpinned and reinforced by the centrality of Maori conceptualization of kinship-based family obligations and responsibilities as core to promoting decision-making by family members rather than professional social workers. This centrality is well acknowledged in much of the writing on FGCs, often seen as the origin of the intervention, but over time it has been possible to acknowledge other interconnected and interwoven strands. These include the developing critical analysis of traditional social casework practices (and especially their Eurocentric and monocultural theories); the increasing voice of Maori activism, finding its expression in the publication of a seminal report on the situation of Maori,

Puao- te- Ata -tu (Ministerial Advisory Committee, 1986); some, perhaps serendipitous, changes of government and ministers; and an underpinning commitment by government to an increased responsiveness to the necessity of Treaty-based principles of a bicultural partnership as central to social services delivery.[2]

The FGC and its creation can best be understood as socially constructed, as a product unique and specific in response to contextual issues of time, place and history in Aotearoa New Zealand in the 1980s. Whilst aspects or threads of the development can be found in other sites and situations, the origin of the FGC remains unique to the mix of circumstances in Aotearoa New Zealand. The significant value shift that took place in child welfare thinking connects to the circumstances of New Zealand context. Questions as to whether and how FGCs work and of portability to other sites, countries and other contexts are then questions which must be considered within this understanding of origins and rationales of development. These are issues I will return to in the next section of the chapter on gender and culture in FGC.

Gender or culture?

The particular mix of forces I have highlighted is notable for the apparent absence of any influence of feminist contribution; especially so as feminist critique was an otherwise dominant force in social work development during this period (Munford and Nash, 1994; Featherstone, 2004). Feminism was especially influential in arguing the extent of the gendered nature of social work but also, more generally, in identifying discriminatory and oppressive practices of social work. It seems that in New Zealand radical critiques of social work were so strongly focused on the extent to which colonization and its associated racism impacted on the practice of child welfare social work that a specific critique (as developed overseas) on the gendered nature of policy and practice in child welfare has not made an impact to the same extent. Feminist activists in New Zealand social work

[2]The Treaty of Waitangi, 1840.

were substantially involved in the critique of the monocultural practices of the state child welfare agency (Dalley, 1998). The Women's Anti Racist Action Group was formed (WARAG, 1984; Dalley, 1998), which spearheaded the investigations into institutional racism that lead directly to the establishment of the review committees from which *Puoa-te-Atatu* emerged and culminated in the CYP& F Act with the FGC as its cornerstone. Thus feminists' critique, whilst anti-discriminatory, was primarily focused on deconstructing the overly monocultural and racist practices of the state child welfare system. Gender issues as such, apart from the obvious focus of concern for vulnerable children, seem to have been sidelined and silenced by this greater problem.

This may account for what seems to have been the surprisingly non-problematized uptake of the notion of family enshrined in the FGC. Undoubtedly the move to foreground indigenous Maori understandings of family, whanau, incorporating extended kin and non-biological but psychologically significant relationships, widened the definitional scope of who was eligible for inclusion in decision-making. But this does not seem to have allowed or provided for due consideration of the not inconsiderable shortcomings of the family as a site of empowerment. How much were the complexity of power dynamics in families and the vulnerability of women and children in situations where there were child welfare concerns subordinated for the greater good of community and family empowerment? The notion of family as undifferentiated and uncomplicated was definitively challenged by indigenous voices. The formally intact barrier between the public and private world was broken down by kin, extended family and those with psychological connection being brought into decision-making roles in the FGC process. However, this became a rather blanket re-categorization of family.

It appears that the redressing of the power imbalances for Maori through the inclusion of traditional forms of decision-making processes became the dominant discourse in revisiting child welfare practices and took precedence over consideration of otherwise extensive concern about the influence of existing gender-power relations in child protection, the complexity of gender dynamics and known vulnerabilities within both indigenous and non-European groups. The shift to family decision making may have carried with it a subordination/subsuming of the feminist critique of the very real potential danger to women and children that the family posed, indeed to the very women and children who were caught up in child protection situations in situations of violence and abuse. It was not that these views had not been aired, as the critique of a child protection focus on mothering carried out by a workforce of middle-class women social workers was well established (Munford and Nash, 1994) but in New Zealand these concerns were simply not seen as the most urgent. Indigenous challenge lined up with official policies privileging biculturalism through partnership. Also, the ideology of empowerment was underpinned by the neo-liberal state's intention to devolve responsibility and, ultimately, fiscal responsibility. The result was that ethnicity in child protection matters overshadowed gender as the dominant issue for attention in child welfare. This can be conceptualized as a situation where macro- and meso-level drivers have been the key to what became fully realized at the micro-practice level as the FGC.

Writing on the impact of similar forces on another iconic New Zealand social service provision, Child Health Camps, historian Margaret Tennant notes that whilst in the mid-1980s feminist concerns had recommended differential responses to boys' and girls' health needs in the same way that special health needs for women had been recognized,

> gender was quickly subordinated to the growing focus on Treaty of Waitangi issues and relationships of Maori to social services. Official policies of biculturalism and the need for accountability with regard to treaty principles saw Maori children become visible . . . as never before. (Tennant 2002: 196)

Researching FGCs – the evidence base in New Zealand

Despite the wide acceptance of and knowledge about The FGC model and its considerable influence internationally it has been difficult to fully evaluate the model in New Zealand. Even with a retrospective gaze of 18 years there remains a dearth of large-scale evaluative research in the child protection area, although the positive impact and value for using family-inclusive practices in the Youth Justice arena has been demonstrated in a number of studies (Maxwell and Morris, 1993).[3]

Whilst the absence of longitudinal outcome data is of concern, some small-scale qualitative evaluation studies have been carried out. These have been focused on hearing the views of participants and have investigated immediate and medium-term effectiveness. Research by the author identified what were labelled critical issues in applying and practicing FGC (McKenzie, 1996; Connolly and McKenzie, 1999), and other early researchers and commentators also raised similar specific concerns: Worral (1996) questioned the taken-for-granted nature of kinship or family care; Tauri (1999) and Love (2000), the incorporation of indigenous culture to meet policy rather than people needs. More generally, each of these authors raised concerns about how the conflicting discourse and inherent contradictions that underpinned the advent of the FGC as a child welfare process impacted upon and constrained everyday practice.

A more recent project has surveyed the views of all care and protection FGC coordinators in New Zealand (McKenzie and Walton, 2005) and Connolly (2006) followed up a small group of long-term Child Protection Coordinators, but no population-based outcome research or long-term effectiveness studies of recipients of the child protection process have been undertaken. This is despite the mandated nature of the process and the contained population size of New Zealand, which would seem to make this potentially feasible and achievable. It may be that the very strength of the favourable international discourse surrounding the empowerment potential of FGC has made the evaluation, and thus potential uncovering of issues, more problematic. It is difficult to broach critique of a model for which our country has received international acclaim and admiration and an iconic status in child welfare circles (Worrall and McKenzie, 2003). As noted earlier, whilst there was widespread debate over a protracted period before the implementation of the Act, much of this remains little known beyond New Zealand (McKenzie, 1996), and since then there has been muted critical comment. Lupton and

[3]In New Zealand, Child Protection and Youth Justice are separate jurisdictions under the one piece of legislation (CYP& F Act 1989), and the FGC functions in a somewhat different manner in each, specifically the incorporation of the victim in the conference with a restorative justice vision in Youth Justice matters.

Nixon (1999) identify a tendency to self-promotion literature underpinning much of the writing on FGC, and whilst this has especially been so in New Zealand it has also occurred overseas. Worrall and McKenzie (2003) suggest that the substantial reputation that has been invested in the process by the government may further contribute to an unwillingness to engage in independent effectiveness research. Certainly any attempts which have proposed such research for the child protection FGC process (Maxwell et al., 1995) have been unable to achieve the required governmental access approval or funding. This problem has exacerbated the tentative nature of both the evidence for and critique against the FGC. Many of those studies available are small-scale and localized, whether in New Zealand or overseas, and can invoke the qualitative/quantitative, credibility/reliability debate. Additionally, and connected to the earlier comment about the largely favourable but perhaps self-promoting literature available, is the question of how difficult it may be for social work itself to critique what has become an iconic practice embedded in the concepts of anti-discrimination and empowerment.

Empowerment and the FGC

It can be argued that by making empowerment explicit as a concept in child welfare and child protection its centrality, or the centrality of power (in social work), is acknowledged. I argue, on the contrary, that the constant foregrounding/use of the term 'empowerment', the very language of empowerment, has instead obscured the existence of ongoing power relations in child protection practice. As indicated earlier, empowerment is the subject of much debate and it is generally accepted (Lupton and Nixon, 1999) that empowerment is at best a slippery and vague notion, at worst an expediency. I do not intend to discuss all the potential definitions and understandings of empowerment as this would take the entire chapter, but rather to work from a starting point that, whilst it is a contested notion, it remains in everyday usage as a concept which should/must inform social work and child protection practice and, importantly, is central to the FGC process. Essentially the term 'empowerment' as used in child protection work implies a handing over of power – from state to community, from social worker to family members. Yet being the one to do the handing over and control who is to be given the power, thus also defining the powerless, is in itself a power relation. The discourse of child protection positions the family in focus as powerless and the social work agency and staff as powerful. The FGC process is said to turn this around. It is said to have transformed child protection practice by empowering family members (Connolly and McKenzie 1999). Ironically, the very language of empowerment can obscure the existence of ongoing power relations, potentially disabling the transformative intent of FGC practice.

If child protection is a gendered practice, how and where does this intersect with the empowering intent of the FGC? Does empowering the family override the intricacies of gendered power relations within families?

Experiences and challenges of FGC in New Zealand

Whilst there can be no doubt that family participatory practice via the FGC is a valuable intervention strategy for child protection, the previous sections have highlighted some underpinning philosophical complexities and macro- and meso-level concerns which remain as dilemmas in New Zealand. This next section of the chapter is concerned with difficulties at the practice implementation level, the micro-level practice. In previous work (McKenzie, 1996; Connolly and McKenzie, 1999) I have argued that a set of critical practice issues needed resolution to ensure that the full intent of FGCs was met. After a further period, and 18 years overall of FGC implementation in New Zealand, I suggest we now need to understand these beyond the level of ongoing practice concerns and conceive of them more fully as sites where empowerment may be obscured. For the purposes of this chapter I will discuss selected sites at the micro-practice level of critical relevance for gender relations and highlight where gender is centrally implicated and intersects with the dilemma under discussion.

What's in a name?

A realistic and critical understanding of family is central to the FGC process. There is considerable debate as to the existence of family networks, with discussion in the literature ranging from suggestions that the extended family is alive and well and still has a prominent role to play to the other extreme, that modern family life with its inherent pressures has pushed family life more and more into increasingly private compartments (Marsh and Crow, 1997; Featherstone, 2004).

This enshrining of the family in legislation is all the more remarkable when we consider the structure of the society in which we live. There is no doubt that our traditional notions of family structure are no longer relevant. Traditional notions have included not just the idea of the two-parent nuclear family, but also that of the available supportive, involved network (or extended family) and the at-home child-raising mother located in a supportive community. Yet we know our New Zealand reality is far from this, and that this is paralleled in most Western countries. (For New Zealand, one-parent families now make up more than 26 per cent of all families and more than 33 per cent of all children will spend time living in more than one family structure before the age of sixteen). This dissonance indicates a need for caution in applying the notion of family as a natural and universal feature of society, given the known diversity of family arrangements and the ways in which personal lives and situations are currently structured. Rather than any ideal perception, family reality is often a proliferation of isolated and isolating arrangements with multiple and frequent re-constitutions (Connolly and McKenzie, 1999), and this may be especially so for those who come to the notice of the child welfare system.

Family relationships and family networks – available? willing?

Whilst a recognized strength of the FGC is flexibility towards inclusive, culturally sensitive definitions of family, FGCs depend on the availability and willingness of family and family networks, both for involvement at the central family decision-making moment and in an ongoing role for practical and psychological support. The process of family decision-making assumes not only the existence of kin networks but that the members are available and willing to become involved around significant difficulties a family member is experiencing, both to be participants in decision-making and then to support implementation of family-based plans.

McKenzie's 1996 study identified the limited nature of the actual family network available for participation in and/or willingness to engage in conferences. Families in this study did not feel they had wide networks, whether kinship or 'friend' networks to call upon. Extensive family networks were not present, and professionals outnumbered family members in each conference reviewed. Given the indicative sparseness of these family networks and our knowledge of fracturing family structures, can we support the underlying assumption of the FGC process that networks, whether kin or psychologically significant others are readily available to assist in decision-making and follow-up support? (McKenzie, 1996). Or is this a continuation of the mythologizing, romanticizing ideology of Family?

In addition to the problem of availability there is the need to access and engage appropriate support systems within a potential network or system. We know that the families who come to notice in child welfare are frequently not those with an intact and supportive network. This is not to dismiss them as 'deficient' or 'dysfunctional' but to recognize that they are less likely to be situated in a context that is resource-rich, whether materially, practically or emotionally. In particular, single parents (single mothers especially) and their children are a significant group in child protection investigations and proceedings. It is imperative that this is not assumed to be a deficit situation, to recognize that these groupings may have been established by choice and with very good reason.

Early studies on FGC in New Zealand (McKenzie, 1996) indicated that for many women alienation from their families had occurred for good reason and they did not view their kin networks as sources of automatic support and care. There were generational (her)stories of violence, neglect and abuse which had led to choices for these women to effect separation and distance from their kin family. Alternatively, women described their family networks as rejecting, uninvolved and distancing them. This stance originated in a number of issues including their lifestyles not being accepted and shame at their involvement in statutory care proceeding. These contradictory conditions point to the need to be cautious of automatically assuming that kin are imbued with altruistic motives and should be mobilized in the interest of reunification for providing superior support and care.

We recognize that single parenthood can be about escaping from dangerous, abusive and violent situations, especially for both women and children. Yet we have legislation that clearly indicates a return of decision-making to the whole family. Does this in fact undermine the positive gains to independence and equality women have made both in daily life and family law? Does it signify a return to former patriarchal arrangements with little status or authority for sole women to make decisions? This, together with the obvious implications for women to take up additional caregiving responsibilities whenever the state devolves caring responsibilities back to family members, are serious issues which have major impact on the lives of (women) clients (see Worrall's 1996 study of kinship care and later studies on grandparents raising grandchildren: Worrall, 2001; Frengley, 2008). There is a danger then that the FGC process can end up using vulnerable women as a dumping ground for child welfare problems – especially those in the complex and dangerous arena – so that a further feminization of care is put in place.

Whilst many Maori whanau have considerable and active family networks, this too can be just as romanticized – for many of the Maori families we work with in child welfare, isolation from descent-based whanau family networks is widespread as a result of geographical, historical, economic and emotional separations (Shannon and Walker, 1996). Maori kin groups can also be as fractured, with some members alienated by choice, and this necessarily limits engagement in decision-making and the provision of resources of support and care.

Gender relations and family power dynamics

It is imperative that the gender-biased possibilities of the FGC be considered so that the process itself does not further disempower women. As previously stated, it is widely acknowledged that child protection is a gendered business: women predominate whether as the givers or receivers or brokers of child protection. This is connected to notions of who provides attachment requirements and of 'good enough' parenting and family life; notions which have strong links to the patriarchy – the idea that bad parenting is about bad mothers. Women appear to retain the ultimate responsibility for protection and are also the first port of call in intervention strategies. It should be no surprise, therefore, to find a predominance of women attending FGCs in New Zealand (though more especially in Pakeha families). Prevailing factors in New Zealand child protection notifications are fractured 'families' and single-parent household arrangements, with sole caregiver women-headed households. Men, and especially fathers, are largely invisible; mothering remains under scrutiny.

Father/male absence is often connected to the problems of complex and dangerous situations rather than a withdrawal of responsibility by fathers. They may well be excluded because of the nature of the underlying family issues, such as violence and abuse – the very issues that lead to the need for a FGC to be called. Unequal power relations are part and parcel of family life, power issues exist within family systems and ultimately these are connected to the types of concerns that come to the notice of child protection work; neglect, abuse and violence, both physical and sexual, are the core business of child protection work. These issues are inextricably linked with power dynamics in family systems.

Violence and power over vulnerable family members go hand in hand. Power sharing and equality can be hard to achieve in stressful conflictual situations such as these, and there is a real danger that the bringing together of all parties can silence the less powerful, most often the women and children. In relation to child sexual abuse there is increased likelihood that these cases will predominately involve male perpetrators and female child victims. An absence of open disagreement and dissent or alternative views can be construed as consensus rather than a product of ongoing gender power relations and or generational dynamics, potentially including both coercion and threat but also loyalty and duty aspects. Family presence should not be construed as providing protection or a sufficient safety net for equality of voice or opinion.

The operation of such power dynamics is further complicated by considerations of cultural custom where the notion of equality between gender and between generations is not automatic. Who is able and enabled to speak? Who can have an opinion and make decisions in the family decision-making process? A recognized hierarchy of valued opinions is in operation between generations in Western culture. How does this operate for non-Westernized cultures, and how much is a hierarchy also present between genders? What happens in mixed-culture families?

The role of FGC coordinators in the FGC process: a gendered profession

In New Zealand, FGC coordinators are recruited from the social work workforce, usually the statutory government child welfare agency who also employs the coordinators. They are therefore not independent practitioners, as is the case in some countries. As a group at large they replicate many aspects of what we consider to be the gendered nature of social work. Walton and McKenzie found in their 2005 study that child protection coordinators are predominately female (78 per cent), social work trained and /or from a social work background (87 per cent), and aged 40 or over (95 per cent). This profile seems to mesh with the feminist critique that child protection service provision is gendered and class-based. The professional background of the coordinators might help to explain the most widely acknowledged problem of family group conferences: namely, the difficulties that occur when coordinators and social workers struggle to relinquish power, and the locus of control moves to the professional regulatory end of the decision-making spectrum. Examples of this occur when there is difficulty in ensuring that the mandatory private time phase of the FGC is maintained and when decisions are made prior to conferencing and merely rubber-stamped in the meeting.

Whilst a significant proportion of coordinators are of Maori or Pacific Island descent (30 per cent and 8 per cent respectively according to Walton, McKenzie and Connolly 2005), their presence is as culturally specific practitioners and has the potential to exacerbate power differences, as traditionally such advising roles carry particular meaning and are often held by those who have authoritative positions in the culture already. This possession of traditional authority can be inhibitive and can increase power differences in situations where the provision of Maori or Pacific staff has not been made with such intention.

Cultural relations /cultural imperatives

It is widely acknowledged that the Maori kin descent-based whanau model and processes of cooperative decision-making were major influences in the development of the concept of the FGC in New Zealand (Cockburn, 1994; Metge, 1995). This incorporation of a decision-making process based on that of the indigenous (Maori) people arose from increasingly strong criticism from Maori that the child protection systems in place had failed them and that culturally sensitive appropriate ways of dealing with Maori children needed to be found. Maori were significantly overrepresented in care statistics, and in particular children in stranger care, that is, care outside their descent line and kinship structure.

Whilst these issues were undeniably crucial to address by changing existing child protection processes, according to McKenzie (1996) two key considerations arise from this with regard to obscuring power relations and empowerment. These are focused at both the local New Zealand and international level.

First are the local questions of the appropriateness of the replacement or substitution of one cultural practice with another. Who benefits? Who loses? And second, at the international level there is the issue of transferability to other cultural contexts. What relevance has a specific practice created for a specific set of cultural relations (settler society with marginalized indigenous culture) to other, and particularly non-settler, societies? Shifting to the blanket use of an indigenous-grounded decision model runs the risk of simple cultural reversal. Formerly we expected Maori (indigenous) whanau to conform to a settler or white Western practice, now we expect pakeha (white European) families to conform to an indigenous model. Have we simply replaced one cultural practice with another? Have we now created practice which is culturally resonant with Maori families but alien to non-Maori? McKenzie's (1996) interviewee families were predominately Pakeha and did not readily avail themselves of kinship support. We need to ask the following questions: first, is the FGC in fact more suited to Maori conceptions of family and kin obligations? And, second, in affirming the values of Maori/indigenous people and enabling these values to be reflected in the decision-making process have we fallen into the same trap we were trying to escape?

At issue here is not just meeting ethnicity and race requirements but also asking the question 'does incorporating an image of Maori whanau into a Pakeha-based system work or is it cultural capture?' Is this a sophisticated assimilation practice? Or have we replaced one cultural practice with another in order to fit a state-driven intention (biculturalism) as much as to achieve an appropriate child welfare practice? Tauri (1999) has named the process that occurred in the incorporation of Maori models such as the FGC into government legislation and policy as a biculturalization of the state rather than an empowerment of Maori. This raises the need to address and understand the diversity of whanau and household structures that Maori also inhabit. To what extent is the FGC process using a historical version of Maori whanau and using assumptive mechanisms based on a one-size-fits-all whanau model, rather than one individually responsive to specific whanau arrangements? This, of course, is paralleled in practices with non-Maori families if individual family arrangements are not accounted for in FGC processes.

The continuing authority of those defined as the expert – social workers, lawyers, teachers, paediatricians, psychologists and psychiatrists – rather than by those with authority in the Maori world, such as Kaumata and Kuia, is also of concern. These concerns reflect power relations: co-option, tokenism and cultural capture are beginning to be raised as problematic aspects of incorporating Maori processes into a practice which is designed for use across cultural groups. However, there are two sides to this, as Pakura, former Chief Social Worker, points out:

> Maori support for the philosophy and principles underpinning family group conferences remains high . . . The Act is a major piece of social legislation, and as it embodies so much of what Maori value and believe about children and families it is dear to them and they embrace it . . . Most children and their families have only one FGC, and their issues are dealt with outside of courts and formal processes, in respectful and private ways. For Maori, faith and optimism in the family group conference process remain. (2004: 120–1)

Humpage, writing recently on how New Zealand social policy appears to operate to include the excluded, acknowledges that the existing literature on concepts of social exclusion and inclusion (which comes largely from Europe and Britain) is fundamentally limited when accounting for 'difference'. She argues that there is a pressing 'need for settler societies to develop policy that reflects their own socio-political circumstances, rather then simply adopt policy discourses that are popular internationally' (Humpage, 2006: 220).

I suggest reframing this. The idea of non-settler societies taking up a concept such as the FGC, which was developed out of a specific indigenous initiative within a settler society context, may be just as tension-laden. The development of the FGC in New Zealand reflects the 'specific relations that exist in countries containing an internally colonised indigenous population' (ibid.: 222). This highlights the risk of applying a policy discourse that developed out of the specific context of New Zealand to other countries which are vastly different, and especially to those that do not have an indigenous population. Humpage (ibid.) contends that New Zealand, like other settler societies, should 'devise its own dance, with steps and a rhythm that best suits its own social-political circumstances'. The development of the FGC fits this notion, but by implication this may not suit and be suitable for conditions in other countries. Additionally, this resonates with my suggestion that the gender agenda in child protection was subsumed to the more important problem for this settler society, one of creating a culturally embedded and ethnically relevant practice.

Conclusion

It has long been recognized and understood that child protection work is difficult and that power issues are central. Successful practice has always relied upon the ability of all involved to negotiate complex, conflicting dynamic processes. We cannot assume that the creation of empowerment practices, such as the FGC, will in itself make this task easier or provide solutions. Moreover, the complexity of ensuring the core qualities of the empowerment process has been highlighted. Power relations and care and protection matters and gender are not only intimately entwined, but I consider they cannot be separated by empowering intents. We must, then, look more stringently beneath the surface intentions of such processes as family-group decision-making and meet these challenges as we work through the application of the concept over a longer term.

The FGC must be seen as an innovative practice development along the journey of child protection policy creation. How can the concept be built upon? The danger would be in viewing it as an end point, in allowing it to become a static routinized practice mechanism or become sidelined as a good idea that was destroyed by disempowering those for whom the process was intended.

References

Barbour, A. (1991). Family Group Conferences: context and consequences. *Social Work Review*, 3 (4): 16–21.

Cheyne, C., O'Brien, M. and Belgrave, M. (1997) *Social Policy in Aotearoa New Zealand*. New Zealand, Oxford

Cockburn, G. (1994). The Children Young Persons and their Families Act. In R. Munford and M. Nash (eds.), *Social Work in Action*. New Zealand, Dunmore.

Connolly M. (2006) Fifteen years of family group conferencing: coordinators talk about their experiences in Aotearoa New Zealand. *British Journal of Social Work*, 36 (4): 523–40.

Connolly, M. and McKenzie, M. (1999) *Effective Participatory Practice: Family Group Conferencing in Child Protection*. New York, Aldine de Gruyter.

Dalley, B. (1998) *Family Matters: Child Welfare in Twentieth-Century New Zealand*. Auckland, Auckland University Press.

Featherstone, B. (2004) *Family Life and Family Support a Feminist Analysis*. London, Palgrave.

Ferguson, H. (2003) Welfare, social exclusion and reflexivity: the case of child and women protection. *Journal of Social Policy*, 32 (2): 199–216

Frengley, S. (2008) Kinship care: roots of grafts. Master of Social Welfare Thesis. University of Otago. Dunedin.

Hassall, I. (1996) Origin and development of family group conferences. In J. Hudson, A. Morris, G. Maxwell and B. Galway (eds.), *Family Group Conferences*. Sydney, Federation Press.

Humpage, L. (2006) An 'inclusive' society: a 'leap forward' for Maori in New Zealand? *Critical Social Policy*, 26: 220–42.

Love, C. (2000) Family group conferencing cultural origins, sharing and appropriation – a Maori reflection. In G. Burford and J. Hudson (eds.), *Family Group Conferencing*. New York, Aldine de Gruyter.

Lupton, C. and Nixon, P. (1999) *Empowering Practice?* Bristol, Policy Press.

McKenzie M. (1996) Family decision-making as a preventative solution in child protection. In N. J Taylor and A. B. Smith, *Investing In Children: Primary Prevention Strategies*. Proceedings Inaugural Child and Family Policy Conference. Dunedin, University of Otago Press.

McKenzie, M. and Walton, E. (2005) *Improving The Family Group Conference: Opinions Of New Zealand Care and Protection Coordinators*. Department of Social Work and Community Development Research Report. Dunedin, University of Otago.

Marsh P. and Crow, G. (1997) *Family Group Conferences in Child Welfare*. Oxford, Blackwell.

Maxwell G. M. and Morris A. (1993). *Family, Victims and Culture: Youth Justice in New Zealand*. Wellington. Social Policy Agency and Institute of Criminology Victoria University.

Maxwell, G. M., Robertson, J., Thom, A. and Walker B. (1995) *Researching Child Protection: A Proposal for a Study of the Outcome Interventions under the Children Young Persons and their Families Act 1989*. Wellington. Office of Commissioner for Children and Social Policy Agency.

Metge, J. (1995) *New Growth from Old: The Whanau in the Modern World*. Wellington, Victoria University Press.

Ministerial Advisory Committee (1986) *Puoa-te-Atatu (Daybreak): The Report of the Ministerial Advisory Committee on a Maori Perspective for the Department of Social Welfare*. Department of Social Welfare, Wellington.

Munford, R. and Nash, M. (1994) A feminist contribution to social work: social work through the eyes of women. In R. Munford and M. Nash (eds.), *Social Work in Action*. New Zealand, Dunmore.

Pakura, S. (2004) The family group conference journey: celebrating the successes, learning the lessons, embracing the challenges. *American Humane Association's Family Group Decision Making Conference and Skills-Building Institute*, 6–9 June 2004, Harrisburg, United States of America.

Parton, N. (1991) *Governing the Family: Child Care, Child Protection and the State*. London, Macmillan.

Parton, N. (2006) *Safeguarding Childhood: Early Intervention and Surveillance in a Late Modern Society*. London, Palgrave.

Scourfield, J. (2003) *Gender and Child Protection*. London, Palgrave.

Shannon, Pat and Walker, Shayne (1996) The New Zealand Children and Young Persons and their Families Act 1989: the need for structural change.

In N. J. Taylor and A. B. Smith (eds.), *Investing in Children: Primary Prevention Strategies. Proceedings Inaugural Child and Family Policy Conference. Dunedin, University of Otago Press.*

Tauri, J. (1999) Family group conferencing: the myth of indigenous empowerment in New Zealand. *Justice as Healing Newsletter*, 4 (1) (Spring).

Tennant, M. (2002) Complicating childhood: gender, ethnicity and 'disadvantage' within the New Zealand children's health camps movement. *Canadian Bulletin of Medical History*, 19 (1): 179–99.

Walton, E., McKenzie, M. and Connolly, M. (2005) Private family time: the heart of family group conferencing. *Protecting Children*, 19 (4): 17–24.

Women's Anti Racist Action Group (1984) *Institutional Racism Report to the Department of Social Welfare.* Wellington. Government Printer

Worrall, J. (1996) Because we're family: a study of kinship care in New Zealand. Master of Social Work thesis. Massey University, Albany, New Zealand.

Worrall, J. (2001) *Grandparents Raising Grandchildren: A Handbook for Grandparents and Other Kin Caregivers.* Auckland, Broughtwood Press.

Worrall, J. and McKenzie, M. (2003) Researching with vulnerable families. In R. Munford and J. Sanders. (eds.), *Making a Difference in Families: Research that Creates Change.* Sydney, Allen and Unwin.

10

Gender in Residential Childcare

Mark Smith

Introduction

Residential or group care for children is described as 'a physical setting in which children and young people are offered care – physical nurturing, social learning opportunities, the promotion of health and wellbeing and specialized behaviour training' (Fulcher, 2001: 418). It is provided across a range of service types from respite units for disabled children, children's homes and residential schools through to secure accommodation. Since the late 1960s, residential care in the United Kingdom has been considered a branch of social work.

Ward stated back in 1993 that the topic of gender was 'virtually invisible in the group care literature (1993: 35). Fifteen years down the line, the topic is slightly more visible but little better understood. The literature that has emerged (for example, Barter, 2006; Green,

Gender and Child Welfare in Society Edited by Brid Featherstone, Carol-Ann Hooper, Jonathan Scourfield, and Julie Taylor.

2005; Green and Masson, 2002; O'Neill, 2007) tends to focus on structural analyses, reflecting an ontological privilege accorded by social work to such accounts, especially when applied to questions of out of home care and gender. Residential care can still be subject to Goffman's (1961) critique of the total institution (Green, 2005). It is similarly stuck in respect of gender. Pollert notes that 'while in sociological writings structures and causes seem to have been taken over by fragments and contingencies, the grand narrative of patriarchy has resolutely survived (1996: 639).

The survival of patriarchy as an organizing construct is especially strong in social work (Scourfield and Coffey, 2002). In the United Kingdom the education and training of social workers has contributed to an oversimplification of discussions around gender (Orme, 2003). The Diploma in Social Work, the baseline qualification across the United Kingdom from 1990 until 2004, sought to address the topic within requirements that students demonstrate anti-discriminatory practice (ADP). This often became reduced to 'standpointism' (Orme, 2003) and, in the 'climate of regulated consensus' (Wilson and Beresford, 2000: 560) that emerged, gender perspectives struggled to move beyond the grand narrative of patriarchy.

Attempts to conceptualize gender through a lens of patriarchy do not capture the complexity or contingency of its enactment in practice, thus denying 'the complex operation of power both within categories and between workers and service users, whatever their gender' (Orme, 2003: 139). This complexity, where power dynamics are multilayered and multidirectional needs to be explored further if gender is to be understood and addressed in ways that are conducive to the development of children in residential care.

This chapter identifies residential childcare as a gendered site of practice both numerically and discursively. I discuss concepts of sex, gender and sexuality, the gendered nature of social work and social care and the ways in which this has acted and continues to act to define caring roles. Whilst, at one level, social work has imposed particular gendered assumptions upon care, at another, it has taken a gender-blind approach and has failed to take sufficient account of the different needs of boys and girls, and of what both men and women can bring, differentially and together, to the caring role. I go on to explore the changing landscape of gender in care, and in particular the discursive possibilities offered by care ethics, which have roots in feminist thinking. As there is very little research into questions of gender in residential childcare some of the ideas are extrapolated from other domains of practice such as the literature on early years, education and criminology.

Oakley (1981) identified a strong gender identification and intersubjectivity that emerged when she, as a woman, interviewed women. As a long-time practitioner in residential school and secure accommodation settings, I was aware at an experiential level of the different relationships I had with boys and girls and the way in which being a male mediated those relationships. My own interests are primarily around masculinity and care, an area that is almost wholly invisible in existing literature. This interest is reflected in the weighting I give to discussion. My background and location in Scotland is also apparent in the data sources and the examples on which I draw.

Defining terms

Arguing that residential childcare is a gendered site of practice raises questions of terminology around what is meant by gender. Language around the terms 'sex' and 'gender' generally can be confusing, and can become confused in both theory and practice. For instance, the way in which the workforce is broken down between male and female is generally represented in terms of gender rather than sex, which might be argued to be more accurate. Sex is generally considered to reflect the biological fact of being either male or female, with gender referring to a more complex notion of how an individual should dress, behave, express him- or herself and relate to others, based upon his or her sex. However, gender identity cannot necessarily be assumed from biology; boys might think and behave in what might be perceived to be feminine ways and girls in masculine ways. Butler (1990) goes further and challenges attempts to differentiate between sex and gender, arguing that they are one and the same thing and that both are culturally constructed.

How a person defines and acts out their gender identity is influenced, to a large extent, by social norms and assumptions. Gender is not a rigid classification, but is in Butler's (1990) term performative:

people 'do' gender. It is achieved 'through repeated, performative iterations which become inscribed on the body and the mind' (Featherstone and Green, 2008). Boys and girls, men and women in residential care 'perform' their gender roles in particular ways, some of which I will touch on as the chapter progresses.

Whilst terminology and conceptualization around gender may be disputed, Warren (2003) argues that terms such as 'masculinity' and 'femininity' continue to be useful sociological concepts, nonetheless, as they reflect the reality of these categories as social imaginaries in the daily lives of boys and girls and men and women. McAra, referring to studies of boys and girls involvement in crime, confirms strong constructions of socially conventional concepts of masculinity and femininity, 'which have a key role to play in shaping their views on popularity and maturity and function as a measuring rod for their own sense of self' (2005: 11). So, in this chapter I hang on to the importance of categories of boy, girl, man, woman and those of masculinity and femininity as conceptual categories for understanding and interpreting behaviours and relationships, whilst at the same time recognizing the crossovers between categories and the exceptions to any generalized claims that might be made for them.

Residential care as a gendered site of practice

Children generally encounter gendered care experiences long before they reach residential care. Whilst mothers undertake most family care, around the turn of the twenty-first century 80 per cent of fathers still lived with all of their biological children and only 13 per cent did not live with any of them. Amongst non-resident fathers, 70 per cent remained in contact with their children (Burghes, Clarke and Cronin, 1997). Most children, then, could count on care from both mothers and fathers. However, this situation changes significantly in respect of children involved in the child protection process. Of these, only 38 per cent lived with both parents; 31 per cent, with a lone mother; 28 per cent, in reconstituted families; and 2 per cent, with lone fathers. The figures for those still with both parents drops sharply as child protection proceedings continue (Daniel and Taylor, 2001). Once children are placed in residential care the likelihood is that a majority will be looked after by their mothers alone or in reconstituted relationships, and many will have little or no contact with their birth fathers.

An early practical problem in discussion of gender in residential childcare is ascertaining accurate figures for the numbers of boys and girls placed and men and women working there. Government figures show that 55 per cent of 'looked after' children are boys (Scottish Government, 2008). However, 'looked after' children can be supervised at home, or placed in foster care or with other family members. Proportionally, more girls than boys are fostered and more boys than girls are placed in residential care. There are no direct figures for children 'accommodated' in residential care, although1,165 boys and 726 girls were 'looked after' in planned short-term placements in 2007–8, perhaps the closest approximation to be gained from the statistics (Scottish Government, 2008).

Most children's homes are mixed-sex, whilst many residential schools continue to be single-sex, catering mostly for boys. Residential care also tends to cater for teenagers rather than younger children, for whom fostering is the provision of choice (McPheat, Hunter and Milligan, 2007). The persistent social class dimensions of residential care (Smith, 2009) also identify it as a resource for the poor. The population of residential childcare is thus skewed towards adolescent boys, almost all of whom come from conditions of poverty and social and emotional disadvantage. The effects of this adversity are often manifest in troublesome or criminal behaviours (McAra, 2005).

The gender split in the residential childcare workforce, is around two females to one male (Scottish Institute for Residential Child Care, 2004). Within this there are some variations in residential schools, perhaps because of their association with control and activity based programmes, traditionally attracting more male staff then the sector in general (Walton 1975). So, whilst the population of residential care is mostly boys, as an occupational field it is dominated by women. In this respect, there are parallels with other 'caring' professions, such as nursing, early years work and primary schooling, reflecting a persistent association of care with women (Hugman, 1991). And because childcare is dominated by women, pay is traditionally low (Thomson et al., 2005), thus contributing to the continuing gender pay gap (Perry and Cree, 2003).

Gender and caring

Childcare is gendered discursively as well as numerically. It is heavily influenced by psychoanalytic and attachment perspectives, which can assert a privileged position for mothering (Buckley, 1997; Orme, 2002; Turney, 2000). Such theoretical orientations have, in the past, been reified in state childcare policies. The Curtis and Clyde reports (1946) specifically sought to base substitute care around what was then a traditional family model. This led to the emergence of family group homes where 'aunties' kept home and 'uncles' went out to work, as the preferred mode of service delivery. A similar model of housemaster/housemother operated in residential schools.

The location of residential childcare in social work brings another theoretical strand to considerations of gender. Social work has been significantly influenced by feminist theory, or at least by second-wave feminism (Orme, 2003; Scourfield and Coffey, 2002). This located many of women's problems at the door of patriarchy, where social relations and political and organizational structures are based around an assumption of the superiority of masculine traits and of the subordination of women to men. Social problems including domestic and child abuse could be argued to be inevitable consequences of patriarchy. From a perspective of patriarchy, the construction of men in caring positions shifted from that of breadwinner to one where they were increasingly identified as a risk to children (Christie 2001).

Orme (2002) identifies how traditional discourses of care can portray it as quintessentially characteristic of women, whilst Scourfield (2003) suggests that social work constructs men in a variety of ways that fail to give them a central role in care and that generally identify them as problematic. Such perspectives can be incorporated into practice cultures that act to exclude men from caring roles to an extent that has been described as a 'pervasive and endemic problem' (O'Hagan and Dillenburger 1995:197). Both the association of care with mothering and that of abuse with men maintains the onus of care with women.

Differences between boys and girls

Biddulph says, 'For 30 years it has been trendy to deny masculinity and say that boys and girls are really just the same. But as parents and teachers know, this approach isn't working' (1997: 3). Most of those who work in residential childcare would attest to differences between boys and girls, some of which can reflect received beliefs, for instance, of girls being more complex and conniving than boys, and hence more difficult to manage. Assumptions, conscious or otherwise, about the differences between boys and girls are also reflected in placement practices. Girls are very often placed in care, and especially in secure accommodation, on account of their sexual vulnerability (O'Neill, 2001), boys, often on account of violence or, increasingly, what is termed 'sexually aggressive behaviour' (Kendrick, Mitchell and Smith, 2004).

In psychological terms, and accepting differences amongst and between boys and girls, they differ, as groups, on just about every dimension that has been investigated (Benenson, 2005). Differences are apparent in the ways in which they respond and are responded to, from a very early age. Girls generally appear more securely attached; boys respond less well to separation, especially from their mothers (Head, 1999).

About 70 per cent of those in special education are boys. Their presenting difficulties in such placements also differ from those of girls. Boys are more likely to have problems with reading and writing, psychosocial problems and attention deficit disorders, whilst girls are more prone to vision, hearing, language and intellectual disabilities (Skarbrevik, 2002).

Boys and girls also appear to demonstrate different patterns of seeking help (Benenson and Koulnazarian, 2008; Daniel et al., 2005), with girls generally better able to ask for adult help and to use friendship networks for support. Boys and girls are also differentially vulnerable to abuse and its consequences. Girls appear more vulnerable to sexually abusive behaviour and sexualized bullying, which, in light of the pre-existing vulnerability of girls in residential care, has implications for their experiences there. Sexual abuse threatens boys' constructions of masculinity and raises fears about their sexual identity (Daniel et al., 2005). In residential care settings this can be manifest in compensatory hyper-masculine behaviours.

Whilst gender-based differences between male and female are apparent, factors other than gender alone need to be borne in mind. There are obvious commonalities between boys and girls in residential care in respect of social class and social adversity, and they can respond to these backgrounds in similar ways. But, even when backgrounds are similar, different patterns of behaviour are apparent: boys are more likely than girls to be involved in serious offences, such as carrying a weapon, housebreaking, robbery, theft from cars (Smith and McAra, 2004); and they are also less likely than girls to grow out of offending behaviour. Moffitt et al. (2001) argue that the neurospsychological patterns that lead to life-course persistent delinquency are much more common in boys than girls, whereas the factors underlying 'normal' offending in adolescence are the same in the two sexes (Smith and McAra, 2004: 21).

Gender wars

Identification of differences in the life courses of boys and girls surfaced through feminist thinking exploring the effects of patriarchy on girls growing up and how expectations around gender role shaped and inhibited their experiences. Historically, girls have been held back educationally by expectations of a domestic future. Demands for equality have led to greater attention being turned to the forces that constrained girls. Pipher (1994) identified that adolescent girls can be obsessed with complicated and intense relationships, have confused and contradictory feelings towards the same people at the same time, and mix up sexuality, romance and intimacy. These concerns, as well as all sorts of mixed messages, such as 'be sexy but don't be sexual', are rooted in cultural and media-driven expectations about what girls and women should be like. Such expectations split adolescent girls into true and false selves. There are some general ways they can respond to these cultural pressures; they can conform, withdraw, be depressed or get angry (Smith and Steckley, 2005).

Reay (2001) identifies similar themes and places girls into four categories according to their responses to cultural pressures. They can present as *spice girls*, *nice girls*, *girlies* or *tomboys*. The Edinburgh Youth Transitions Study found that to attain status, girls 'were required to be good-looking. Wearing designer labels, short skirts and high heels adds to popularity as does heavy use of make-up. Being blonde and thin are also key attributes' (McAra, 2005: 12). Recent years have seen the emergence of what has become known as raunch culture, whereby girls are less inhibited, but perhaps no less shaped by societal forces. They have become more sexually assertive and, in some cases, more aggressive, a trend that is made manifest in the increased numbers of girls coming to the attention of the authorities. 'Hard' girls seem to attract some status with other girls, although not necessarily from boys (McAra, 2005). Whilst both boys and girls in Reay's study saw girls as harder working, more mature and more socially skilled, all of the boys and most of the girls nevertheless believed that it was better being a boy. For those girls placed in residential care, the social pressures to conform to particular ways of being a girl are likely to be intensified as many will lack the mediating influences of a supportive family or peer group.

The boys' turn

Feminism's success in drawing attention to the long-term under-representation and repression of women and in bringing their experiences to the surface prompted men – starting around the early 1990s – to explore what it was to be a man, something that until that point had been, largely, taken for granted. The resultant 'men's movement' took different forms, some drawing on a mytho-poetical reclamation of 'traditional' manhood (see Bly, 1990), others focusing a critical gaze on what was termed 'hegemonic masculinity' (Connell, 1995), a dominant expression of masculinity which depended for its continued sway on subjugating alternative ways or expressions of being a man. Boys became part of these debates (Weaver-Hightower, 2003), and it was seen that they weren't faring too well. They were more prone to a whole range of physical and emotional problems than girls (Head, 1999), who are, in fact, generally more resilient (Daniel, 2007). Boys' educational underachievement is increasingly a cause of concern across the developed world. They also account for more than 80 per cent of school exclusions (Brodie, 2001). In Scotland, 75 per cent of those referred to the Reporter to the Children's Panel on offence grounds are boys (Children in Scotland, 2008). Involvement in crime can be seen by some boys as a way of 'doing masculinity'. 'Being hard' was valorized by the adolescents in the Edinburgh Youth Transitions Study (McAra, 2005).

Yet, their bravado may mask an insecurity at the heart of boys' existence. Much of their identity is constructed around not being a girl. When boys describe themselves it is often in terms of not being 'sissy' or 'girly' in any way, rather than around any more positive image of emerging masculinity. Assertions of boyhood are often expressed in sexist or homophobic language and behaviours (Frosh, Phoenix and Pattman, 2002). They police each other in relation to dominant constructions of masculinity, which imply, for example, that 'telling' about one's troubles is to behave like a 'wimp' (Daniel et al., 2005).

There are different schools of thought as to why boys experience some of these difficulties. Pollack (1999) suggests that they are pushed by societal pressures to subscribe to the set of behavioural expectations he calls 'The Boy Code'. Pressure to subscribe to the boy code, and in particular not to express any sissy or girly qualities, inhibits them from expressing more caring and emotional sides. Hoff Sommers (2000), however, takes another view. The title of her book *The War Against Boys: How Misguided Feminism is Harming our Young Men.* She argues that boys are suffering because Western culture devalues manhood and seeks to feminize boys. Both these writers share a belief, from different ideological positions, that the problem with boys is that they are not allowed to get in touch with their inner selves; 'One camp wants to reform masculinity, the other to restore it; one seeks to rescue boys from patriarchy, the other from feminism' (Young, 2001: 1).

Doing gender in residential childcare

If gender is performative, residential care can focus a spotlight on its enactment, bringing together boys and girls, men and women in an intense and intimate setting. Differences between boys and girls and their differential responses to male and female staff used to be acknowledged in residential care. For example, boys' angry responses to female staff could be understood as a transference reaction, where anger at their mothers' failure to protect them was projected onto caring adults whom they might see as representing their mothers. Such psychodynamic meaning-making has become subsumed since the early 1990s beneath increasingly technical rational constructions of social work (Ruch, 2005). Alongside this, the Anti-discriminatory Agenda, by privileging structural considerations around equality and patriarchy, allowed the emergence of professional orthodoxies that sought to challenge what might be perceived to be any expressions of maleness. In residential care, activities such as football, which might be considered a 'male' preserve could be frowned upon or opened up to boys and girls in ways that failed to take into account their different interests or aptitudes.

Boys and girls in residential care respond differentially to adult traits and dispositions. Girls seem to prefer staff who are friendly and nice, who make it safe for them to show how they feel and who are sensitive to them when they are experiencing hard times. Boys prefer staff who will talk and joke with them, who play sport and who are deemed to be fair (Nicholson and Artz, 2003). A European study looking at the difference between male and female teachers or pedagogues (the profession working in residential care settings across most of Europe) towards the behaviour of 'unruly' boys, suggest that males can distinguish better between playing and aggression amongst boys than can their female colleagues, who tend to view unruly play more as aggression whilst males are more likely to regard it as typical boyish behaviour (Tavecchio, 2003). This might make sense of some of the aversion to horseplay that has emerged in residential care settings in recent years. Whilst men might view this as a legitimate and healthy way to interact with children, women perhaps identify it as being based on physical power and leading to further violence.

Boys and girls 'doing gender' will influence the experience for those around them. Acting out particular male or female ways of being can set a tone that gives the message, 'This is how we do things around here', with attendant implications for those who might want to do things differently. Green (2005) identifies boys in residential care as being sexually demanding and dominating, whilst O'Neill

(2007) identifies them as disproportionately involved in bullying. However, both boys and girls are capable of negative and antisocial behaviour. Both are capable of bullying and being bullied, as well as being abusive and being abused (Children in Scotland, 2008). Girls as well as boys are also capable of taking the lead sexually. Sexually active and demanding boys or girls can affect the culture of residential homes by placing pressure on other residents to be similarly sexually active.

But gender relations are not all characterized by power imbalances, and residential care is not defined by bullying, sexual or otherwise. Emond (2003) notes that relations amongst resident groups in children's homes are characterized far more by acts of kindness and consideration than by bullying. In fact, bullying as a trait did not confer status within groups of residents of children's homes.

Men and women caring

Whilst there are differences between boys and girls there are also differences between the men and women caring for them (Hollway, 2006). Ways of caring are forged by life histories that have traditionally been heavily gendered (ibid.) and which are reproduced in the ways men and women go about caring (Cameron, 2006). In early years education (and likely too in residential childcare), men are often deployed as substitute and more appropriate father figures (ibid.). Strong social forces, largely unarticulated, push men towards adopting particular roles with children, especially around the activities in which they become involved. This happens even when they are aware of and trying to resist stereotypical expectations (ibid.). Cameron argues that underlying gender divisions in childcare can remain based around 'ideas about domestic divisions of labour, with male workers positioned as performing stereotypical male tasks in families' (ibid.: 74). Smith, Macleod and Mercadante (2005), in a study of men recruited to work in a residential school, identify a similar preoccupation with domesticity and the practical rather than the emotional aspects of care. Doing the dishes and laundry was a common theme for new workers keen to be seen to be breaking down gender barriers.

Aspects of the care role relating to comforting, 'reading children's thoughts', 'being patient', are largely ascribed to female workers in Cameron's account of men in the nursery and in a study of males coming into work in residential care (Smith, MacLeod and Mercadante, 2005). Whilst this might suggest some fairly essential differences between male and female ways of caring, and Hollway indeed suggests that such differences are inevitable based around early experience, there is also a context. Cameron notes that male workers' 'possibilities to use physical comfort were sometimes limited by rules, either self-imposed or institutional, about contact with the children' (2006: 76).

Another significant practice in residential care that can take on a gendered dimension is that of physical restraint. Traditional models of caring might identify male staff as disciplinary figures or as having a heavy-handed and over-bearing approach in contrast to a more sensitive, feminine response to difficult situations. Social work constructions of men (Scourfield, 2003) can reinforce such assumptions. Yet there is little evidence on which to base them. Research into parenting indicates that men are no more likely to physically chastise children than are women, whilst experience in residential childcare would suggest that patterns of discipline and restraint are far more nuanced than to lend themselves to explanations based around patriarchy. Factors such as age, experience, confidence and indeed what particular adults may represent for particular children can all be implicated in staff's involvement in situations of restraint.

Role models

Increasingly, social problems around absent fathers and unsocialized boys are identified in political discourse with a lack of appropriate gender role models. In residential childcare there is an emerging or resurrected expectation that men act as role models for the boys they work with, perhaps supporting a 'compensatory model' where contact with male workers can substitute for the absence of fathers. In situations where a majority of boys cannot count on the presence of a stable father figure in their lives this argument would posit that male care staff can assume a crucial role in the ways that boys begin to identify themselves as men. This is essentially a rites-of-passage type argument. Burns claims that, 'when young males are initiated into their respective cultures by men who have acquired healthy attitudes, behave in a responsible manner, and express their full range of emotions, they are given the opportunity to grow into mature manhood' (2003: 1). Recalling the purposes of residential care from the opening paragraph, one of which is to provide social learning opportunities, the intimacy and intensity of the setting lends itself to possibilities for adults modelling particular ways of acting and being around gender roles.

However, role model theory is not that simple. It raises questions about *what* role male workers are to model. This becomes increasingly muddy in light of increased awareness and tolerance of non-traditional sexualities. Are men to model traditional masculinity or are they to challenge this and to provide models of a range of different masculinities? (Owen 2003a). Moreover, as Cameron says, 'in situations where only one male worker is employed he cannot hope to embody all the different possibilities of "maleness", to be a universal, all-purpose, comprehensive model of being a man' (2006: 75).

Perhaps it matters less what particular gender images are modelled than that both boys and girls are given access to male carers. Some men may present a 'traditional' masculinity, others more nurturing ways of responding. Both may have their place. What seems to be important is that men are available for children as they grow up, and their active presence in children's lives is likely to bring about positive outcomes so long as it is non-abusive (Newstone, 2000). This fits with a perspective that sees children and workers as co-constructing knowledge and learning from each other. Role modelling is thus about providing resources for children to make their own discoveries and identities (Cameron, 2006). The task for residential care is to ensure that the images of gender presented to children are positive and healthy ones and that they are also multidimensional; masculinity and femininity are not single entities but involve a range of expressions that are context dependent.

Sexuality

The intimacy of residential childcare makes it inevitable that questions of sexual attraction between children, and indeed between adults and children, will exist, openly or otherwise. Fewster (2001: 12) points out that 'sexuality, in the broadest sense, is a powerful and persistent theme that, in one way or another, implicitly or explicitly, plays itself out within and between both participants' (worker and child). Freel (2003) identifies a significant proportion of workers in childcare settings (15 per cent of males and 4 per cent of females) acknowledging a sexual interest in children, figures likely to be under-reported in light of the social undesirability of admitting such an interest. Yet sexuality is not well managed in residential care (Green, 2005). This may be because for the most part it is treated instrumentally and externalized from the experiences of the social actors who live and work in care settings. Thus, it is expected at a policy level that staff in residential care engage at an appropriate level with young people, providing neutral advice and guidance around some of the most intimate areas of their lives. Yet, as Fewster observes, sexuality makes us feel uncomfortable and practitioners 'find compelling reasons to place their own sexuality in cold storage when it comes to working with their 'clients'. Sexuality, as a result, becomes split off from 'self', a situation which is neither conceptually nor practically feasible and one that hinders the building of authentic personal relationships. For staff in residential childcare to engage safely and authentically with children requires a preparedness to explore and accept sexuality as integral to 'self'.

Gender and abuse

The recent history of residential childcare has been defined by sexuality (generally masculinity) gone wrong, with revelations of children having been abused in care. Berridge and Brodie (1996) found a 'macho' or masculine culture to be a factor in inquiry reports they examined. Residential schools in particular are open to concerns that they operate 'macho' cultures with an emphasis on control (Barter, 2003; 2006) and that programmes reinforce traditional conceptions of masculinity. The Scottish Government's systemic review of abuse in residential care (Shaw, 2007; Sen et al., 2007) resurrects questions of the relationship of masculinity to abuse. Almost all identified perpetrators of sexual abuse in residential childcare settings are, indeed, men (Gallagher 2000, Colton, 2002). This has resulted in considerable ambivalence over men's involvement in care work, leading some authors (for example, Pringle, 1992) to argue that men should not be employed in the sector, a position subsequently modified (Pringle, 2001). But whilst almost all reported allegations of abuse are against men, this is in the context of very few recorded incidents of sexual abuse by carers. Moreover, residential childcare is no more implicated in abuse than other institutional or community settings where adults have access to children (Gallagher, 2000).

The association of men with abuse has led to attempts to identify and select out aberrant sexuality within the recruitment process (for example, Edinburgh Inquiry, 1999). Some views, however, do not locate abuse with individual men but view it as an expression of hegemonic masculinity (Cowburn and Dominelli, 2001). Featherstone and Lancaster (1997) point out that men who abuse are indistinguishable from those who do not. Freel notes that 'despite a prevalent male sexual interest in children, a much smaller number of men actually abuse children . . .[than] express a sexual interest in children' (2003: 485). Whilst it might be argued that protecting children requires greater consideration of the link between masculinity, sexuality and child sex abuse (Cowburn and Dominelli, 2001), on the other hand, coupling men with abuse can be tantamount to 'whole gender blaming'.

It is too easy to hide the complexity of gender relations in residential care behind glib and pejorative assertions of macho cultures. In contexts in which practice cultures are in fact heavily feminized (Scourfield and Coffey, 2002) such claims raise questions as to what a macho culture is and how it might manifest itself, and indeed whether such cultures might be possible independent of the presence of men. Given the small number of men implicated in abuse, Cameron, Moss and Owen (2001) suggest the need for men and abuse to be uncoupled and for protection strategies for children and staff to be separated from the wider desirability of ensuring a gender balanced workforce. Nevertheless, the tendency to maintain this link within the culture of social work appears to be one of the factors inhibiting the recruitment of men into social professions (Perry and Cree 2003, Owen 2003b). There is an undoubted 'fear on the part of many men that their motives will be impugned and that they would be leaving themselves open to charges of being nascent sexual predators or potentially abusive' (Children in Scotland, 2008). It may also foreclose different expressions of masculinity (Smith, 2003).

Rethinking gender in residential care

If boys and girls demonstrate significant differences over a number of dimensions and men and women bring different qualities to the provision of care then simplistic attempts to apply equal opportunities policies and practices, decreeing that everyone be treated the same, are misconceived. European models of social pedagogy increasingly recognize the need for practice to take into account the different needs and responses of boys and girls. Jensen (1996) advocates a gender pedagogy rather than a gender-neutral culture. Gender pedagogy is premised on a belief that 'boys and girls and men and women behave in different ways, and all children should have the experience of both male and female ways of caring – a gender blind approach ignores important differences' (Owen, 2003a: 102).

Addressing the gender imbalance in the workforce

Adopting ideas of gender pedagogy requires that the pronounced imbalance in the current workforce be addressed. The lack of male carers in particular is increasingly identified as problematic (Rolfe, 2005). Institutional processes, nonetheless, can operate to perpetuate the gender imbalance. Women, perhaps because of their long association with care, seem to more readily speak a language of care (Bubeck, 1995). This appears to translate to their better performance in recruitment processes. McPheat's (2007) study of an initiative to recruit residential childcare staff notes a significant difference in the success rates of male and female applicants, with 89 per cent of female candidates being successful at recruitment events as opposed to only 69.7 per cent of males. Figures such as these raise questions as to whether traditional recruitment processes serve to filter out men from care positions. Rolfe (2005) argues that these disadvantage men, who are often less connected to childcare circles, and suggests that training may have a greater potential to attract men than jobs alone. Indeed, initiatives that include training do seem to be able to attract men into childcare, suggesting that there is an untapped pool of men who want to be involved in childcare as a career (Smith Macleod and Mercadante, 2005).

Arguments about a language of care and about men and women exhibiting different caring preferences seem to have some substance. In a residential school senior staff discovered that if they changed the wording of advertisements from childcare to youth work they attracted more male applicants (Smith, Macleod and Mercadante, 2005), reinforcing Cameron's (2006) observation that men seem to prefer working with older children. Men also seem to prefer activity-based ways of working. Introducing sports and outdoor education on social pedagogy courses in Northern Europe led to an increase in male applicants (Peeters, 2007).

Policy developments

The policy landscape has become more sensitive to gender issues of late. The Gender Equality Duty (GED) is a legal obligation, which came into force in the United Kingdom in April 2007, that requires that public authorities and publicly-funded services to promote gender equality and tackle sex discrimination. This ought to mean that they take steps to address the differential needs of boys and girls and provide support to both mothers and fathers to parent their children. The GED may establish a framework whereby approaches to gender that are more sensitive and sophisticated than heretofore can be brought to bear on work with children.

Conceptual shifts

It is not just at policy level that shifts in thinking about gender in care are apparent. As previously noted, social work discourse in relation to gender has been stuck in second-wave feminist assumptions based around patriarchy (Orme, 2003; Scourfield and Coffey, 2002). However, feminist theory is, as Orme (2003) argues, far more diffuse and sophisticated than this, and many of its ideas resonate with social work practice, as it does is in relation to understandings of care and in particular the growing interest in care ethics.

The literature on care ethics can be located within a feminist tradition that can be traced back to Carol Gilligan's book *In a Different Voice* ([1982]1993). Gilligan was a student of Lawrence Kohlberg, who provided us with what has become the standard model of human moral development. Gilligan challenges Kohlberg's model as reflecting predominantly male ways of thinking and acting on questions of morality. Gilligan deems men to speak and act from a 'justice' orientation, where qualities of objectivity, rationality and general principle predominate; women, from a 'care' orientation, drawing on 'softer' attributes of intuition, connection and compassion when coming to moral decisions.

There is some dispute around whether Gilligan's thesis reflects essentialist characteristics of men and women or whether it merely provides a framework within which to conceptualize different orientations towards moral issues, the actual 'voices' being applicable to either men or women. Tronto challenges essentialist identifications of care as resting with women, describing care as a practice involving 'a general habit of mind' to care that should inform all aspects of a practitioner's moral life' (1994: 127). This habit of mind to care does not rest exclusively with women. Care, according to Tronto, shifts from being a private concern to become a social one, and one which is not gender specific.

What Gilligan has done is open up spaces through which to differentiate between the relational and intuitive aspects and more rule-bound ways of conceptualizing care. Caring relationships 'are predicated upon an expressive rather than instrumental relationship to others'. (Brannen and Moss 2003: 202). A feminist approach to care is essentially relational, requiring a stepping in to encounters with the other rather than a stepping back into a 'rational' and objective position where 'self' becomes distanced from the other by means of rules and procedures (Ricks, 1992). Within a managerial rubric, however, care can be conceived as a technical/rational commodity, a male voice, privileging reason and objectivity. The kind of managerial cultures that have emerged in the past couple of decades (Clarke and

Newman, 1997) speak with a hyper-masculine voice, even though the exponents of managerial ways of working may be women as well as men. Those who make it up the management ladder generally have to speak with a male voice to get there and stay there. The results of this are evident in organizational cultures driven by legalism and procedure that sap the moral purpose of those who live and work there (Bauman, 2000). Critics of the direction social work has taken in recent years (for example, Meagher and Parton, 2004) explicitly draw upon care ethics to provide a conceptual base from which to challenge managerialism.

Care, if it is to have any impact on children's lives, needs to be understood as an irredeemably relational practice. Bureaucratically conceived care is an unequal relationship in which the worker stands above the object of their concern. Care ethics, on the other hand, are rooted in attending to and feeling for the other. They take 'professional caring into the personal realm and require that both parties show up, be present, be engaged at a feeling level for each other. The presence of feeling(s) provides the link, which connects the worker and client' (Ricks, 1992). Again, this might be thought of as a female voice, but one that many men might be happy to claim or develop. They can be inhibited from doing so by constructions and associations in social work and in particular in child protection discourses of men with abuse.

Conclusion

This chapter has sought to take discussion of gender in residential childcare beyond the biological essentialism of traditional models of care and the sociological reductionism of accounts based around the concept of patriarchy. The capacity to care is not wholly natural, nor is it wholly social (Hollway, 2006). Narratives of male power, whilst they might apply at some level, mask the complexity of power dynamics, within what is a heavily gendered and in many respects heavily feminized field of practice. Shibboleths around gender equality are misconceived. So too are expectations that men suddenly take on the kind of caring roles previously ascribed to women. Both social conditions and also the 'skin bond' that women experience in bearing and suckling children 'have forged [in women] capacities to care different from men's' (Hollway, 2006: 122). Residential care needs to explore and celebrate some of these differences and nuances if it is to provide a healthy environment for children to grow up in, where both male and female have an equal if different responsibility to care. The nature of residential care, through its emphasis on social learning, provides powerful opportunities to both affirm and to extend the range of gender models available to children. Care ethics may offer a conceptual framework through which to engage such debates, but this needs to be taken forward conceptually and empirically in ways that have been largely absent to date. Progress 'in the ethic of care debate lies in the direction of detailed discussion rather than that of programmatic and simple oppositions' (Bubeck, 1995: 241).

References

Barter, C. (2003) Abuse of children in residential care NSPCC Inform
Barter, C. (2003) Abuse of children in residential care NSPCC Inform
<www.nspcc.org.uk> accessed 21 November 2008.

Barter, C. (2006) Discourses of blame: deconstructing (hetero)sexuality, peer sexual violence and residential children's homes. *Child and Family Social Work*, 11 (4): 347–56.

Bauman, Z. (2000) Am I my brother's keeper? *European Journal of Social Work*, 3 (1): 5–11.

Benenson, J. F. (2005) Sex differences. In B. Hopkins, R. Barr, G. Michel and P. Rochat (eds.), *The Cambridge Encyclopedia of Child Development*. Cambridge, Cambridge University Press.

Benenson, J. F. and Koulnazarian, M. (2008) Sex differences in help-seeking appear in early childhood. *British Journal of Developmental Psychology*, 26 (2): 163–9.

Berridge, D. and Brodie, I. (1996) *Children's Homes Revisited*. London, Jessica Kingsley.

Bly, R. (1990) *Iron John: A Book About Men*. New York, Addison-Wesley.

Biddulph, S. (1997) *Raising Boys*. London, Thorsons.

Brannen, J. and Moss, P. (eds.) (2003) *Rethinking Children's Care*. Buckingham, Open University Press.

Brodie, I. (2001) *Children's Homes and School Exclusion: Redefining the Problem*. London, Jessica Kingsley.

Bubeck, D. (1995) *Care, Gender, and Justice.* Oxford, Clarendon Press.
Buckley, H. (1998) Filtering out fathers: the gendered nature of social work in child protection. *Irish Social Worker*, 16 (3): 7–11.
Burghes, L., Clarke, L. and Cronin, N. (1997). *Fathers and Fatherhood in Britain.* Family Policy Studies Centre (Occasional Paper No. 23).
Burns, M. (2003) Red knight errantry: the first step towards mature masculinity. *Relational Child and Youth Care Practice*, 16 (4): 22–7.
Butler, J. (1990) *Gender Trouble: Feminism and the Subversion of Identity.* London, Routledge.
Cameron, C. (2006) Men in the nursery revisited: issues of male workers and professionalism. *Contemporary Issues in Early Childhood*, 7 (1): 68–79.
Cameron, C., Moss, P. and Owen, C. (2001) *Men in the Nursery: Gender and Caring Work.* Edinburgh, Chapman.
Children in Scotland (2008) *Making the Gender Equality Duty Real for children, Young People and their Fathers.* Edinburgh, Children in Scotland.
Christie, A. (ed.) (2001) *Men and Social Work: Theories and Practices.* Basingstoke, Palgrave.
Clarke, J. and Newman, J. (1997) *The Managerial State: Power, Politics and Ideology in the Remaking of Social Welfare.* London, Sage.
Clyde Report (1946) Report of the Committee on Homeless Children (Cmd 6911). HMSO.
Colton, M. (2002) Factors associated with abuse in residential child care institutions. *Children and Society*, 16 (1): 33–44.
Connell, R. W. (1995) *Masculinities.* Berkeley, University of California Press.
Cowburn, M. and Dominelli, L. (2001). Masking hegemonic masculinity: reconstructing the paedophile as the dangerous stranger. *British Journal of Social Work*, 31: 399–414.
Curtis Report (1946) Report of the Care of Children Committee (Cmd 6922). HMSO.
Daniel, B. (2007) The concept of resilience: messages for residential child care. In A. Kendrick (ed.), *Residential Child Care: Prospects and Challenges.* London, Jessica Kingsley Publishers.
Daniel, B., Featherstone, B., Hooper, C. A. and Scourfield, J. (2005). Why gender matters for every child matters. *British Journal of Social Work*, 35 (8): 1343–55.
Daniel, B. and Taylor, J. (2001) *Engaging with Fathers.* London, Jessica Kingsley Publishers.
Edinburgh Inquiry (1999) *Edinburgh's Children: Report of the Edinburgh Inquiry into Abuse and Protection of Children in Care.* City of Edinburgh Council.
Emond, R. (2003) Putting the care into residential child care: the role of young people. *Journal of Social Work*, 3 (3): 321–37.

Featherstone, B. and Green, L. (2008) Judith Butler. In M. Gray and S. Webb (eds.), *Social Work Theories and Methods.* London, Sage.

Fewster, G. (2001) Morality, empathy and sexuality. *Journal of Child and Youth Care*, 14 (4): 1–16.

Freel, M. (2003) Child sexual abuse and the male monopoly: an empirical exploration of gender and a sexual interest in children. *British Journal of Social Work*, 33: 481–98.

Frosh, S., Phoenix, A. and Pattman, R. (2002) *Young Masculinities: Understanding Boys in Contemporary Society.* London, Palgrave.

Fulcher, L. (2001) Differential assessment of residential group care for children and young people. *British Journal of Social Work*, 31: 417–35.

Gallagher, B. (2000) The extent and nature of known cases of institutional child sex abuse. *British Journal of Social Work*, 30: 795–817.

Gilligan, C. ([1982] 1993) *In a Different Voice: Psychological Theory and Women's Development.* Cambridge, MA, Harvard University Press.

Goffman, E. (1961) *Asylums: Essays on the Social Situation of Mental Patients and Other Inmates.* New York, Doubleday.

Green, L. (2005) Theorizing sexuality, sexual abuse and residential children's homes: adding gender to the equation. *British Journal of Social Work*, 35: 453–81.

Green, L. and Masson, H. (2002) Adolescents who sexually abuse and residential accommodation: issues of risk and vulnerability. *British Journal of Social Work*, 32: 149–68.

Head, J. (1999) *Understanding the Boys: Issues of Behaviour and Achievement.* London, Falmer Press.

Hoff Sommers, C. (2000) *The War against Boys: How Misguided Feminism is Harming Our Young Men*, New York, Simon & Schuster.

Hollway, W. (2006) *The Capacity to Care: Gender and Ethical Subjectivity.* London, Routledge.

Hugman, R. (1991) *Power in Caring Professions.* Basingstoke, Macmillan.

Jensen, J.J. (1996) *Men as Workers in Childcare Services: A Discussion Paper.* (Produced for the EC Childcare Network). Brussels, EC Equal Opportunities Unit.

Kendrick, A., Mitchell, R. and Smith, M. (2004). The development of a residential unit working with sexually aggressive young men. In H. G. Eriksson and T. Tjelflaat (eds.), *Residential Care: Horizons for the New Century.* Aldershot: Ashgate.

Lamb, M. E. (2003) *The Role of the Father in Child Development*, 4th edn. New York, John Wiley & Sons.

McAra, L. (2005) Negotiated order: gender, youth transitions and crime. *British Society of Criminology* <www.britsoccrim.org> accessed 2 October 2008.

McPheat, G. (2007) Evaluation Residential Child Care Recruitment and Development. Centre. MSc thesis, University of Strathclyde.

McPheat, G., Milligan, I. and Hunter, L. (2007). What's the use of residential childcare? Findings of two studies detailing current trends in the use of residential childcare in Scotland. *Journal of Children's Services*, 2 (2): 15–25.

Meagher, G. and Parton, N. (2004) Modernising social work and the ethics of care, *Social Work and Society*. <www.socwork.net> accessed 2 October 2008.

Moffitt, T. E., Caspi, A., Rutter, M., and Silva, P. A. (2001). *Sex Differences in Antisocial Behaviour*. Cambridge, Cambridge University Press.

Newstone, S. (2000) Male foster carers: what do we mean by 'role models'?, *Adoption & Fostering*, 24 (3): 36–47.

Nicholson, D. and Artz, S. (2003) Preventing youthful offending: where do we go from here? *Relational Child and Youth Care Practice*, 16 (4): 32–46.

Oakley, A. (1981) Interviewing women: a contradiction in terms? In H. Roberts (ed.), *Doing Feminist Research*. London, Routledge and Kegan Paul.

O'Hagan, K. and Dillenburger, K. (1995) *The Abuse of Women within Child Care Work*. Buckingham: Open University Press.

O'Neill, T. (2001) *Children in Secure Accommodation: A Gendered Exploration of Locked Institutional Care for Children in Trouble*. Jessica Kingsley, London.

O'Neill, T. (2007) Gender matters in residential child care. In A. Kendrick (ed.), *Residential Child Care: Prospects and Challenges*. London, Jessica Kingsley.

Orme, J. (2002) Social work: gender, care and justice. *British Journal of Social Work*, 32: 799–814.

Orme, J. (2003) 'It's feminist because I say so!' Feminism, social work and critical practice in the UK. *Qualitative Social Work* 2 (2): 131–53.

Owen, C. (2003a) Men in the nursery. In J. Brannen and P. Moss (eds.), *Rethinking Children's Care*. Buckingham, Open University Press.

Owen, C. (2003b) *Men's Work? Changing the Gender Mix of Childcare and Early Years Workforce*. Thomas Coram Research Unit, Institute of Education, University of London.,

Peeters, J. (2007) Including men in early childhood education: insights from the European experience. *NZ Research in Early Childhood Education*, 10: 1–11.

Perry, R. and Cree, V. (2003). The changing gender profile of applicants to qualifying social work training in the UK. *Social Work Education*, 22 (4): 377–83.

Pipher, M. (1994) *Reviving Ophelia: Saving the Lives of Adolescent Girls.* New York: Ballantine Books.

Pollack, W. S. (1999) *Real Boys: Rescuing Our Sons from the Myths of Boyhood.* New York, Henry Holt and Company.

Pollert, A. (1996) Gender and class revisited; or, the poverty of 'patriarchy'. *Sociology*, 30 (4): 639–59.

Pringle, K. (1992) Child sexual abuse perpetrated by welfare personnel and the problem of men. *Critical Social Policy*, 36: 4–19.

Pringle K. (2001) Men in social work: the double-edge. In A. Christie (ed.), *Men and Social Work: Theories and Practices.* Basingstoke, Palgrave.

Reay, D. (2001) 'Spice girls', 'nice girls', 'girlies' and 'tomboys': gender discourses, girls' cultures and femininities in the primary classroom. *Gender and Education*, 13 (2): 153–66.

Ricks, F. (1992) A feminist view of caring. *Journal of Child and Youth Care*, 7 (2): 49–57.

Rolfe, H. (2005) *Men in Childcare Occupational Segregation: Working Paper Series No. 35. Manchester, Equal Opportunities Commission.*

Ruch, G. (2005) Relationship-based and reflective practice: holistic approaches to contemporary child care social work. *Child and Family Social Work*, 10: 111–23.

Scottish Government (2008) *Children Looked After Statistics 2007–08.* <www.scotland.gov.uk/Publications/2008/11/25103230/36> accessed 2 October 2008.

Scottish Institute for Residential Child Care (SIRCC) (2004) Residential child care: audit of qualifications. SIRCC. <www.sircc.strath.ac.uk> accessed 20 December 2004.

Scourfield, J. (2003) *Gender and Child Protection.* London, Palgrave Macmillan.

Scourfield, J. and Coffey, A. (2002) Understanding gendered practice in child protection. *Qualitative Social Work*, 1 (3): 319–40.

Sen, R. Kendrick, A. Milligan, I. and Hawthorn, M. (2007) *Literature Review for Shaw, T. (2007) Historical Abuse Systemic Review: Residential Schools and Children's Homes in Scotland 1950 to 1995.* Edinburgh: Scottish Government <www.scotland.gov.uk/Publications/2007/11/20104729/20>.

Shaw, T. (2007) *Historical Abuse Systemic Review: Residential Schools and Children's Homes in Scotland 1950 to 1995.* Edinburgh: Scottish Government www.scotland.gov.uk/Publications/2007/11/20104729/0 accessed 9 July 2009.

Skarbrevik, K. J. (2002) Gender differences among students found eligible for special education. *European Journal of Special Education*, 17 (2): 97–107.

Smith, D. J. and McAra, L. (2004) Gender and youth offending, *Edinburgh Study of Youth Transitions and Crime Research Digest*

No. 2. <http://www.law.ed.ac.uk/cls/esytc/findings/digest2.pdf> accessed 2 October 2008.

Smith, M. (2003) Boys to men: exploring masculinity in child and youth care. *Relational Child and Youth Care Practice*, 16 (4): 12–21.

Smith, M. (2009) Residential care and social justice. In S. Moore and R. Mitchell (eds.), *Power, Pedagogy and Praxis: Social Justice in the Globalized Classroom.* Rotterdam, Sense Publishers.

Smith, M., Macleod, I. and Mercadante, I. (2005) *Men Can Care: An Evaluation of an Initiative to Train Men for Work in Child and Youth Care.* Glasgow, Scottish Institute for Residential Child Care.

Smith, M. and Steckley, L. (2005) Working with boys and girls. In M. Smith (ed.), *Secure in the Knowledge: Perspectives on Practice in Secure Accommodation.* Glasgow, Scottish Institute for Residential Child Care.

Tavecchio, L. (2003) Presentation at the 'Men in Childcare' conference. Belfry, Ghent, November.

Thomson, E., McKay, A., Campbell, J. and Gillespie, M. (2005) *Jobs for the Boys and the Girls: Promoting a Smart Successful and Equal Scotland.* Glasgow, Glasgow Caledonian University and Equal Opportunities Commission.

Tronto, J. C. (1994) *Moral Boundaries: A Political Argument for an Ethic of Care.* London, Routledge.

Turney, D. (2000) The feminizing of neglect. *Child and Family Social Work*, 5: 47–56.

Walton, R. G. (1975) *Women in Social Work.* London, Routledge and Kegan Paul.

Ward, A. (1993) *Working in Group Care.* Birmingham, Venture Press.

Warren, S. (2003) Is that an action man in there? Masculinity as an imaginative act of self-creation. *Discourse: Studies in the Cultural Politics of Education*, 24 (1): 3–18.

Weaver-Hightower, M. (2003) The 'boy turn' in research on gender and education. *Review of Educational Research*, 73 (4): 471–98.

Wilson, A. and Beresford, P. (2000) 'Anti-oppressive practice': emancipation or appropriation? *British Journal of Social Work*, 30 (5): 553–73.

Young, C. (2001). *Where the Boys Are. CYC-Online.* <www.cyc-net.org/today2001/today010221.html> accessed 20 November 2008.

11

Therapeutic Options in Child Protection and Gendered Practices

Trish Walsh

Introduction

A significant body of research now exists from different Western child welfare and child protection systems suggesting that similar themes and issues emerge across different fields of practice despite local political, cultural, legal and social policy contexts. Two related issues in child protection have received increased attention in recent times: the concentration of interventions focused at women as mothers, and the apparent reluctance/inability/failure of workers to engage with men as fathers in child protection work (Daniel and Taylor, 2001; Ferguson and Hogan, 2004; O'Hagan, 1997; Ryan, 2000). Central to these issues is the acknowledgement that gender roles are diverse and shifting and that more men now are increasingly involved in active parenting and

Gender and Child Welfare in Society Edited by Brid Featherstone, Carol-Ann Hooper, Jonathan Scourfield, and Julie Taylor.

value their role in their children's lives (McKeown, 2001). In general, there appears to be a consensus that, despite the linguistic shift from 'mothering' to 'parenting' in the professional rhetoric of child welfare, certain factors influence or even predetermine intervention practices being heavily weighted towards women as mothers. These include:

- the acceptance that, in the majority of families, women are still the primary caregivers;
- the over-representation of men as the perpetrators of physical and sexual abuse of children, and the persistent evidence that issues of domestic violence frequently co-exist with, and often underpin, patterns of neglect and abuse of children, with men again most often implicated as the main culprits (Hearn, 1998; Johnson and Sacco, 1995).

These factors, coupled with the predominance of women as front-line workers, are thought to contribute to gendered patterns of practice whereby the primary relationships workers forge are most often with mothers, while men as fathers or partners are either avoided or ignored, especially if there are suggestions of violence or dangerousness (Daniel and Taylor, 2001; Milner, 1994; Humphreys, 1999). Not that this necessarily works in women's favour as undue emphasis may be placed on women to be the primary agents of change. Despite often significant structural and social disadvantages women are likely to be expected to exercise 'agency' in their relationships with problematic men or in their own engagement in problematic behaviours. 'More is expected of women, but when they fall they fall from a great height' (Scourfield, 2001: 85), whereas 'men, when seen as abusers, are beyond subjectivity and therefore beyond clienthood' (Scourfield, 2002: 10).

The child protection discourse

Despite attempts over time to rebalance services away from the child protection model towards broader family preservation, family support, or child welfare paradigms, the child protection discourse has generally remained stubbornly resistant to change. Whilst differences obviously exist in the specific forms and practices of child protection services globally, most systems share the following features:

1. a focus on the identification of specific forms of maltreatment and neglect and projected risk of reoccurrence into the future at the expense of a broader concern with child and family welfare and functioning (Walsh, 1999);
2. a system of assessment dominated by defined procedures within tight time frames in which the primary emphasis focuses on the identified immediate safety needs of the child/children; alongside a scrutiny of the capacities of care-givers;
3. a tightly monitored decision-making process broadly spanning the options of reception into care for a child/children and/or medium-term interventions focused on achieving family functioning change or permanent substitute placement if it is thought that sufficient change is not possible within an acceptable time span;
4. the formalization of the state's role through the involvement of the legal system as the ultimate authority and decision-maker in matters of child welfare law: most often through expensive adversarial legal systems where the judiciary presides and decides between two or more competing parties (Cooper, 1999);
5. child protection practices which have become shaped by '*fear of failure*' (Cooper, Hetherington and Katz, 2003: 10) in part because of the disproportionate influence of extreme, high-profile cases followed by formal inquiries and detailed demands for changed practices (for example, Arnold et al., 1987, Laming, 2003; McGuinness, 1993).

Problematizing the child protection discourse

None of the defining features of modern child protection systems are unproblematic. Indeed, all of them are conditional on perceived expert knowledge at a particular point in time, involving agreed or disputed definitions of such social constructs as 'acceptable parenting', 'bad parenting', 'significant harm' and 'capacity for change'. Yet the evidence bases for such expert knowledge are not only perpetually incomplete but also notoriously difficult to disseminate effectively in usable forms to workers, managers and teams embedded in practice contexts. In addition, notwithstanding the profusion of work which highlights the contested nature of much social work practice and the conflicting and problematic tasks with which social workers are charged, there is often an erroneous expectation that evidence-based practice can be seamlessly introduced into 'the swampy lowland' of child protection, where 'messy, confusing problems defy technical solution' (Schon, 1987: 3). Not only that, but practices are also heavily influenced by occupational discourses and local cultural norms (Pithouse, 1987), in addition to the myriad of local and national protocols and guidelines which increasingly shape social work practices in state services.

Moving specifically to the questions that key workers invariably need to ask themselves when charged with the responsibility of acting in a child protection 'case', two in particular are central to the construction of an individual case scenario: '*What is the matter?*' and '*what is to be done?*' (Howe, 1987: 7, my emphasis). For the practitioner for whom real-life problems present, in Schon's (1987) words as 'messy, indeterminate situations', other forms of knowledge bear an influence. Mattaini (1995) suggests that social workers draw on a range that can include practice wisdom derived from narrative experiences of the profession and professional colleagues; personal experience of the practitioner; a knowledge of the professional literature; a knowledge of history and current events; research issues that inform practice; theoretical and conceptual analyses; and information that is provided by the case itself.

Two of these are particularly hard to access in standard research reviews and studies: the personal experience of the practitioner, and information that is provided by the case itself. How, therefore, might we advance an understanding of how these elements interplay with others to influence interventions in child protection? In particular, what can we learn about how gendered practices are either reinforced or destabilized in practice scenarios in child protection?

Destabilizing discourses from psychiatry

Although it is sometimes assumed that the current focus on gendered practices and gender relations in child welfare work is a new development, researchers and practitioners have, over a far longer time span, worked to investigate and incorporate aspects of family life beyond the dyad of mother–child into their work. Featherstone, Rivett and Scourfield (2007) summarize the influences, both positive and harmful, of psychoanalytic theory and developmental psychology on our engagement with men as fathers. Lamb and Lewis are credited with 'paying attention to the complexity of family relationships' (2004: 83) and Flouri with emphasizing the need for systemic frameworks 'highlighting the interacting influences of . . . different factors on father involvement' (2005: 84). Some of this work is also undoubtedly historically rooted in the empirical stream of psychiatry which has consistently challenged the notion that any one overarching theory or meta-narrative might provide the holy grail for effective work in child welfare. For example, researchers in the Maudsley Hospital and, latterly, the Institute of Psychiatry in London sought to uncouple the roles of primary caregiver and attachment figure from the mother established in Bowlby's influential early work and automatically assumed since then (Bowlby, 1951; 1953; 1969). Rutter concluded that:

> For some aspects of development the same-sexed parent seems to have a special role, for some the person who plays and talks most with the child and for others the person who feeds the child. The father, the mother, brother and sisters, friends, school-teachers and others all have an impact on development, but their influences and importance differ for different aspects of development. A less exclusive focus on the mother is required. *Children also have fathers!* (1972: 125, my emphasis).

Subsequent work provides further insights into the significance of men as fathers and partners both in contributing to and in protecting against adverse outcomes for vulnerable women (Brown and Harris, 1978; Quinton and Rutter, 1988). Although these studies could be criticized for failing to locate men's potential as parents in a more central and less subsidiary role they were never intended to provide a base for a general theory of men's role as parents; rather, they were studies focused specifically on women's depression and adult outcomes for children raised in institutional care, respectively. In identifying factors which influenced outcomes, they also emphasized broader components of vulnerability: class, bad housing, insecure employment, financial problems and social isolation. Familial components, such as the quality of family relationships and the number and ages of children, were incorporated with elements of personal biography and identity, such as experiences of loss and other adverse life events, to provide multifactorial explanations both for female depression and mothering capacities of women reared in institutions.

Work on parenting capacity and parenting outcomes continues to build dynamic and interactional explanatory theories, ones which challenge more simplistic and uni-directional theories such as those focused on attachment behaviours alone. It is precisely such combinations of individual and structural dimensions, as identified by Flouri (2005), that need recognition if child welfare workers are to avoid overly blaming and pathologizing mothers whilst ignoring or minimizing the potential of men as fathers and carers.

Vulnerable mothers and discontinuities of adversity

Whilst the concept of 'parenting' can be rightly criticized for being gender-neutral and often as conflating mothering and fathering practices into a seemingly homogenous category, it appears necessary to locate breakdowns in parenting practices as being a central issue in child welfare work. 'It is important to consider what is involved in parenting in order to determine what might be affected when parenting fails' (Quinton and Rutter, 1988: 8).

Quinton and Rutter begin from the position that

> parenting must be seen in an ecological perspective that recognises the family as a functional system, the operation of which will be altered by its internal composition and by external forces. This means that parenting must be assessed in terms of the emotional resources available to the parent, together with the material resources that can be drawn on and the physical environment in which parenting takes

place ... it makes no sense to view parenting as a uni-dimensional variable, or as a personal attribute. (1988: 10).

Their review of a retrospective and prospective study of both children and women who had come into residential state care or matured out of it and subsequently became parents themselves identifies the importance both of the quality of the relationship between the women in their study and their partners and what they term 'spousal characteristics' (which cover co-habiting relationships). 'A lack of support in the ... relationship was associated with high rates of poor current social functioning' whilst 'high rates of satisfactory social functioning [were found] for women with a currently supportive or non-deviant spouse. This was true for parenting also, where half the supported mothers were in the good outcome category.' They conclude that the findings suggest that for women who had poor parenting experiences themselves, their partners' 'good qualities exerted a powerful ameliorating effect leading to better parenting and better functioning' (ibid.:184). Furthermore, they incorporate the element of women's agency in their choices of partner and life-planning in that 'the choices or changes that lead to more satisfactory circumstances in adulthood are major breakpoints in the continuity of adversity across generations' (ibid.: 191). Egeland, Jacobvitz and Sroufe made similar findings in their study of mothers who had suffered abuse as children: 'Emotional support from a partner may help provide parents with the emotional resources necessary to give adequate care to their children' (1988: 1087).

There has been an increasing consensus since that no assumptions can be made that intergenerational cycles of abuse and maltreatment are either fixed or immune to change, and, allied with this, an increasing recognition of the multiplicity of factors which influence parenting behaviours (Buchanan, 1996). Alongside a more developed understanding of how stressful experiences can build resilience has come greater understanding of the different features involved in the development of resilience, 'including prior experiences, how the individual deals with stress at the time, inherent qualities of the individual, and subsequent experiences'(Rutter, 2002: 10). These studies challenge child protection workers to appreciate more fully that poor childhood experiences do not in themselves create poor parents, mothers and fathers.

The therapeutic potential of a child protection 'crisis'

For families that become the focus of a child protection investigation, the encounter may be experienced and constructed as a 'crisis'. That a child protection worker is engaging with a family to assess parenting capacity, levels of risk and potential for change, and, furthermore, is mandated to do so with the backing of statutory powers, triggers a shift in the family's boundaries and creates a family–professional system. For a time or permanently, depending on the outcome of assessments and interventions, a child or children removed from family and placed with alternative carers will be located in a transitory space, in time and place. So, too, will family members, who must cooperate with, negotiate with and frequently just accept interventions from professionals who, in the main, first identify whether problems exist, second, what those problems are, and, third, specify the interventions which need to be put in place to improve parenting, reduce risk, counteract harm and/or build in systems of surveillance of families and parenting practices.

Crisis intervention theory suggests that with crisis comes potential for change (and this is assuming that change needs to take place). With the questioning of old, established patterns of being and behaving comes the potential for new patterns and practices to be developed. In therapeutic terminology, crises represent opportunities. Drawing on the classic work of Caplan (1965), crises have been defined as 'turning points in people's lives when precipitating hazardous events lead to rising distress, upsetting the steady state in which previous coping mechanisms dealt with problems' (Payne, 2005: 98).

It is often on this belief that therapeutic interventions rest: the hope for change and the belief that change is possible. Of particular importance, then, are both the mindsets and actions of the child protection worker, team and system with this family at this point in time. How is the family perceived? How are their actions and behaviours construed? How is the family defined? Who is to be engaged with, included in an assessment and interventions and how?

Traditionally, therapeutic skills were an integral part of the repertoire that child welfare workers were expected to develop and sustain. This is seen to have changed in the reconstruction of social work in the latter part of the twentieth century: 'No longer are social workers constructed as caseworkers drawing on their therapeutic skills in human relationships, but as care managers assessing need and operationalising packages of care where notions of monitoring and review are central' (Parton, 1996: 12). Nowadays, therapeutic interventions in child welfare more often occupy a curious place between statutory services defined by assessment and protection roles, mental health services which are primarily defined by diagnostic and therapeutic roles and legal systems which are defined by another discourse of public protection and personal rights, although there have also been consistent calls for frontline child welfare workers to be re-equipped with such skills (see, for example, Batty and Cullen, 1996; Cooper, Hetherington and Katz, 2003).

The 'window of opportunity' that can emerge in that temporary space and place between family and professional systems at the time of initial assessment and engagement can be a powerful time of change, yet investigation systems now dominate, leading to 'a sharp reduction in the investment of interagency time and resources at the stage of working with children and parents to help solve their problems once the crisis, and possibly the excitement, of investigation and initial conference has passed. Yet the intervention phase is precisely the point where interagency effort needs to be concentrated' (Hallett, 1996: 8).

In many contemporary child welfare systems it seems that following the initial case conference the key worker acts as coordinator and manager of continuing assessment and therapeutic services. But what interventions are chosen? Why? And what does this tell us about the possibilities of such services offering gender-sensitive interventions which honour the heterogeneity of parenting practices across diverse and unique situations? One small step forward might be to take a hypothetical case of child protection assessment and intervention and consider how it might unfold and with what impact, using a gender-sensitive analysis.

'Let's suppose' – unpacking the practitioner's dilemma

'Let's take a case': these are words familiar to students on social work and child welfare courses. 'Let's look at how this might unfold in practice.' Adopting Howe's (1987) mantra that 'there are many ways to skin a cat' it *is* possible to create scenarios and try out different approaches to see what might unfold. Intended and unintended consequences emerge in role plays and hypothetical work – but in the 'let's suppose' space created re-imagining can take place and new possibilities can emerge. So let's take a case – and see how different intervention types and packages might play out.

Ben Carroll: the initial picture

Ben is a 3-year-old child who is taken to hospital by his mother, Betty, and stepfather, Clive, with bad burns covering most of his body one Monday mid-afternoon. He is gravely ill and remains in intensive care in the hospital for three weeks, following which he will need at least eight months of treatment consisting of surgery, painful skin grafts, and protective bandaging over much of his body. The doctors calculate that the burns occurred more than 12 hours prior to his arrival to hospital. The mother explains that she only noticed the burns that morning, after she had organized her older five children for school and went up to wake Ben. Clive had gone to work. Ben told her that his oldest half-sibling, Charles, had accidentally burnt him whilst giving him a shower the evening before. This is what she tells the doctors. They are sceptical, and think it is 'inconsistent'; they think the burns were inflicted deliberately. Child protection services are called.

The doctors are adamant that the burns were deliberately inflicted. They point to the presence of bruising and possible finger-marks on Ben's shoulder, indicating that he was held under the water. The police and social workers are called and a criminal investigation and child protection assessment are started. The police interview Charles and take a statement in which he retells how he was showering Ben down in the bath, did not realize how hot the water was or that Ben was injured and just put him to bed. They interview Clive and take a statement from him. Clive recounts how he came back from his work late in the evening; all seemed well, and the children were all in bed. The police confirm that they have inspected the water heater in the house and that the heater thermostat was broken. The police take no further action.

The family have no record of previous involvement with social services. Ben remains in hospital and the child protection team start their assessment. A social worker is allocated to the case, a young woman with 18-months' post-qualifying experience. She is preparing to go travelling in about three months, a common trend for many newly-qualified social workers, many of whom move on from initial post-qualifying child protection employment in the first two years (Loughran and Walsh, 1998).

Hypothetical situation one – the initial assessment

Betty is the mother of seven children from four relationships: Charles (15), Hugh (12), Louise (10), Lisa (8), Bettina (5), Ben (3), and Clive junior (6 months). She lives with Clive in a four-bedroomed house on a public housing estate in a navy town in a rural setting. Five of her seven children now live with her: Ben is in hospital and Charles has been sent back to live with his father in a distant city in another country. Betty works full-time in the home, Clive has shift work in a local factory. Money is tight. Details of the relationships and names of the children's fathers are taken. Enquiries about their whereabouts are made, but the worker is most concerned with Betty, her history and her account of what happened to Ben.

Betty is interviewed and her family history is taken. She does not elect to have Clive there and the worker does not think to ask whether she would like him with her. Betty describes herself as a local girl whose parents have both died, her father only nine months earlier. Betty had cared for him for the last three years of his life. She had successfully managed to get the council to build another bedroom for him downstairs after he lost his mobility. She has one brother who lives in a neighbouring town, but she does not have much contact with him.

When Betty was 16 years old she left home and moved to a distant city where she married when aged 18. Her eldest son, Charles was born when she was 19. She describes her relationship with her first partner as violent and abusive. She separated from him and returned to her home town when Charles was 3.

Betty started a new relationship with Matias in her home town. They started living together and she had children Hugh, Louise and Lisa within a four-year span. This was a happy time, but after being together for six years they started arguing and Betty became involved with another man, Christy. Matias moved out of their home, leaving Betty caring for the children, but he was frequently in contact and committed to his children.

Christy was, in Betty's words, a 'mad-man' who drank too much and was terribly violent to her. She did not realize this fully until after she had had two children with him, Bettina (now 5) and Ben (3). She broke off contact with him after a particularly violent incident when he tried to run her over in his car. Christy neither had any more contact with her nor showed any interest in the children.

Then she met Clive, and she describes him as being 'great', somebody who really looks after her and the children. She says that she is finished with gadding about, that she had a bad time since her father died and she had been drinking heavily but now she realizes that she was really depressed. But she resisted taking anti-depressants because she had seen family members and neighbours become dependent on them.

She explains how Ben ended up with burns. She was, as usual, in the house making the dinner for the kids at six. Clive was out working. Ben, who was getting toilet-trained, had 'an accident' and Betty told Charles to take him upstairs and clean him up and put him to bed. The other children went to bed later that evening. She knew nothing of what happened until the following morning when she went to get Ben up at about ten o'clock, after the older children were gone to school. She and Clive slept in the downstairs bedroom with their baby, Clive junior.

A pause

At this point a key worker has many dilemmas and urgent choices to make. The primary focus will be on Ben's burns: does this account add up? What does it say about Betty's parenting? If the account is believed, what does it say about Charles? Does this matter, since Charles is now out of the country, with his father in a distant city? What else does the key worker need to do: should she interview the other children? arrange a case conference? get feedback from the hospital staff on how Betty interacts with Ben, and her visiting patterns? find out how the other children are doing from their schools? involve Ben's father?

Clive does not enter into the equation because he is rarely around and he seems to the worker to be a mild, timid man, quite a bit older than Betty. Betty doesn't suggest involving him and the local police have no concerns about him; he is known and respected locally.

At this stage we can all feel sympathy for the worker – she has a lot on her plate. To her relief, Betty is cooperative and accepts the social worker's visits and interviews, but she is very anxious about Ben and what might happen. Keeping an engagement with Betty is her primary focus.

The case conference

Across some but not all child protection systems, the case conference is an event of some significance. Originally developed as a forum for professionals from a range of agencies and disciplines to come together and share information about a particular family and child with a view to making decisions about how to proceed, it has subsequently also become the focal point for a formal interaction between state services and a family, reconstructed around principles of partnership.

The case conference on Ben takes place. The female social worker reports that the family have had no previous social work contact; that the schools in general are positive about the children, although they note that the children are a little unkempt sometimes; they have no real concerns about Betty's mothering abilities. The health visitor has no concerns about the baby, although there is a query over his hearing and he is being referred for hospital tests. The social worker has spoken to nurses in the hospital who have observed the interactions between Betty and Ben. They report that Ben is always pleased to see her and his siblings when she brings them, and Betty demonstrates care and concern for her son but can be a bit 'over-the-top', bringing him too many or inappropriate presents. Nurses are worried too about how traumatized Ben was for a long time following admission. The key worker's report draws on her training: the importance of attachment theory (Ainsworth et al., 1978; Bowlby, 1969; Brandon et al., 1999, Howe, 2005); the importance of a multidisciplinary perspective on a family's functioning; the significance of trauma and its impact on children.

She writes what she knows about. She also voices a concern about the 'rights' of Ben's father, Christy, and whether the service has a legal responsibility to inform him of the situation given recent court judgements made about 'fathers' rights'. Her male team leader is concerned that the service be seen to be 'inclusive'. His recent team-leader training has emphasized the need to ensure that he keeps to the principle of 'working in partnership' with parents, keeping them informed and involved.

The hospital paediatric consultant and registrar, both male, voice clear professional opinions that Ben has suffered an intentionally-inflicted non-accidental injury; that the injured boy was not brought sufficiently quickly to the hospital for urgent medical treatment and that this has increased his suffering and chance of a good recovery. He was seriously ill when admitted, with severe dehydration. There were finger-mark bruises on his shoulders suggesting that force had been used.

Betty attends for part of the conference. She is there by herself. Clive is minding the baby in the car. No one thinks to ask her if she would like him to accompany her, or to offer practical assistance such as someone to mind the baby. She gives her account of what happened to Ben. She tells how she has sent Charles back to live with his father, as 'it was not working out'. She neither confirms nor denies the narrative that Charles was responsible for Ben's injuries. She does not see why a fuss is still being made, because Charles will not be coming back to live with them again. She is clear that she wants only one outcome: her child, Ben, returned. She emphasizes that her children are more important to her than anything else in the world. She leaves the meeting to wait whilst decisions are made.

A long discussion ensues between conference participants. The focus is the issue of how Ben got his injuries. Following the strong beliefs on the part of the doctors that this was a non-accidental injury, that there was neglect in the delay in bringing him for hospital treatment and that the mother, even if she did not inflict the injury herself, 'must have' known that the child was subsequently in pain, the message is clear: this mother is not to be trusted. Risks are not to be taken.

The legal advisers worry that Betty, already distressed and anxious about Ben, might attempt to remove him from the hospital, and that the hospital staff would have no way of stopping her without legal protection. She is being viewed as irrational and possibly dangerous. The decision is made to apply for an emergency care order to make it possible to keep Ben in hospital legally until it is possible to hold a court hearing. A second decision is made that further assessment of this family and its ability to provide future safe care for Ben is required. The team leader and social worker are charged with commissioning this work. 'The family's ability' is automatically interpreted as 'Betty's ability'. Though this is not explicitly articulated, Betty is now effectively viewed as a vulnerable single parent, with an unfortunate pattern of choosing unsuitable partners. That her current partner is apparently unproblematic is neither commented upon, nor, indeed, noticed.

With the focus now shifted to the management of Betty as a problematic parent, Charles, and his possible culpability in the issue of Ben's injuries, slips out of view. That he is no longer 'on the scene', nor indeed in the country, is tacitly taken to mean that he need no longer preoccupy the child protection services. No one refers to him.

A third decision is made that Ben's father, Christy, needs to be contacted and informed of the situation, although he is known not to have had any contact with the two children since his separation from Betty almost three years ago. The team leader undertakes to carry out this task.

Betty, now accompanied by Clive and the baby, when informed of these decisions becomes angry and upset. She blames the social worker and her team leader for not believing her; for taking her child. She is incredulous that they are going to contact Ben's father, Christy, when he has not displayed the slightest interest in the two children since they separated on bad terms three years previously. She is fearful that her child will not be returned. She leaves the meeting abruptly, pouring her scorn on the team leader whom she is blaming for keeping her child from her.

A pause

Cooper, Hetherington and Katz note that child protection systems 'encourage social workers to protect their own position, in a way which runs counter to the lessons and principles they learnt during their training' (2003: 11). However, in reviewing how this hypothetical case conference played out, it is possible to see how dynamics of power and gender, authority and trust are also at play. It is at the multidisciplinary case conference that the most significant decisions are made. Inputs from expert systems based on notions of certainty and science are powerful authoritative voices. Social workers' own initial tentative analyses of a situation are often vulnerable to being overshadowed by these more definitive discourses. Otley has suggested that men have tended to dominate both the discourse and positions of power in the child protection field leaving female practitioners 'marginalised and isolated' (1996: 171). This may, in addition, be a factor here.

The fear of making the wrong decision dominates the discussions. Safety is played for whilst the focus remains on only one dynamic in this situation: poor mothering and damaged children. The core components of a therapeutic child protection system – those of trust, authority and negotiation (Cooper, Hetherington and Katz, 2003) – are singularly missing in this case at this time. The relationship between the key worker and the family has now become strained. Although Betty continues to cooperate with what is asked of her she is demoralized and angry.

'There appears to be a self-reinforcing cycle in which mothers expect to be the focus of attention, fathers expect not to be involved, and childcare practitioners expect to engage with mothers' (Daniel and Taylor, 2001: 23). At this case conference, the combination of choices made in relation to topics discussed and decisions made in relation to future interventions, as well as the language used in framing the specific incidents and objects of concern, all reveal heavily-gendered assumptions about parenting practices and responsibilities as well as the sites of potential for change. The self-reinforcing cycle is evident.

A concerning cynicism about the extent of the remit of child protection services is also discernible in the setting aside of Charles both as a focus of concern in this scenario, as a possibly violent young man, and also as a subject of concern himself, as, potentially, a vulnerable adolescent male with significant problems of his own. He is, after all, not their problem any longer now that he lives outside the country. In the context of the seemingly universal pressures inherent in overstretched contemporary child protection systems the pragmatic disregard for a potential client or even young person in need now 'gone missing' may be understandable, but is it defensible? Is it also possible that to keep Charles in the frame, as potentially culpable for Ben's injuries, and as a worrisome young male in need of services himself, might quite simply introduce too much complexity and ambiguity for the workers at the centre of this case? Might it also challenge the gendered nature of existing services, which may not, after all, have anything to offer this teenager?

The impact of the public debate on the rights of fathers, and particularly unmarried and non-resident fathers, is also evident in the concern about Ben's father and his 'right' to be consulted or included. Legal child welfare and public child protection services have been heavily criticized by radical father's rights groups for some time now. Social workers, possibly anxious to demonstrate their ability to be even-handed and anti-oppressive in their approach to mothers and fathers, may equate the demand for father's rights with the need for equal treatment (Scourfield, 2002). By doing so, Scourfield argues, they run the risk of ignoring important historical and contextual elements to the construction of parenting, mothering and fathering roles in a particular case. Nonetheless, the legal advice is that despite his absence as an active parent to date, Ben's father is to be contacted and interviewed.

The recruitment of additional expert systems

Following the case conference, all trust is broken between the social work department and the mother. Further assessment is required; the team leader and social worker agree that rather than leave the young social worker exposed, expected to cope with Mrs Carroll's anger, other agencies will be recruited to carry out this work. The local child mental health service will be approached to assess her parenting capacities further, assess the welfare of the other children, and advise on whether additional therapeutic interventions are indicated; the agency monitoring the access visits will be asked to provide a report on the relationship and 'attachment pattern' between Ben and his mother. Betty is to be advised to seek help for her self-admitted alcohol misuse problem, and she is provided with names of local addiction counsellors to contact. A foster-family living in a neighbouring town is identified that can take Ben once he is ready for discharge. The foster-mother is encouraged to start visiting him to build up a relationship.

The team leader and social worker carry out a joint visit to the family home to inform Betty of these decisions. The visit takes place during the daytime when Clive is at work. Betty hears what they have to say; accepts passively the recommendations made and agrees that she will await further contact regarding appointments. The only concern she voices is whether her weekly access visits to Ben will continue and when she might be allowed to host those visits at home. This last query is not picked up on by the workers, who wish to avoid any suggestion of progress towards a return home, at least until a more detailed assessment is carried out. Clive remains a figure of no evident relevance to the situation.

Hypothetical Situation Two

Let's pretend that the first worker now leaves this job to go travelling, as she had already planned, and is replaced by an 'old hand' returning from a career break. This worker reviews the file three months later, before making contact with Ben or his family. The case files tell her that:

- Temporary care orders continue to be made in court as assessment is 'continuing' but the judge and legal teams are becoming impatient at the continued delays and are pushing for a final resolution. The service's administrators are also concerned at the mounting legal costs.
- Ben's father was notified of the situation and has applied for legal aid, is represented at the care hearings and has stated a wish to care for Ben. The team leader who interviewed him has formed the opinion that he has an active chronic drug problem and so far has delayed any moves to offer him access or contact. However, his legal representatives have applied to court for access rights and the judge wants a decision on this soon.
- Ben has just moved from hospital into foster-care. New recruits to foster-parenting, the foster mother and her husband do not want Betty visiting their home so Betty has access visits in a local health centre once a week. Ben stills needs daily dressings and wears protective clothing; he still has some skin graft operations outstanding. Ben's foster-mother has voiced concerns about him going home whilst his medical needs are still time-consuming. She has only met Betty once at the hospital before Ben was discharged.
- Betty is on the waiting list for a parenting assessment. She has not yet got around to making contact with the addiction counsellor, but she has started a parenting course at the local school and keeps all her access visits to Ben. The access worker reports that she sometimes upsets Ben by telling him that he will be coming home soon, although she has been warned not to do so. Otherwise, the visits go well and Ben continues to enjoy the visits with his mother and siblings.

A pause

Let's suppose that this worker completed a family therapy course whilst on her career break. Having read the family file she decides to 'map out' the dynamics and interactions between the different family members. She knows enough from systemic reviews of child death cases (Reder Duncan and Gray, 1993) not to restrict this to family members living together; emotional and parenting bonds transcend distance. She maps out the family relationships on a genogram and charts an eco-map of support networks and their strengths and weaknesses (Wilson et al., 2008). She looks at the gaps in information and knowledge.

She is worried about the lack of any follow-up on Charles; where is he and what care is he receiving? She wonders how this family works – not just how Betty functions as a mother but also how she and Clive work as a set of parents, and also how Hugh, Louise and Lisa relate to their father, who lives locally and is involved. She wonders what role Ben's father sees himself playing – and, more importantly, what he has to offer this vulnerable, damaged child? She wonders what impact the dramatic event of Ben's injuries and subsequent disappearance from family life has had on all the children and how they are dealing with Ben's absence – how do they understand the situation?

She maps out a plan: meet with Betty and Clive and work with them to fill in some of the missing gaps in the genogram and eco-map; get their views on which are strong relationships, and who are supports. Also, use the opportunity to observe how Betty and Clive relate: what are the power dynamics in their relationship? how do they view their roles, especially in relation to parenting? This worker knows that she is going to have to re-engage the family and offer them a fresh start, to involve them in her work and regain their trust.

'Making progress'

Their first meeting is strained, but working on the charts together gives them a shared task; the worker uses this opportunity to find out more about Betty's own parenting and also Clive's family and past. Betty becomes tearful as she recounts her own childhood: both her parents were alcoholics who died of cirrhosis of the liver; her mother had no time for Betty and doted only on her sons; Betty adored her father but he was physically abusive to her mother when they were both drunk. Betty ran away from home when she was 15 because there was 'nothing at home' for her. The worker and Betty spend some time identifying Betty's positive actions in escaping difficult situations: not only then, but also making the brave choice to leave the relationship with Charles's father when that too became abusive; returning to her home town, even though there was a stigma in doing so as a single parent; and then again when she realized she had made a mistake by getting involved with Christy, Ben's father. Betty said she'd had enough of making the wrong choices: she now had a good man she was going to settle with.

These revelations allowed the worker to turn the talk to Betty and Clive – how had they met, how had they got together. She observed the warm interactions between them; the obvious admiration that Clive had for Betty; his gentleness towards her when she became upset. She also observed how Clive looked to Betty for directions, and how he was the one to attend to the children and change nappies. He was very proud of his baby son, but also talked about how Ben needed to come home, for them all but especially for Betty, who was heartbroken without him.

Clive's family history showed an uneventful childhood with parents in the local barracks town; the youngest of three children, he followed his father into the navy as a teenager; married when he was 22 years old and had two children, both girls who are now adult and live in nearby cities. His marriage, he said, had faltered at the point that he had taken early retirement from the navy; he and his wife had grown apart. He knew Betty to see from a distance, and although she was twenty years younger than him had found her attractive. He said that he 'couldn't believe his luck' when they got chatting and then fell in love. He was committed to a life with Betty, wanted to be involved in his parenting of the children and was already taking an active role in doing so.

A pause

*In this second hypothetical situation, the worker has managed to start rebuilding a relationship with the two primary carers: she is focusing on trust, negotiation and the therapeutic use of authority. By taking a systemic and ecological approach (*Germain and Gitterman, 1996; Vetere and Dallos, 2003*) and using creative tools in her work, she has* *managed to re-open a space with this family. She is interested in how Clive is motivated and engaged in playing an active part in finding solutions to the childcare issues. He has already reorganized his working schedule to fit in more hands-on parenting work; not only is he supporting Betty in her parenting but he is also quietly bringing in new daily life routines which are providing structure and stability for the other children.*

She knows that further changes are necessary if she is to argue for a return home at the next case conference. She is also aware that time is running out. Ben is forming a new relationship with his foster-mother. The family is systemically reforming without Ben's presence. Betty is over-focused on one goal only and that is the return of Ben. The other children are suffering, and what has happened to Charles?

Moving this forward, the worker argues successfully for workload time on this case to be doubled in order to complete this assessment and put in place a package of care:

1. *A session to sit in on the family at home one morning: to observe Betty's parenting of the five children together – how does she manage?*
2. *A session to observe an access visit – how are the family dynamics playing out?*
3. *Charles needs to be discussed with Betty – how does she think he experienced his return to his father? What might it be like for him if he did punish Ben for soiling by holding him under the hot water for too long?*
4. *Betty needs to connect with the addiction counsellor and work on her tendency to self-medicate; to reflect on her fear that she too might die at a young age from cirrhosis and to work on her own identified aim to develop a controlled drinking pattern.*
5. *A short series of joint sessions with Betty and Clive to develop their joint parenting practices; to promote Clive as being quite an expert on parenting because he had such good experiences himself in childhood; to help them work out a more systematic approach to meeting the needs of all the children.*
6. *A family meeting with Matias and his new partner to work out a less chaotic arrangement of shared care for the children Hugh, Louise and Lisa.*

Reflecting on the case

These hypothetical scenarios demonstrate two quite radically different forms of engagement and interventions in a fairly typical child protection scenario.

The first is premised on a combination of implicit explanatory theories, gendered thinking and contextual factors which result in practices overly-concentrated on the mother in this family, with a simultaneous disregard for the potential strengths of her partner once he had been assessed as posing no danger. Interventions are framed as relating to the mother alone; she carries the exclusive responsibility of persuading the authorities that she is worthy of a second chance and can be entrusted again with the care of her child. Focusing too strongly on attachment-based theories and interventions without being informed by a systemic analysis and a gender-aware approach to family interactions will not allow diverse patterns of role-fulfilment to emerge. This is not new knowledge: 'It should be appreciated that the chief [attachment] bond need not be with a biological parent, it need not be with the chief caretaker and it need not be with a female' (Rutter, 1972: 125).

In this hypothetical case the non-resident father of the injured child, who has been absent from his children's lives for some time, is perceived to have legal rights which may need to be facilitated on demand. The other non-resident father in this case is ignored; he is neither demanding attention nor offering anything, yet he is actively involved in parenting behind the scenes. The older teenage boy, who is central to this scenario, is discounted as an object of concern: 'out of sight, out of mind'. Individualizing explanations and remedies are utilized to allow a package of care to be constructed which reinforces the narrative of maternal failures and mistakes being central to the child's injuries; nowhere is there a space for a more nuanced and multidimensional assessment.

In the second scenario, the application of a systemic perspective from the onset allows for a form of engagement which invites participation from a broader range of actors. An effort is made to approach the family with a more neutral curiosity: how does this family work? Less of an attempt is made to fit the family into a particular type; the mother and her partner are viewed as two adults who, along with the other actors actively engaged in parenting roles to these seven children, have formed their own working model of how to do parenting. The dilemma for the worker which invariably remains is that this model did not work, in that it failed to protect a small child from painful and life-threatening injuries. So, alongside the efforts to build a relationship-based engagement with these parents, the worker has to retain her focus on resolving the question of what's best for Ben, as well as attending to questions of justice and potentially conflicting rights for the various people in this extended and blended family.

Conclusions

> Child protection is perhaps the most demanding, conflict-ridden, worrying and controversial of modern public services. That is because in exercising its responsibilities to safeguard children, the state uses its power to become involved in the most intimate and sensitive family relationships. (Cooper, Hetherington and Katz, 2003: 16)

The intervention scenarios developed in this chapter are, of necessity, brief, overly-simplistic and insufficiently nuanced to depict fully the real-life difficult situations in which families find themselves, and which child protection workers are expected to bring to a successful resolution – whatever that may be determined to be. It can be argued that the sketches are unfair to younger, mainly female, newly-qualified workers, the foot-soldiers of most child protection systems, in depicting them as less powerful and authoritative in their work both with other disciplines and with families and children themselves. Yet that is often the case, and it is not a failure at individual level but a systemic problem. At a higher level, a choice has been made to select younger, less experienced and often less confident workers to become the foot-soldiers of the child protection system, responsible not only for managing complex and often highly-charged scenarios but also for creating effective interventions in them.

The case can also be made that these scenarios overstate the case for 'experienced' workers and implicitly suggest that such workers are more effective and skilled than younger workers. This is not the intention; rather, the point is being made that some element of confidence and ease with the authoritative role that child protection work invariably entails is necessary if workers are to destabilize gendered practices. Authority need not be a dirty word: 'Authority can be accepted and indeed welcomed if it is used openly and sensitively and within a context of some level of trust' (Cooper, Hetherington and Katz, 2003: 45).

The case is made in this chapter that practitioners' chances of combining therapeutic work at the coalface of child protection interventions with a gender-sensitive approach can be improved by a knowledge of systemic and ecological theories and skills in systemic formulations and practices (Germain and Gitterman, 1996; Vetere and Dallos, 2003) in addition to an awareness of studies of significance on parenting outcomes from the fields of developmental psychology and psychiatry (Reder and Lucey, 1995; Reder, Duncan and Lucey, 2003). Some such studies offer a deep base in acknowledging the interplay of factors in the creation of individual circumstances: 'a consideration of individual actions and the psychological processes underlying them is entirely consistent with the study of wider social forces in the explanation of social phenomena, and indeed ... the inclusion of both is often essential' (Quinton and Rutter, 1988: 217). Alone, systemic theories and reference to research literature will, obviously, not be sufficient to address the social conditions and processes which lead to heavily-gendered constructions of parenting practices, but they might just assist workers in building a more nuanced, gender-sensitive form of practice in child protection work. 'What is required is a combination of respect for the inevitability of complexity, allied to purposeful work in the interests of children and continual attention to questions of rights and justice. We argue that systems theory is the best foundation from which to conceptualise and mobilise change' (Cooper, Hetherington and Katz, 2003: 12).

References

Ainsworth, M., Blehar, M., Waters, E., and Wall, S. (1978) *Patterns of Attachment: A Psychological Study of the Strange Situation.* Hillsdale NJ, Lawrence Erlbaum.

Arnold, E., Bogle, M., Fernando, F., Howells, R., Ramsay, L., Sedley, S. and Warmington, A. (1987) *Whose Child? The Report of the Panel Appointed to Inquire into the Death of Tyra Henry.* Brixton, London Borough of Lambeth.

Batty, D., and Cullen, D. (1996) *Child Protection: The Therapeutic Option.* London, British Association for Adoption and Fostering.

Bowlby, J. (1951) *Maternal Care and Mental Health.* Geneva, World Health Organization.

Bowlby, J. (1953) *Child Care and the Growth of Love.* Harmondsworth, Penguin.

Bowlby, J. (1969) *Attachment and loss. Vol. 1. Attachment.* New York, Basic Books.

Brandon, M., Hinings, P., Howe, D. and Schofield, G. (1999) *Attachment Theory, Child Maltreatment and Family Support: A Practice and Assessment Model.* Basingstoke, Palgrave Macmillan.

Brown, G. and Harris, T. (1978) *Social Origins of Depression.* London, Tavistock.

Buchanan, A. (1996) *Cycles of Child Maltreatment: Facts, Fallacies and Interventions.* New York, Wiley.

Caplan, G. (1965) *Preventative Psychiatry.* London, Tavistock.

Cooper, A. (1999) Anxiety and child protection work in two national systems. In P. Chamberlayne, A. Cooper, R. Freeman and M. Rustin (eds.), *Welfare and Culture in Europe: Towards a New Paradigm in Social Policy.* London, Jessica Kingsley.

Cooper, A., Hetherington, R. and Katz, I. (2003) *The Risk Factor: Making the Child Protection System Work for Children.* London, Demos.

Daniel, B. and Taylor, A. (2001) *Engaging with Fathers.* London, Jessica Kingsley.

Egeland, B., Jacobvitz, D. and Sroufe, L. A. (1988) Breaking the cycle of abuse. *Child Development,* 59 (4): 1080–8.

Featherstone, B., Rivett, M. and Scourfield, J. (2007) *Working with Men in Health and Social Care.* London, Sage.

Ferguson, H. and Hogan, F. (2004) *Strengthening Families through Fathers.* Waterford, Waterford Institute of Technology.

Flouri, E. (2005) *Fathering and Child Outcomes.* Chichester, Wiley.

Germain, C. and Gitterman, A. (1996) *The Life Model of Social Work Practice,* 2nd edn. New York, Columbia University Press.

Hallett, C. (1996) From investigation to help. In D. Batty and D. Cullen (eds.), *Child Protection: The Therapeutic Option.* London, British Association for Adoption and Fostering.

Hearn, J. (1998) *The Violences of Men.* London, Sage.

Howe, D. (1987) *An Introduction to Social Work Theory.* Aldershot, Avebury.

Howe, D. (2005) *Child Abuse and Neglect: Attachment, Development and Intervention.* Basingstoke, Palgrave Macmillan.

Humphreys, C. (1999) Avoidances and confrontations: social work practice in relation to domestic violence and child abuse. *Child and Family Social Work*, 4 (2): 77–87.

Johnson, H. and Sacco, V. (1995) Researching violence against women: statistics of Canada's national survey. *Canadian Journal of Criminology* (July): 281–304.

Lamb, M. E. (ed.) (2004) *The Role of the Father in Child Development*, 4th edn. Chichester, Wiley.

Lamb, M. E. and Lewis, C (2004) The development and significance of father–child relationships in two-parent families. In M. E. Lamb (ed.), *The Role of the Father in Child Development*, 4th edn. Chichester, Wiley.

Laming, H. (2003) *The Victoria Climbie Report*. <www.victoria-climbie-inquiry.org.uk> accessed November 2008.

Loughran, H. and Walsh, T. (1998) Newly-qualified Irish social workers: what work worlds are they entering? *Irish Social Worker*, 16 (5): 4–7.

McGuinness, C. (1993) *The Kilkenny Incest Investigation Report.* Dublin, Stationery Office.

McKeown, K. (2001) *Fathers and Families: Research and Reflection on Key Questions.* Dublin, Department of Health and Children.

Mattaini, M. (1995) Knowledge for practice. In Meyer, C. and M. Mattaini (eds.), *Foundations of Social Work Practice.* Washington, DC, NASW.

Milner, J. (1994) Avoiding violent men: the gendered nature of child protection and practice. In H. Ferguson, R. Gilligan and R. Torode (eds.), *Surviving Childhood Adversity.* Dublin, Trinity College Social Studies Press.

O'Hagan, K. (1997) The problem of engaging men in child protection work. *British Journal of Social Work*, 27 (1): 25–42.

Otley, O. (1996) Social work with children and families. In N. Parton (ed.), *Social Theory, Social Change and Social Work.* London, Routledge.

Parton, N. (1996) Introduction. In N. Parton (ed.), *Social Theory, Social Change and Social Work.* London, Routledge.

Payne, M. (2005) *Modern Social Work Theory*, 3rd edn. Basingstoke, Palgrave Macmillan.

Pithouse, A. (1987) *Social Work: The Social Organization of an Invisible Trade.* Aldershot, *Avebury.*

Quinton, D. and Rutter, M. (1988) *Parenting Breakdown: The Making and Breaking of Inter-generational Links.* Aldershot, Avebury.

Reder, P., Duncan, S. and Gray, M. (1993) *Beyond Blame: Child Abuse Tragedies Revisited.* London, Routledge.

Reder, P., Duncan, S. and Lucey, C. (2003) *Studies in the Assessment of Parenting.* Hove, Brunner-Routledge.

Reder, P. and Lucey, C. (1995) *Assessment of Parenting: Psychiatric and Psychological Contributions.* London, Routledge.

Rutter, M. (1972) *Maternal Deprivation Reassessed.* Harmondsworth, Penguin.

Rutter, M. (2002) Nature, nurture, and development: from evangelism through science toward policy and practice. *Child Development*, 72 (1): 1–21.

Ryan, M. (2000) *Working with Fathers.* London, HMSO.

Schon, D. (1987) *Educating the Reflective Practitioner.* San Francisco, Jossey-Bass.

Scourfield, J. (2001) Constructing women in child protection work. *Child and Family Social Work*, 6 (1): 77–87.

Scourfield, J. (2002) Reflection on gender, knowledge and values in social work, *British Journal of Social Work*, 32 (1): 1–15.

Vetere, A. and Dallos, R. (2003) *Working Systemically with Families.* London, Karnac.

Walsh, T. (1999) Changing expectations: the 'impact' of child protection on Irish social work. *Child and Family Social Work*, 4 (1): 33–42.

Wilson, K., Ruch, G., Lymbery, M. and Cooper, A. (2008) *Social Work: An Introduction to Contemporary Practice.* Harlow, Pearson Longman.

Index

Note: The abbreviation FGC refers to Family Group Conference

